The Politics of Globalisation and Polarisation

For Eileen, Alexander, Harry and Poppy, Emma and Christopher

The Politics of Globalisation and Polarisation

Dr Maurice Mullard

Reader in Public and Social Policy, University of Hull, UK

Edward Elgar
Cheltenham, UK • Northampton, MA, USA

Published by
Edward Elgar Publishing Limited
Glensanda House
Montpellier Parade
Cheltenham
Glos GL50 1UA
UK

Edward Elgar Publishing, Inc.
136 West Street
Suite 202
Northampton
Massachusetts 01060
USA

A catalogue record for this book
is available from the British Library

Library of Congress Cataloging in Publication Data

Mullard, Maurice, 1946–
    The politics of globalisation and polarisation / Maurice Mullard.
        p. cm.
    Includes bibliographical references and index.
        1. Globalization—Political aspects. 2. Globalization—Political aspects—
    Developing countries. 3. Polarization (Social sciences) 4. Democracy.
    5. Citizenship. I. Title: Politics of globalization and polarization. II. Title.

    JZ1318.M83 2004
    327.1—dc22

                                                                    2004043318

ISBN 1 84376 579 9 (cased)

Typeset by Cambrian Typesetters, Frimley, Surrey
Printed and bound in Great Britain by MPG Books Ltd, Bodmin, Cornwall

Contents

Preface

This book is about the 'politics' of globalisation. In the aftermath of the fall of the Berlin Wall, Friedman (1999) offered a vision of the opportunities of a new globalisation:

> 'It was born when the Wall fell in 1989. It's no surprise that the world's youngest economy – the global economy – is still finding its bearings . . . Many world markets are only recently freed, governed for the first time by the emotions of the people rather than the fists of the state. From where we sit, none of this diminishes the promise offered a decade ago by the demise of the walled-off world . . . The spread of free markets and democracy around the world is permitting more people everywhere to turn their aspirations into achievements. And technology, properly harnessed and liberally distributed, has the power to erase not just geo-graphical borders but also human ones'. (Friedman, 1999, pp. xiii–xiv)

Understood in this way, the concept of globalisation seemed to offer the hope that free markets, technology and democracy would lead to a re-distribution of power founded on free markets, individuals and competition. Globalisation was implicitly connected with ideas of meritocracy and opportunity. The promise was that globalisation would create 'real markets' of consumer sovereignty and individual choice and where multinational corporations, business lobbyists, the financial community, governments and political elites would be eclipsed by great transparency, accountability and democracy. The new globalised world was supposed to shift power and influence to the individual.

The emphasis of this book is to make connections between economic globalisation and the politics of citizenship and democracy. Globalisation involves political priorities and political choices. Michael Moore (2003), when secretary general of the WTO, argued that globalisation and the market economy provided the framework for personal freedom, democracy and equal opportunity and represented the bulwark against protected, powerful and privileged forces. The rules of free trade and open markets provided the best means for increased global democracy. Moore (2003) criticised the anti-globalisers for seeking to undermine the potential of globalisation for underestimating the peaceful years associated with more free trade of the post-war decades.

Globalisation is at present defined as something which is inevitable, an exogenous event that is happening to the world and where the role of government is primarily to ensure that their policy frameworks correspond to the needs of the external challenges and opportunities. The concept of political choice implies deliberate policy decisions. To be critical of present forms of globalisation is not necessarily to be against globalisation, but rather to be against present forms of globalisation. Present forms of globalisation do not necessarily benefit developing countries. The attempt to enforce a specific definition of globalisation a 'one-fits-all' policy, as constructed by the IMF, the World Bank and the WTO, has been criticised for harming the economic development of countries that should have been allowed to 'evolve' towards economic integration at their own pace, recognising their own needs. Political choice indicates that things can be changed and there are alternatives to the free market liberal views that dominate present thinking. Intervention, regulation, awareness of poverty, commitments to social justice and a better re-distribution of income could be part of the agenda of globalisation.

Globalisation is neither inevitable nor inescapable. Governments are not the prisoners of globalisation. The major increases in capital flows in financial markets, decisions on world trade and deregulation of labour markets represent deliberate policy decisions. Markets are social constructs, fashioned, shaped and defined in the policy process. There is no such thing as a market for labour, but there are histories, rules and regulations that define labour markets:

> 'neo-conservatives argue that corporate-led globalisation is inevitable and the most we can therefore hope to do is make the process just a little bit kinder and gentler. Such crude economic determinism is neither politically acceptable nor intellectually tenable . . . Globalisation, unlike gravity or the pull of the tides, need not be with us forever. Rather, it is a set of policies shaped by corporate lobbyists and enacted by politicians. It is, therefore, possible to replace it with a different end-goal for the world economy, and to design a different set of trade rules in order to achieve that goal'.(Lucas, *The Guardian*, 20 May 2003)

Lee (2003) has divided the economic history of the last 60 years as belonging either to the Bretton Woods era, which he dates as lasting between 1950 and 1972, and the era of the Washington Consensus, which began in 1973, when the then President Richard Nixon abandoned the policy of fixed exchange rates. The Bretton Woods period, according to Lee, was associated with commitments to full employment, managed currencies and capital controls. By contrast, the period of the Washington Consensus has been associated with slower economic growth, more frequent recessions and high levels of unemployment:

> 'Most of the Bretton Woods era was characterised by recessions which averaged 1.1 years. A total of 94.4 per cent of these recessions were only 1 year in length. In overall terms, only 5.6 per cent of the Bretton Woods era was spent in recession. The post-Bretton Woods era (1973–2000) has witnessed recessions averaging 1.5 years . . . While 60 per cent of these recessions were 1 year in length, no fewer than

32.5 per cent were 2 years in length and the remainder 3 years or longer'. (Lee, 2003, p. 287)

'Economic events' do not stop. A number of issues raised in this book reflect a series of events that continue to shape and define the global landscape. The military side of the war in Iraq might be finished, but the future of Iraq is still being formed. Furthermore, the fall out from that War, including the relationships between the United Nations and the USA, between the Eurozone and the USA and between the UK and the EU, are also highly insecure and uncertain. All these factors will have major influences on the future prospects of the global economy. It seems therefore, that after the failure in Cancun of the WTO meeting (September 2003) it is a paradox to be writing about globalisation, when events point towards uni-lateralism, retreat and isolation, especially by some leading US politicians, who seem to be disenchanted by the world of rules which they helped to create in the aftermath of the Second World War. The War in Iraq and the criticisms of the UN by the USA have overspilled into questions about the future of the WTO – the institution set up to provide global governance on trade and economic integration. The recent WTO ruling on US steel tariffs, subsidies on agriculture and tax breaks on US export industries have been described as an unnecessary intervention by the USA. The decision by President Bush to take action against the EU on Genetically Modified Foods, which the US administration described as protectionist, will have a major impact on the WTO. These are the beginnings of a mood disenchantment with global integration, especially on the part of the USA, but also the EU, which also seems to show reluctance in phasing out agricultural subsidies. The refusal by the US government to recognise the Kyoto protocol on the environment and the initiative to create an International Criminal Court are seen as further examples of the global breakdown:

> 'In our present circumstances, those who dream of tearing down the institutions of global governance – imperfect though these institutions may be – would be wise to show a little more care and a lot less indifference to the implications of their demands . . .They are putting at stake a system of international interdependence and decision making through painstaking consensus building that has for the most part stood the test of time'. (Peter Sutherland, 'Reflections of a frustrated global governor', *The Financial Times*, 22 April 2003).

The widely held view is that the sharp fall in stock markets represent the weaknesses in economic fundamentals. The increases in stock market prices in the 1990s represented the over priced new technology sectors. The sharp declines in stock prices experienced in 1929 did not recover until 1960. Since the mid-1990s, many US savers have been persuaded to put their savings and their pensions into the stock market. The people who were due to retire within the next year have had to postpone their retirement:

'between 1996 and 2001 there was a rise of $1653 billion in corporate tangible assets, dwarfed by a rise in financial assets of $3603 billion. Almost $3000 billion of this increase is accounted for by 'goodwill' accrued in the deal making binge of the late 90s. For the most part, as the merger of AOL and Time Warner exemplified, the 'goodwill' has proved worthless and symptomatic of the long term trend in which organic growth of businesses was replaced by mergers and takeovers'. (Elliott, 'Bubble blowers run out of puff', *The Guardian*, 13 March 2003)

The concern for many economists is no longer the problem of inflation. The worry now is the problem of deflation – a world of falling prices and falling consumer demand, especially within the advanced economies. During the month of April 2003, the US Production Price Index for a series of consumer goods fell by 1.9 per cent. It was the sharpest fall in prices since 1949. The fear in the USA is that inflation is now too low. During 2002, a number of Eurozone countries experienced their lowest levels of growth in the post-war years. The economy in Germany grew by 0.4 per cent, Italy by 0.4 percent and France by 1.2 per cent. German unemployment continues to be stuck at around 5 million – an unemployment rate of 11.1 per cent. Despite a number of attempts by the governments of Japan to reflate the economy through lower interests rates, higher levels of public expenditure and lower taxation, the Japanese economy has continued to under-perform, with the economy only growing at around 1.4 per cent per annum during the last decade. This is in contrast to the previous two decades, when the Japanese economy was growing at an average of 4.5 per cent per annum. Equally, interest rates in the USA are at their lowest level, at 1.25 per cent. Falling stock prices can explain most of the decline in consumer optimism, as consumers looking at their savings portfolios feel they are less safe. There is increased uncertainty. However, in the context of contemporary globalisation failing consumer demand in the USA, Japan and Europe are also likely to influence the economies of India, Pakistan and China, since all these countries are increasingly geared to exporting cheaper consumer products to the industrialised West.

The tax reduction package of approximately US$550 billion over the next 10 years as outlined by President Bush in January 2003, was justified as being the necessary stimulus to the US economy. Meanwhile, critics of the package have pointed to worries about increases to the US budget deficits, which have been estimated to rise to between 1.5 and 3 per cent of GDP. These critics have also pointed out that over half the package will go to the top 0.01 per cent of income-earners who are likely to receive tax windfalls of US$98 000, compared with ordinary households, who are estimated to receive US$420 a year. The new millionaires are likely to save their tax windfalls, when what is needed is to direct a tax reduction to low income groups and to states that are likely to spend these reductions (Krugman, 2002).

> 'Millionaires would receive approximately $139 billion in tax cuts through 2013. This is essentially the same amount of tax cuts that would be received by the entire bottom 89 per cent of households combined. In 2003, there will be 184,000 million-aires comprising 0.1 per cent of households. Millionaires would receive average tax cuts of about $93,500 this year, far in excess of those received by other groups. The middle fifth of households would receive tax cuts averaging $217 in 2003'. (Shapiro, 2003)

This debate also reflects a debate that is taking place at the global level. In a world population of 6 billion, it is estimated that over half of that total are living in extreme poverty, trying to live on less than US$2/day. At present, under the EU Common Agriculture Policy – cows in Europe receive a subsidy of the equivalence of US$2/day (UNDP, 2001). It is estimated that the subsidy to agri-culture within the OECD totals some US$320 billion. The UN has asked the industrial countries to donate the equivalent of 1 day's subsidy to agriculture – an estimated US$10 billion – to the world HIV/AIDS programme. The USA at present donates 0.15 per cent of their GDP to overseas aid. It made a commit-ment to the UN to donate, along with other countries, 0.7 per cent of GDP to overseas development. Despite recent increases, the UK is now donating 0.35 per cent of GDP to overseas aid, against the commitment of 0.7 per cent.

One common theme to emerge since the early 1980s, has been the increase in income inequalities. With hindsight, it would seem that the period between 1950 and 1970 could be described as a Golden Age, while the period since the 1980s has been described as a return to the Gilded Age of the years in between the two World Wars (Krugman, 2002):

> 'For the America I grew up in – the America of the 1950s and 1960s – was a middle-class society, both in reality and in feel. The vast income and wealth inequalities of the Gilded Age had disappeared . . .Yes, of course, some wealthy businessmen and heirs to large fortunes lived far better than the average American. But, they weren't rich the way the robber barons who built mansions had been rich . . . The days when plutocrats were a force to be reckoned with in American society, economically or politically, seemed long past'. (Krugman, 2002, p. 1)

The twin commitments to full employment and expenditures on public provi-sion contributed to the reductions of income inequalities. Those in work expe-rienced secured employment and rising wages while expenditures on health, education, pensions and social security provided access to improved education and health services. The Golden Age also helped to bring prosperity to the world economy. Countries in Africa and South East Asia became part of that increased prosperity.

By contrast, economic and social policies, since the early 1980s, have put some of those achievements into reverse. In the context of rising inflation and unemployment, economic and political arguments shifted towards arguments towards 'less government'. The ascending paradigms of monetarism and supply side economics have replaced Keynesian economic and social policies. The new monetarist paradigm emphasised the need to reduce taxation and government spending, in order to reduce inflation and increase employment. In the global context, the policy prescriptions adopted by the IMF and World Bank also put an emphasis on their agenda of 'less government'. Governments seeking help from the IMF since the mid-1980s have had to subscribe to the policy prescriptions of reducing their social spending and reducing taxation. They had to show a commitment to privatisation and liberalisation of public sector utilities and financial markets. Mexico, Brazil, Argentina, Thailand and Indonesia came to the IMF with different economic problems and social contexts and yet met with common policy prescriptions, defined by the Washington Consensus (Stiglitz, 2002a):

> 'The IMFs policies, in part based on the outworn presumption that markets, by themselves, lead to efficient outcomes, failed to allow for desirable government interventions in the market, measures which can guide economic growth and make everyone better off . . . My research on information made me particularly attentive to the consequences of the lack of information. I was glad to see the emphasis during the global financial crisis in 1997–98 of the importance of transparency, but saddened by the hypocrisy that the institutions, the IMF and the US Treasury, which emphasized it in East Asia were among the least transparent that I had encountered in public life'. (Stiglitz, 2002a, p. xii)

In the global context, this combination of policies of tax reductions, reductions in social spending, privatisation and liberalisation has contributed to increases in income inequalities. While in 1950, the top 1 per cent of income earners had 15 times more income than the bottom 10 per cent, this had increased to 48 times in 2000. While average wages have increased by around 10 per cent in the last 30 years, the average compensation for the top 100 CEOs went from US$1.3 million – 39 times the pay of an average worker – to US$37.5 million – more than 1000 times the pay of the ordinary workers (Krugman, 2002). In the UK, as in the USA, the Gini coefficient has increased from 0.25 in 1979, to 0.35 in 2002 (IFS, 2003). Income inequalities in Britain, which had accelerated during the Thatcher years of 1979 to 1992, have again increased during the years of the Blair Government. Income inequalities in 2000 have returned to those of pre-First World War. The New Deal in between the two World Wars in the USA and the commitments to Beveridge and full employment in Britain after the Second World War, have been put into reverse (Krugman, 2002). Atkinson (2002) has shown that since 1984, the differences between market incomes and disposable incomes increased in the UK after the Thatcher Government shifted taxation towards VAT and reduced expenditure on social provision. The author's comparative studies of the USA, the EU and developing countries, have shown that while market income inequalities have increased, expenditure on social policies have continued to be the best mechanism by which to re-distribute income.

The shift in income inequalities is towards a very specific 0.01 per cent of earners.

> 'Most of the gains in the share of the top 10 per cent of taxpayers over the past 30 years were actually to the top 1 per cent rather than the next 9 per cent. In 1998 the top 1 per cent started at $230,000. In turn 60 per cent of the gains of the top 1 per cent went to the top 0.1 per cent those with incomes of more than $790,000. And almost half these gains went to a mere 13,000 taxpayers, the top 0,01 per cent who had an income of at least $3.6 million and an average income of $17 million'. (Krugman, 2002, p. 3)

This 0.01 per cent of the population is described as the new plutocracy – the new elites that are able to make major financial contributions to politicians and political parties, provide for the financing of professional lobbyists and academic think tanks that promote their interests in the making of public policy decisions:

> 'Not to put too fine a point on it: as the rich get richer, they can buy a lot of things besides goods and services. Money buys political influence, used cleverly, it also buys intellectual influence . . . economic policy caters to the interests of the elite, while public services for the population at large – above all, public education – are starved of resources' (Krugman, 2002, p. 11)

The concerns of this book are three-fold. First, there is the issue of defining and explaining the nature of contemporary globalisation and the questions of how and who is defining and shaping contemporary globalisation. Increasingly, globalisation has become conflated with markets' liberal prescriptions about governments and social policies. Globalisation has become connected with market liberal views on labour markets, flexibility, wages and rewards (Beck, 2000c). In the global context, the focus becomes the new individual, the individual as a consumer and as a seller of ideas. In the new global economy, there is no role for collective resistances or for collective social provision. It is a globalisation that advocates an anti politics:

> 'My core argument is that by the 1990s society has become more depoliticised, more lacking in the spirit of civic engagement and public obligation, than at any time in recent history with the vast majority of the population increasingly alienated from the political system that is commonly viewed as corrupt, authoritarian. . . .

This deterioration has occurred ironically and ominously, at a time when deepening social problems will surely require extensive and creative political intervention'. (Boggs, 2000, p. vii)

Politics is becoming increasingly connected with corrupted public spaces. The safety is to retreat into the private. It seems paradoxical that as economies become globalised at the same time, political decisions become more removed and more remote. The politics of globalisation encourages retreat. The pointing out of injustices or the arguments that life can be different is dismissed:

'You can read my chapters up to here and get damned depressed: the big boys, the bullies, the brutal always seem to win. When your daddy was a president and your brother, the governor of Florida, counts the ballots, you don't have to win an election to become president. They don't call the 'privileged' class for nothing. Corporate cash beats democracy every time. So it seems. But not always. It may seems like a battle of bears versus bunnies but sometimes we little critters stand on our hind legs, fight it out and win'. (Palast, 2002, p. 182)

This leads to the second point, which is the need to re-visit democracy and citizenship. Globalisation is at present shaping a democracy, which is minimalist and thin (Barber, 2000). Democracy is limited to elections and voting. Choosing a government every 4 years is deemed as democracy. Politicians, lobbyists, policy advocates and business interests occupy the public space. The idea of government of the people is relegated to the quiet audience sitting in the political auditorium. However, democracy is more than the 'is' of elections (Sartori, 1987). It is also the 'ought' of optimism and hope. Democracy reinforces the idea of political equality, accountability and transparency (Beetham, 1999). Globalisation can be made to be democratic in the sense that decisions are made to be transparent and accountable.

Finally, globalisation is at present defining and shaping a consumer view of citizenship. Our citizenship is satisfied in terms of material well being; the ability to buy and wear designer-labelled clothes is a way of creating a sense of belonging. However, citizenship is also connected with ideas of political rights, with ideas of vigilance, of being awkward, of seeking dialogue for change. Citizenship is also about belonging and membership of a political community. Belonging means access to public services, such as education and health. However, belonging also means an awareness of the other – the stranger, the migrant and the asylum seeker. Citizenship is therefore about a universal language of human rights and also an equal commitment to the idea of the right to be different.

Globalisation is at present being shaped and defined within the specific discourse of market liberalism. Implicitly, it is a discourse that encourages views about the limits of government and the retreat from the public space.

Resistances and protests are described as illegitimate or of belonging to some bygone age. Accordingly, the new globalisation is about the knowledge economy, where the power has shifted from the organisation to the individual. It is the individual with ideas who now has power, because ideas are used to sell products as concepts. In this brave new world, there is no need for trade unions, or collective struggles. However, the new globalisation is accompanied with increased income inequalities. The discourse of market liberalism and the policies of liberalisation and privatisation have contributed to the shaping of a new economic elite – a new plutocracy that buys influence into the political and intellectual process, which undermines the democratic process.

1. The politics of globalisation

DEFINING GLOBALISATION

The War in Iraq has contributed to increased global uncertainties. In the USA, the War in Iraq has been accompanied by a distinct change of mood among some senior politicians who advocate a break with multilateral agreements and argue against the interventions and regulations of the UN, NATO or the WTO. There is resistance to review the subsidies to US agriculture and steel making, instead the focus is put on unfair competition from China. In this context, it is therefore difficult to talk about globalisation without taking into account a changing mood about the commitments to the concept of a global economy. The commitment to free trade, the promise of cheaper goods and more choice for US consumers is being increasingly eclipsed by arguments that favour protection and tariffs and bilateral agreements rather than the multi-lateralism of the global economy.

In making the point that globalisation has to be located in an historical perspective Michie (2003) provided the following quote from Marx and Engels (1848) Communist Manifesto. Marx and Engels wrote:

> 'All old-established national industries have been destroyed or are daily being destroyed. They are dislodged by new industries, whose introduction becomes a life and death question for all nations, by industries that no longer work up indigenous raw material, but raw material drawn from the remotest zones, industries whose products are consumed not only at home, but in every quarter of the globe. In place of the old wants, satisfied by the production of the country, we have new wants, requiring for their satisfaction the products of distant lands. We have universal inter-dependence of nations. And as in material, so also in intellectual production'. (Michie, 2003, p. 4)

The concept of globalisation is a contestable concept. This chapter outlines the three interpretations of globalisation, including the hyper-globalists, the globalisation sceptics and those who argue the case of global transition (Michie, 2003). According to the hyper-globalists (Ohmae, 1990, 1995) globalisation is reinforcing a view of a borderless economy. Horsman and Marshall (1994) have linked globalisation with the concept of the borderless economy:

> 'Effortless communications across boundaries undermine the nation-state's control: increased mobility and the increased willingness of people to migrate, undermine

its cohesiveness. Business abhors borders and seeks to circumvent them. Information travels across borders and nation-states are hard pressed to control the flow . . . The nation-state is increasingly powerless to withstand these pressures'. (Horsman and Marshall, 1994, p. 60)

The nature of trading between and in between corporations and their impact on trade and employment contribute to the making of the borderless economy. The concept of the borderless economy points to the nature and influence of multinational corporations. Multinational corporations make decisions on foreign direct investment. Sub-contracting allows car manufacturers to import shock absorbers from Taiwan, electronics from Korea, engines from Germany while assembling the final model in Dagenham. Increasingly corporations are becoming weightless in the sense that relationship with production has become one step removed due to the practice of sub contracts. Corporations are no longer direct employers. Workers are hired through sub contracts and employment agencies.

World exports relative to world gross domestic product (GDP) increased from 7 per cent in 1950 to 23 per cent in 2000, while Foreign Direct Investment (FDI) has also grown from 4 per cent of world GDP in 1950 to over 19 per cent in 2000 (Epstein, 2003). By contrast, globalisation sceptics (Glyn and Sutcliffe, 1992; Hirst and Thompson, 1999) have argued the case that the process of globalisation has always been with us and that it would be misleading to argue that present globalisation represents something which is qualitatively different to what has happened in the past (Michie, 2003). According to Hirst and Thompson,

'Globalisation has a history. The 50 years between 1950–2000 are not remarkable when compared with the period 1850–1914 – in that period flows of merchandise trade, capital investment and labour migration were all comparable to or greater than those of today'. (Hirst and Thompson, 2003, p. 2)

Hirst and Thompson (1999) point to the concentration of Foreign Direct Investment (FDI) in the Triad of USA, the EU and Japan and to the argument that 80 per cent of Multi National Corporations (MNCs) are located within the borders of the advanced economies:

'Our point in assessing the significance of the internationalisation that has occurred is to argue that it is well short of dissolving distinct national economies in the major advanced industrial countries or of preventing the development of new forms of economic governance at the national and international levels'. (Hirst and Thompson, 1999, p. 4)

Hirst and Thompson have adopted a narrow approach to globalisation by concentrating too much on economic indicators including the inflows of foreign direct investment, exports, trade and the geographic location of MNCs. By contrast the arguments outlined in the following sections seek to analyse and evaluate the language of globalisation, the conflation of globalisation and ideas of markets, the acceptance of the logic of globalisation at the level of politics and the influence of business and the financial community in the defining and the shaping of globalisation. The IMF, World Bank and WTO are central to the making and shaping of globalisation by enforcing agreements on free trade, ensuring that developing countries adopt policies of liberalisation of financial markets and privatisation policies. Hirst and Thompson seem to discount the impact of liberalisation and privatisation on the global economy and the connections between mobile financial capital and the privatisation of assets. While acknowledging that MNCs are responsible for 80 per cent of all exports and internal trade and are also responsible for the employment of 60 per cent of the workforce in all of the advanced economies, Hirst and Thompson fail to make the connection between the interests of MNCs and their relationships with governments. Their only conclusion is that business needs governments and communities:

'The national economic bases from which most companies operate actually contribute to their economic efficiency and just in the sense of providing low cost costs infrastructure. Most firms are embedded in a distinct national culture of business that provides them with intangible but very real advantages. Companies benefit not just from national business cultures from nation-states and national communities as social organisations'. (Hirst and Thompson, 1999, p. 272)

However, globalisation is being continually defined and shaped by deliberate policy decisions. Both the EU and USA continue to make political decisions to subsidise their agriculture, while the USA had increased tariffs on steel imports. According to Hirst and Thompson (2003) the problem of globalisation is that there is not enough trade between nations. Economic globalisation is at present being negotiated between the triad of trading blocs, the USA, Japan and the Eurozone.

While it can readily be acknowledged that globalisation needs to be put into historical context; it is also important to argue the case that the nature of present day globalisation is qualitatively different and that it represents a new watershed and a break with past histories. Globalisation is not some end-state but needs to be understood as an ongoing process:

'In this sense, the boundaries between domestic matters and global affairs become increasingly fluid . . . Globalisation is not a singular condition, a linear process or a final end point of social change. Globalisation can thus be understood as involving a shift or transformation in the scale of human social organisation that extends the reach of power relations . . . It implies a world from which developments in one region can come to shape the life chances of communities in distant parts of the globe'. (Perraton, 2003, p. 38)

Critics of globalisation including Strange (1995, 1996) have argued that a major implication of globalisation has been the hollowing out of politics and the narrowing of political autonomy of the nation state. Strange (1995) has pointed to the concepts of the 'defective' and the 'hollowed' state arguing that governments have become victims of a shift in power in the relationships between globalisation, the ascendancy of neo-liberal ideas and the state:

> 'state authority has leaked away, upwards, sideways and downwards. In some matters, it seems even to have gone nowhere just evaporated. The realm of anarchy in society and economy has become more extensive as that of all kinds of authority has diminished'. (Strange, 1995, p. 56)

The histories of economic contexts confirm the view that the Industrial Revolutions of the nineteenth century were firmly located within the boundaries of the nation state. Equally, resistance, demands for change were located in factories, textile mills, coal mines and engineering workshops. Democracy, political parties, demands for political and social welfare reforms were equally located within the geographic spaces of the nation state. Economic, political and social contexts were located in a common public space. By contrast contemporary globalisation is increasingly defined in the cyber spaces of financial transactions, financial markets and the weightless corporation. The weightless corporation does not employ people directly but sub-contracts or outsources production to sub-contractors. There is therefore an ethic of disavowal of responsibility for employees or production.

The new globalisation is shaped and defined by financial flows between the major financial centres in New York, London and Tokyo, where the daily turnover has reached more than US$1500 billion, 97 per cent of which are speculative transactions, but which at the same time, make domestic macroeconomic policy wholly dependent on global market sentiments.

A direct result of these major financial flows has been for governments to construct macroeconomic policies that focus on monetary policy, the commitments to low inflation and low interest rates and policies that are transparent to the financial markets. Commitments to low inflation, an independent central bank, low government borrowing and low interests have become the acceptable policy prescriptions. This in turn has implications for the making of social policy but also restricts the autonomy of government in their attempts to use public sector deficits as a means to deal with problems of rising unemployment. Financial markets have become an important industry not just for the wealthy since they also carry the hopes and aspirations of millions of savers around the globe. Castells (1997) in his book *The Information Age* explained:

'observations and analyses seem to indicate that the new economy is organised around global networks of capital, management and information, whose access is technological know-how is at the roots of productivity and competitiveness. Business firms, and increasingly, organisations and institutions are organised in networks of variable geometry whose intertwining supersedes the traditional distinction between corporations and small business, cutting across sector and spreading along different geographic clusters of economic units. Accordingly the work process is increasingly individualised, labour is disaggregated in its performance and reintegrated in its outcome through a multiplicity of interconnected tasks in different sites ushering in a new division of labour bases on the attributes and capacities of each workers rather than the organisation of the task'. (Castells, 1996, p. 27)

The globalised networks reinforce the view of a corporate liberalism (Craypo and Wilkinson, 2003) of organised business interests including the expansion of Transnational Corporations (TNCs) and their influence on world trade and financial flows. Lee (2003) estimates that in 2000 there were 60 000 TNCs and about 800 000 overseas affiliates responsible for approximately US$1.3 trillion of global FDI. According to this approach the new globalisation is about the understanding of networks and the ability of those with influence to switch and transform these networks. Finance networks are switched to become global financial networks; business networks also become media networks. The result is an increasing discrepancy between those who make networks and those who work in these networks, a widening gulf between a politics, which continues to be located in geographic spaces and the borderless global economy of switches and networks that operate outside the limits of national governments:

'Deregulated markets, short-term corporate performance objectives and overriding shareholder and executive claims on resources non dominate the US productive system. These, together with the increasing globalisation of this system, encourages corporations to cut pay and worsen conditions of works – moves that workers are increasingly powerless to resist. When dominant firms drive down labor costs in the way, others are forced to follow suit . . . Within the global productive system, US employers increasingly resort to importing low-wage labor and emigrant jobs have become the hallmark of US labor relations and production strategies'. (Craypo and Wilkinson, 2003, p. 284)

The 'weightless' corporations involved in outsourcing and sub-contracting of production create pressures on wages, demand for de-regulation of labour markets and reducing labour costs. The continuous movements in the production chain to cheaper markets, regions and countries result in continuing labour shake-outs in manufacturing and their impact on industrial communities:

'The garment industry provides an example of the changes in manufacturing. Starting in the 1960s and '70s European and US companies outsourced to countries like Hong Kong, Singapore and South Korea. As wage levels and labour conditions improved in these countries, they moved to Indonesia, the Philippines, Thailand and Mexico. More recently production has shifted to Bangladesh, Central America, Vietnam and China. The effects of competition and the complicated patterns of contracting and sub-contracting means that there is intense pressure on prices and therefore on wages and hours'. (Brosman, 2003, p. 107)

During the 100 years from 1870 to 1970, hourly wages for US workers increased by 2 per cent per year in real terms. This meant that over the lives of two generations, income doubled for each generation and they experienced continued employment and higher incomes. This could be described as the 'golden age'. By contrast, over the last three decades, wages have actually stagnated and for the bottom 10 per cent of earners, wages have actually declined by around 10 per cent. These trends have parallels in Europe (Atkinson, 2002). The increases in wage inequalities have been blamed on the decline in the overall demand for low-skilled workers in the advanced economies while at the same there has been an increase in the demand for high-skilled labour especially in the new technology sectors. The low-skilled jobs in the advanced economies have been displaced by those in the developing economies. The globalised world is described as having a dual labour market of a core of skilled workers in the advanced economies and the periphery workers who are now located in the developing economies:

> 'developed countries have become increasingly open to trade with developing countries. The latter are rich in unskilled labour, it is argued, they can supply goods where production is 'unskilled-intensive' such as T-shirts from China, at a fraction of developed countries costs. Hence unskilled wages in developed countries must fall'. (CEPR, 1999, p. 5)

Atkinson (2002) has described this as the 'Transatlantic Consensus' to explain wage inequalities as being inevitable and located in market forces:

> 'I take issue with the assertion that rising inequality is inevitable. It may in fact turn out that the 21st century sees rising inequality but this is not inescapable. . . . The Transatlantic Consensus can be described as a triumph of 'supply and demand'. A major economic phenomenon is explained by nothing more than the supply and demand curves which are learned by a first year student'. (Atkinson, 2002, pp. 25 and 36)

It is difficult to put the blame on developing countries for the loss of jobs in the advanced economies since the import penetration from the South only makes up some 1.5 per cent of the GDP for the OECD countries, while the advanced economies still have a surplus in trade with the developing countries. Atkinson (2002) has criticised the assumption that present inequalities are market driven, arguing instead that the rise in income inequalities has been due to the major increases of incomes for the top 10 per cent of earners especially the top 1 per cent:

> 'Empirically the (Transatlantic) Consensus does not readily explain the tilt in the upper part of the distribution (to understand which a simple unskilled/skilled distinction does not seem adequate). The alternative approach described here argues that the relation between skill and pay reflects social conventions, where adherence to the pay norm is endogenously determined . . . If, as I am suggesting widening wage dispersion in part arises on account of shifting norms, the same shift may have educed the willingness of governments to redistribute'. (Atkinson, 2002, p. 44)

Atkinson is implicitly arguing in favour of an endogenous approach to explain inequalities that include the policies of government that contribute to inequality. It is also an argument that seeks to explore the influence of changing expectations and about social norms on pay and wage dispersions of what is acceptable. Phelps Brown's (1977) studies pointed to ideas of wage league tables based on expectations and relativities between skilled and unskilled workers and wage differentials which were decided mainly through wage bargaining and the willingness of government to use social policies and public expenditure to redistribute income. The shift towards greater income inequalities since the 1980s can be explained in terms of changing expectations, that is of workers accepting the idea that markets decide wages and therefore passively accepting wider wage inequalities. The issue is to ask what has contributed to this shift in expectations and social norms that make larger wage inequalities more acceptable in 2003 than they were during the 1960s and the 1970s?

In the following sections, it shall be argued that the increased inequalities can be explained in terms of how present globalisation is being defined and shaped, so that it generates a discourse of globalised inevitability – a model of globalisation that puts an emphasis on inevitability and that argues that the need is for less government intervention and to allow for markets to work.

POLICY CHOICES AND GLOBALISATION

The WTO Development Round that met in Doha (Qatar) in November 2002 emphasised the need to address the problems of more access to markets by developing countries. Recent decisions by the USA and EU trade negotiators would suggest that the agreements on the production of generic drugs and also on subsidies on steel and agriculture have now been reversed. The lack of an agreement in Cancun in 2003 can be partly explained by the advanced economies to make the concessions that were promised at Doha. Monbiot

(2003) has pointed out that major interest groups in the USA and Europe have had a major influence on the undermining of the WTO agreements reached in Qatar:

> 'On Wednesday (19 February 2003) the US took a decisive step towards the destruction of the World Trade Organisation. The WTO current trade round collapsed in Seattle in 1999 because the poor nations perceived that it offered them nothing while granting new rights to the rich world' corporations. It was re launched in Qatar in 2001 because those nations were promised two concessions; they could override the patents on expensive drugs and import cheaper copies when public health was threatened and they could expect a major reduction in the rich world's agricultural subsidies. At the WTO meeting in Geneva last week, the US flatly reneged on both promises'. (Monbiot, 2003)

The Pharmaceutical Industries in the USA made major financial contributions to President Bush election campaigns in 2000 and 2002. In the Presidential Election campaign the top Pharmaceutical Companies including Research and Manufacturers of America, Pfizer Incorporated and Eli Lilly contributed some US$27 million of which 20 million went to the Republican Party, while in 2002 Congressional and Senate Election they contributed US$25 million dollars with 18 million going to the Republican Party (Centre for Responsive Politics January 2003 (www.opensecrets.org). According to Monbiot (2003):

> 'The Republicans victory in the mid-term elections last November was secured with the help of $60 m from America's big drug firms. This appears to have been a straightforward deal; we will buy the elections for you if you abandon the concession you made in Qatar. The agri-business lobbies in both the US and Europe appear to have been almost as successful, the poor nations have been forced to discuss a draft document which effectively permits the rich world to continue dumping its subsidised products in their markets'.

Donors make donations to politicians and political parties because they can gain access to the policy process. The bigger the donors the more likely they are to be invited to give advice to government on policy making thus making sure that their concerns are addressed when policy is made. In providing testimony to the McCain-Feingold campaign on finance reform Alan K Simpson who served as a US senator explained how donations and donors were corrupting democracy in the USA:

> 'I served as a United States Senator from Wyoming from 1979 to 1997 . . . I have seen firsthand how the current campaign financing system prostitutes ideas and ideals, demeans democracy and debases debate. When I was in the Senate, the Republican leadership would take us off to Capitol Hill give a list of heavy hitters and tell us to make phone calls to get more money from donors . . . The more money one donates the higher-level players he or she has access to . . . At these events it was not uncommon for the donors to mention certain legislation that affected them.

Large donors of both hard and soft money receive special treatment . . . Too often members' first thought is not what is right or what they believe, but how it will affect fundraising'. (Declaration of Alan K Simpson in the United States District Court of Columbia Civil Action No 02-0582 and quoted in the *Washington Post* 4 December 2002, p. A23)

At present there seem to be two forms of resistance to globalisation. First, there is the resistance located within the politics of modernity. According to this approach globalisation is located within the universal discourse of market liberalism and therefore argues that resistance equally requires a discourse that seeks to provide a universal response to globalisation. The concepts of universal rights and global citizenship represent examples of resistance. In addition, resistance is often defined in terms of social democratic politics, social movements located in the workplace, including trade unions and voluntary organisations working alongside the poor such as OXFAM, CAFOD and SHELTER. According to this approach, the aim is to create greater political transparency and political accountability while seeking to separate the interests of governments from those of business. The concern is still the role of government in the delivery of universal social policies that seek to address issues of poverty and income inequalities.

By contrast, the politics of postmodernity recognises problems of increased ideas of fragmentation diversity and pluralism. Within a post modern framework resistance has to reflect that plurality. Coalitions that seek to reform the globalised economy are different to those that seek to address the globalised environment. Equally global oppressions of women and the exclusion of migrants require different coalitions and different resistance. The World Social Forum that met in Port Allegre in 2002 and 2003 introduced the concept of 'Boca Fundamentalism' and the resistance to the fundamentalism mouth that includes religious fundamentalism and a neo-market liberal fundamentalism. The coalition against fundamentalism implies the recognition of pluralities and differences and thus allowing for a thousand social movements to bloom. Protests against evictions, cuts in electricity and protests against privatisation that are at present seeking to shape politics in South Africa (Desai, 2002) and Argentina (Klein, 2003) reflect the multiplicity of resistances to globalisation.

'The precondition for human emancipation is seen to be the recovery of the voices of the oppressed. Oppression, occurring in myriad tangible forms, is understood as an effect of different configurations of power and of discursive regulation. It is seen as the outcome of both exploitative economic relations and cultural practices, which construct oppressive subject positions and identities'. (O'Brien and Penna, 1998, p. 55)

The differences between modern and postmodern forms of resistance are reflected in discussions of citizenship and democracy. While the cornerstone of citizenship continues to be the universal discourse of human rights there is equally the claim of citizenship as a form of resistance to multiple forms of oppressions and therefore claims to citizenship that are founded in demands around identity and the right to be different, the nature of gender oppressions, the nature of racism and different forms of exclusion. Citizenship in this context is best understood as a process of dialogue of being awkward and continually challenging what is. The challenge of democracy is the attempt to break with oligarchy and the rule of the plutocracy and to create a democracy of public spaces, committed to involvement and participation. The resistances to the globalised economy depend on the continuing re-definitions of citizenship and democracy. Resistance however is never easy:

> 'To fall out of step with one's tribe; to step beyond it into a world that is larger mentally but smaller numerically – if alienation or dissidence is not your habitual or gratifying posture – is a complex, difficult process. It is hard to defy the wisdom of the tribe, the wisdom that values the lives of its members above all others. It will always be unpopular – it will always be deemed unpatriotic – to say that the lives of the members of the other tribe are as valuable as one's own. It is easier to give one's allegiance to those we know, to those we see, to those with whom we are embedded, to those with whom we share – as we may – a community of fear'. (Susan Sonntag, *The Guardian* 26 April, 2003)

To resist is therefore to have the courage to step out of line to join a minority against the majority. To be part of a minority can be isolating, the resistance of Rachel Corrie in her yellow jacket who was killed in Rafah while standing as a human shield alongside Palestinians trying to stop the bulldozing of housing by the Israeli Army confirms the moral courage but also the isolation of those who resist against the powers of government. Peace activists who stood up for peace in New York and London have been labelled as being unpatriotic. Anti globalisation protesters have been described as the enemies of the poor.

GLOBAL CHALLENGES – DIFFERENT RESPONSES

The Coalition of Immokalee Workers (CIW) represents the interests of tomato pickers in South Florida. They are mainly immigrants from Mexico and earn about US$7500 a year, which is well below the US poverty line of US$14 500. The coalition has recently embarked on a campaign of consumer boycotts targeted at the Taco Bell restaurants. Taco Bell belongs to the Tricon Group, which has some 30 000 food outlets worldwide and an estimated turnover of US$1.2 billion. The CIW is seeking to highlight the plight of tomato pickers who are mainly migrants from Mexico. Taco Bell and their sub contractors have refused to meet with CIW. The response of Taco Bell has been to disavow responsibility. The tomato pickers are on sub-contracts to the Six Ls Packing Company:

'Our position hasn't changed in regards to this. We think it's unfortunate they're targeting our restaurant. We're being targeted because we buy tomatoes from Six Ls. But this is a labour dispute between Six Ls and its employees . . . If they'd spend the same amount of time targeting Six Ls as they do targeting us, they might be able to get something accomplished'. (Laurie Gannon, Taco Bell Spokeswoman, Human Rights Watch, 11 February, 2002)

The members of CIW have no rights to belong to trade unions, to overtime pay, sick or holiday pay. Recently the Sheriff of Collier in Tampa, Florida, has asked for the right of access to immigration data. While the Sheriff points out that this is due to the 11 September attacks, the CIW has protested that innocent Mexican workers and protest leaders will be targeted as illegal immigrants. Most of the tomato workers have no regular visas or immigration papers. Surveillance will result in a chilling effect on the protest movement.

The Governments of Ecuador and Brazil are involved in debt re-scheduling negotiations with the IMF and the World Bank. Both countries need to finance their public debt. The IMF letters of intent have as usual provided the one cap fits all policy of privatisation, de-regulation and liberalisation of financial markets as conditions of economic restructuring. The Government in Ecuador has given the go ahead for the construction of a new oil pipeline that will run from the Amazon delta to the Pacific coast in the hope that the oil revenues will be used to deal with the problems of external debts. The US$1 billion pipeline is owned by Agip, Repsol and Occidental Petroleum and is financed by German Bankers. In Brazil, the Cardoso Government decision to phase out subsidies to agriculture displaced some 4 million small farmers, which in turn resulted in increased land centralisation and higher income inequalities. In Brazil, 1 per cent of the population owns 46 per cent of the land. While the bottom 50 per cent of the population received 10 per cent of the total income, the top 10 per cent received 50 per cent of income. Brazil has the highest levels of poverty, with 22 per cent of a total population of 170 million being defined as below the poverty line. In 1999, the High Court in Brasilia declared that the Monsanto Corporation could not introduce GM Crops unless they had provided the impact studies of genetic crops. Defending the principle of precaution, Judge Prudente stated:

'The questions raised by genetic engineering will not be resolved by the laws of the market alone, rather they will be resolved by the rigorous respect to the legislation which protects life, as established by our laws and Constitution'. (Judge Prudente as quoted in *Public Citizen*, September 1999)

In the meantime, the Movement for Landless People (MST) has been involved in direct action taking over unused land, which is legal under the Constitution of Brazil – and resettling small farmers. It is estimated that some 1169 people have lost their lives in the landless campaigns.

Unocal Corporation, a US Construction company is at present accused by Burmese workers in the Supreme Court of California of aiding and abetting the Military in Burma in human rights abuses and have used the Burmese military to protect the construction of the Yadana Oil pipeline. The Burmese military are also accused of forced evictions and using forced labour. In a hearing in September 2000, the US Supreme concluded that there was:

> 'Evidence demonstrating that before joining the Yadana pipeline project, Unocal knew that the military had a record of committing human rights abuses and that the project had hired the military to provide security for the project, a military that forced villagers to work and entire villages to relocate for the benefit of the project'. (http://www.laborrights.org)

In the case of Unocal, university students in the USA have continued to campaign for their universities to remove their share holdings in an attempt to bring pressures on the multinational corporation. It is estimated that the Universities of Wisconsin, Minnesota, Washington and Virginia have divested some US$3 million worth of shares from Unocal since the student protests started. In the case of Virginia, seven Nobel Prize Winners, including Desmond Tutu, joined the student campaign. Since the campaign for better human rights started in Burma, some 28 large corporations have now moved out including Sara Lee, Wal-Mart, IKEA, Tommy Hilfinger and Spiegel. Student protests have also put pressures on Universities to stop buying student clothing from Nike.

These three case studies highlight the nature of contemporary globalisation. Governments in developing countries seeking to attract FDI are reluctant to introduce minimum labour standards or minimum wages as they come under pressure from the IMF to liberalise and reform their labour markets. Second, there are the challenges of MNCs and the weightless corporations involved in sub-contracting, not directly involved in employment and disavowing responsibility for working conditions and wages and pointing instead to the blurred relationships between government officials and corporate interests. Nike sub-contracts sports shoes and shirts to contractors in China, Indonesia, Thailand, Mexico and Cambodia. In each of these countries, the contractors have dismissed and harassed workers who have tried to organise independent trade unions, yet Nike is a signatory of the UN Global Compact, which is founded on principles derived from the Universal Declaration of Human Rights and the ILO Convention on rights of workers. Article 23 of the Declaration of Human Rights points to the rights of people to organise into free and independent trade unions. Despite the commitments made by Nike, there is little evidence of enforcement of good practice by Nike on their sub-contractors to recognise trade unions. The CIW campaign is seeking to copy campaigns that were launched against Nike and Gap by Anti Sweatshops campaigns by student groups on US Campuses and the AFL CIO Campaign 'Working Families for Global Justice'.

Contemporary globalisation is at present being defined by globalised financial flows and liberalised financial markets, by international financial institutions including the IMF and the World Bank and by large corporations and their ability to access policy making at the global and national levels. Total world trade in goods and services has increased from 19 per cent of trade GDP in 1990 to 29 per cent of trade GDP in 2001 (Perraton, 2003). The ratio of merchandise exports in relation to GDP in Europe growing from 9 per cent in 1950, to 21 per cent in 1973, to 30 per cent in 1992. Furthermore, for the 15 EU countries, trade increased at 5.1 per cent per annum between 1970 and 1999, while the GDP during the same period grew at 2.4 per cent per annum. The top 100 MNCs are responsible for over 13 per cent of the world's FDI (World Investment Report, WIR, 2002). The UNCTAD Report (UNCTAD, 2001) confirms that the top 100 MNCs increased their FDI in developing countries from 17.1 per cent of total FDI in 1990 to 21.4 per cent in 2001. China accounts for about half of the developing countries' FDI. Developing countries share of world exports in manufactured goods increased from 17 per cent to 27 per cent during the same decade. Finally, UNCTAD estimated that the top 100 MNCs invested 41.7 per cent of their assets overseas, had 49 per cent of their sales overseas and 46 of their employed workforce overseas (UNCTAD, 2001, pp. 94, 256).

Developed and developing countries have become involved in a bidding process to reduce taxations and review regulations in order to attract FDI. The OECD Report (OECD, 1998) concluded:

'Globalisation and the increased mobility of capital has also promoted the development of capital and financial markets and has encouraged countries to reduce tax barriers to capital flows resulting in harmful preferential tax regimes . . . undermining the integrity and fairness of tax structures discouraging compliance by all taxpayers, reshaping the desired level and mix of taxes and public spending'. (OECD, 1998, p. 14)

However, it would be misleading to argue the case that it is the top 100 or top 200 MNCs that are dictating the shape of globalisation. Using the measure of total sales estimates have shown that the turnover of the top 200 MNCs have increased from 24.2 of world product in 1982 rising to 31.2 per cent in 1995. This estimate has in turn led to the view that top 200 MNCs control over one third of the world' production. However, Sutcliffe and Glyn (2003) have pointed out that such figures include double counting, since the sales include products and materials an MNC would have brought from other suppliers. A better estimate according to the authors would be to measure the MNCs contribution to the national product or by value added to sales which means taking out the value of imports. According to these estimates Glyn and Sutcliffe come to the conclusion that the contribution of the top MNCs to World Product is closer to 10 per cent rather than the 10 per cent which is often quoted:

> 'Applying this to the estimates of the importance of the 200 largest firms we would arrive at the conclusion that they accounted for about 10 per cent or less of World Product instead of the frequently heard estimate of nearly one third. This figure is broadly consistent with the estimate that in the year 2000 the 100 largest firms ranked by values of foreign assets worth about $6,300 billion which amounts to a little under 10 per cent of the world's capital stock'. (UNCTAD, 2002)

The World Investment Report (WIR, 2002) also pointed out during the period 1991–1999 approximately 94 per cent of policy changes favoured foreign investors with many countries moving towards increased liberalisation in financial markets and de-regulation. In the meantime MNCs have become increasingly involved in providing 'advice' to governments on policies of de-regulation of labour markets, de-regulation of rules on conditions of work, the environment and health and safety. Business organisations including the International Chamber of Commerce (ICC) and Business Action for Sustainable Development (BASD) have argued the case for more self-regulation and for the retreat of government. In the meantime the IMF and the World Bank have continued to exert external pressure on governments in developing countries to remove trade barriers, de-regulate financial markets and privatise government utilities. In addition there are pressures for governments to reduce their social spending.

Over the past two decades, global income inequalities have continued to accelerate. This has been mainly because the global economy has actually slowed down in the last 20 years. While between 1960 and 1980 *per capita* income in Latin America increased by 75 per cent, between 1980 and 2000, income *per capita* increased by only 7 per cent. In Africa, during the period 1960 to 1980, incomes increased by 36 per cent, while in the last 20 years, incomes have actually fallen by 15 per cent. In addition, there have been reversals in public policies including subsidies on food, water and cooking oils that had previously contributed to the reduction in income inequalities especially for the poorest countries. Privatisation policies and the phasing out of subsidies on essentials have affected the lives of the poor (Reddy and Pogge, 2003). However, the increases in income inequalities have not been a common experience for all countries. For example, in the advanced economies of the OECD area, while Britain, the USA and New Zealand have experienced the largest increases in inequality, Sweden and Germany have experienced slower moves towards inequality. Cornia and Kiiski (2001) have found that in a study of 73 countries, which account for four-fifths of the world population, 48 of these countries, experienced greater inequalities between 1980 and 2000. The determinants of that inequality have been mainly attributed to deliberate political decisions including government macro economic policies such as interest rates, the decision to de-regulate labour markets and the liberalisation of financial markets:

> 'The main source of the recent inequality is to be found in the adoption of Washington Consensus-type policies – liberalisation-globalisation often have adverse effect . . . Unless the orthodox economic paradigm evolves in a distributionally favourable manner in the years ahead, in several countries current inequality trends are likely to depress growth and prevent the achievement of the growth and poverty alleviation targets. Commitments to pro poor growth requires therefore that alternative structural, macroeconomic, distributive and external policies with a more favourable distributive impact'. (Cornia and Kiiski, 2001, p. 37)

Politics still make a difference. Growth in income inequality is not inevitable. The role of government is still central in responding to income inequalities. Government policy can mitigate income inequalities and they can equally contribute to make inequalities wider. There is always political choice provided there is the political will. Taxation policies on higher incomes, corporation tax, inheritance taxes, capital gains tax can all be utilised to generate pro poor policies to finance public health, sanitation, clean water, primary education provision and primary healthcare policies that can have an impact on world illiteracy, infant mortality rates and illness. Equally, privatisation policies on water and other utilities have often resulted in government corruption, high profits for private contractors and higher prices for the poor. Universal social welfare, public provision in health, education and social security are still judged to be the best mechanisms that mitigate against growing income inequalities:

> 'the Chilean experience also indicates that 'policy matters'. Income distribution did improve massively with the progressive distributional policies of the first democratic government (1989–1993) even though this government continued the process of greater integration of the Chilean economy into the world economy, however when the second democratic government (1993–1999) formed by the same political coalition abandoned these progressive distributional policies, the ratio of decile 10 to 1 returned to where Pinochet left it in 1989'. (Palma, 2003, p. 78)

The influence of the IMF, the World Bank, large business organisation and present government policies are defining and shaping present forms of globalisation. There are at present major problems of political accountability, transparency and involvement. Oligarchy, plutocracy, the narrowing of political spaces, political elites, bureaucracy and experts are at present defining the nature of the democratic process. Globalised struggles, cosmopolitan connections and global citizens are still emerging as forms of new resistances. Peace campaigners who go to Gaza, Iraq, Kosovo and work alongside people with no voice but provide testimonies of their sufferings reflect these new globalised connections.

AIMS OF THE BOOK

The central theme of this book is to make connections between citizenship, democracy and globalisation. It is to move away from an abstracted debate about the nature of globalisation but instead to understand the processes that are influencing peoples lived experiences. There is therefore an urgent need to understand the nature of contemporary globalisation and to ask whether present forms of globalisation are qualitatively different to what happened in other periods. There is a need to explain the politics, economics, social and cultural forms of globalisation. In the EU, all member states are committed to reduce their deficits to below 3 per cent of GDP, which in turn restricts national government's ability to finance public investment and respond to problems of unemployment. Recent attempts by the German and French Governments to increases the levels of their budget deficits and respond to problems of unemployment reflect the tensions between national interests and the monetary policy framework established by the European Central Bank (ECB). In the meantime, European economic convergence has been defined as being essential to Europe's response to the challenges of globalisation. Global agreements on trade in services (GATS) and intellectual property rights (TRIPS) threaten the abilities of government in developing countries to purchase generic medicines while small farmers in Thailand and India are unable to buy patented seeds. There is also concern as to the impact of new global cultures of music, TV broadcasting and designer labelled clothing. Protests and forms of resistance are at present fragmented. Resistance at present involves a multiplicity of concerns including environmental degradation, labour standards and the right of workers to join independent trade unions, to the undermining of the local economy by TNCs.

At present (2003) globalisation represents a series of paradoxes. While on the one hand there is an increasing concern that contemporary economic globalisation lacks accountability and transparency there is at the same a retreat from the public space. Furthermore, there is a tendency on behalf of governments to encourage passivity and retreat. Stories of sleaze, financial contributions to policy makers, the influence lobbyists and policy captured by business interests have a corrosive influence on the public spaces and politics. They result in an anti-politics, distrust for politicians, which in turn result in declining electoral turnouts.

Globalisation is at present being defined as some exogenous variable, something, which is beyond the control of people and that there is no alternative. Neo-liberal policy prescriptions on privatisation, de-regulation and liberalisation of financial markets are resulting in high water charges in Ghana, higher electricity prices in Mexico and an increase in the number of people experiencing severe poverty and deprivation. Dealing with globalisation becomes a policy response. There is, therefore, an implicit denial that globalisation is being defined by political choices. The implication of such a denial is that there is a lack of any attempt to evaluate who is doing the defining, who benefits and who loses. In a recent article, Kofi Annan the UN Secretary General stated:

> 'Personally I do not believe that the poor are victims of globalisation. Their problem is not that they are included in the global market but, in most cases, they are excluded from it. It is not enough to say, though it is true that without business the poor would have no hope of escaping their poverty . . . They (business) are the ones, who, as the leading taxpayers, can argue most persuasively for debt relief and official assistance to developing countries'. (Kofi Annan, 'The bottom line is hope', *The Financial Times*, 4 February 2002)

According to the UN Secretary General, the 1.2 billion people living on less than US$1 a day are victims of a lack of globalisation. There is no attempt to evaluate the impact of globalisation on world poverty when there is ample evidence that poverty and income inequalities have increased on a global level since the mid-1980s. Instead, the statement represents an acceptance of the view that whatever jobs multinationals create these should be always seen as a benefit. Children and women sewing clothing for Gap or Nike are better off than those who are seeking subsistence engaged in farm labour. The poor have no hope without business. It is only business that creates wealth. There is no possibility that business needs workers and they do not exist without labour. Business needs to make goods and to sell those goods to somebody. Those who invest their pensions in business do so in the belief that that business will continue to succeed, which in turn depends on making things and selling them.

Democracy puts the focus on the public space including issues of participation and involvement. One major political concern of present globalisation is the influence of TNCs on the democratic process. In the recent Enron case, there was ample evidence that the energy company contributed some US$6 million in political donations to both the Democrat and the Republican Parties and also that Enron executives have been involved in the making of the Bush administration Energy policy. Enron has favoured a policy of greater de-regulation of the energy business. There is therefore a clear and urgent need to avoid policy capture by business interests. In this context, policy making needs to be more transparent. This requires the commitment by governments and their civil servants to properly record all meetings between politicians, officials and those who are co-opted to give policy advice. This policy advice should then be open to public scrutiny. The concept of anonymity in policy making is at present being using to make the argument against accountability. Ministers and civil servants argue that open and honest advice will not be given to ministers if there is a threat of scrutiny that overhangs the decision making process. Advisers need to be protected. However, there is equally the strong case that increased transparency would reduce suspicion and increase the credibility of policy makers. Furthermore, the commitments to involvement and participation where all groups have a chance to make their views in policy formulation, are also essential pillars in making democracy.

Both the World Bank and the IMF have, since the mid-1990s, committed themselves to the concept of participation. The IMF Poverty Reduction and Growth Facilities (PRGF) and the World Bank Poverty Reduction Strategy Papers (PRSPs) have outlined arguments for governments to make commitments to greater openness to communities in submitting strategies for debt rescheduling and debt relief programmes:

> 'Participation is the process through which stakeholders influence and share control over priority setting, policy making, resource allocation and access to public goods and services. Participation is the key to long-term sustainability and leverage. We must never stop reminding ourselves that it is up to the government and its people to decide what their priorities should be. We should never stop reminding ourselves that we cannot and should not impose development by fiat from above'. (President James Wolfenson's Opening Address, The World Bank Report, 1998).

By contrast, Christian Aid (2003) and other aid organisations have pointed out that the hopes of the PRSPs have fallen well short of the promises. Studies have confirmed that very often participation has been limited to consultation very often after Governments and their officials had agreed the policy outcomes with the World Bank and the IMF so that groups involved in the participation process complained that their involvement was to rubber stamp' PRSPs, while at the same time their domestic governments could argue the case that the policy was the product of involvement:

> 'At first PRSPs appeared to be an exciting new development. Non-Government groups in many countries were being offered the opportunity to influence policy making . . . The reality of participation processes in PRSPs thus far has clearly not lived to the optimistic rhetoric. In the majority of countries participation by civil society in the PRSPs has as yet been limited and superficial'. (Christian Aid, The Limits of Participation, April 2003)

There is an inherent conflict between the PRSPs submitted to the World Bank and the conditions outlined by the IMF. Poverty Reduction Strategies have to be made compatible with the IMF conditions on macro economy issues. Priority is therefore given to macro economic policy including the reductions in government expenditure commitments even when this policy is likely to impact the lives of the poor. Aid agencies and voluntary organisations working alongside the poor are therefore very often being asked to endorse policies, which are most likely to impact the groups they represent. However, in discussions on PRSPS, IMF conditions are kept separate from these discussions. Policies on interest rates and privatisation are also very often part of the strategy developed by Governments with the IMF. The IMF economic model is presented as a given during PRSPs discussions. The PRSPs becomes a form of tinkering around the edges. Macro economic targets and strategies are not open for discussion.

Participation as defined by the World Bank and the IMF is not working. Consultation with civil society groups has only been consultation. Civil society is not involved in policy formulation. Governments make policy and then community groups are consulted and asked to endorse the policy. This approach gives legitimacy to governments in presenting their programmes to the IMF and the World Bank. Equally both institutions can also argue that policies are emerging from below and not being imposed by the Bank and IMF:

> 'The problem with having rules of the game dictated by the IMF – and thus by the financial community – is not just a question of values (though that is important) but also a question of ideology. The financial community's view of the world predominates – even when there is little evidence in its support. Ideology enables IMF officials not only to ignore the absence of benefits but also to overlook the evidence of the huge costs imposed on countries'. (Stiglitz, 2002a, p. 7)

Citizenship is a potential form of universal discourse in that it allows people to connect as global citizens demanding equal treatment and therefore the claims for citizenship implicitly provides the potential to politicise globalisation. At present, globalisation is being de-politicised in the sense that it is defined as an event and therefore empty of ideology. There is a denial that public spaces are increasing by politicians, bureaucrats, large multinational corporations, financial communities professional trade lawyers and their ability to lobby and articulate their demands. There is unequal access to the policy process. International organisations including the World Bank, the IMF and the WTO are one step removed from democratic accountability and transparency.

The Campaigns by tomato pickers, in Florida, resistance to the oil pipelines in Ecuador and Burma, trade union action against Benetton in South Africa and Mozambique and riots against water privatisation in Ghana and electricity privatisation in Mexico, all provide examples of global connections. The consumer boycott against Apartheid in South Africa, Taco Bell Restaurants, Shell Oil and Nike confirm these new forms of global awareness, global connections and new forms of resistance.

The decline of manufacturing and industrial communities in Europe have over the last 20 years contributed to the steady decline in trade union membership, since the new jobs in the service sector have been more individualised and therefore more difficult to unionise. During the years 1964 to 1973, the EU unemployment rate was around 2.7 per cent of the working population. By contrast, for the decade 1990 to 1999 the EU unemployment rate increased to 10.3 per cent of the working population. The decline in trade union membership throughout Europe reflects the decline of jobs in manufacturing. For the period 1980 to 1990, trade union membership in France declined from 19 to 12 per cent of the workforce; in Italy from 50 to 39 per cent; the Netherlands from 40 to 26 per cent and for the UK from 50 to 32 per cent (Singh and Zammit, 2003). The implication is that the shared and collectivist experiences of industrial communities have been replaced by increased fragmentation, diversity and plurality. The consequence has been the increased retreat into private lives where forms of traditional collective resistance and protest seem to be a thing of the past. Advocates for the New Economy have celebrated the new found individual and the new economy of technology, major productivity gains and the knowledge economy where power had shifted from the owners of organisations to the new owners of knowledge:

> 'It is a quantum leap because the essence of the economy has changed. What matters isn't how or where goods are manufactured, but the definitions of the 'product' that is bought and sold. It is the idea that sells, not the material built into its construction. Human capital counts for far more than anything else in giving companies a competitive edge . . . Even if we were talking about selling cars, a good deal of what is sold is in style and image'. (Giddens, 2001, p. 24)

However, it is never the end of history. The ongoing fire fighters dispute in the UK, together with recent elections of trade union leaders that are willing to oppose the UK Government, would confirm that trade unions continue to be an important agency for collective resistance.

In the New economy, production and manufacturing are no longer important. Materials and production techniques tend to be similar in the production of cars or the making of clothing. What is important is the attempt to make the difference – to make the product unique – to give it meaning, image and identity, whether it is a pair of jeans, a perfume, running shoes or T-shirt. It is the making of images that make Gap, Nike and Starbucks. The invention of the computer is equated with the inventions of steam, railways, electricity and the telegraph. The new uses and productivity gains of the computer are still in their infancy.

In the new economic landscape, work and employment become individualised experiences. It is the new risk society of Beck (2000c) and the doing-it-your-self (DIY) biography (Sennet, 2000), of people selling their knowledge and the ownership of human capital. It is the political economy of uncertainty (Bauman, 2000) because jobs are no longer for life; where there are no longer attachments of identity between work and the individual. Unemployment and world poverty are a continuing reminder of the political economy of uncertainty:

> 'The political economy of uncertainty is good for business. It makes bulky, unwieldy and costly instruments of discipline redundant, replacing them not so much with the self-control of the trained, drilled and disciplined objects, as with the inability of privatised and endemically insecure individuals to act in a concerted way, an inability made all the more profound by their disbelief that any such action may be effective and that private grievances may be recast into collective issues'. (Bauman, 2000, p. 174)

The discourses of globalisation are at present occupied by neutral concepts that make specific connections in the uses of the languages of 'governability', 'employability', 'underclass' and 'social exclusion', to name but a few. These words are given legitimacy and have become the norm – the language that helps to define and shape the world of options and possibilities. In the context of these discourses therefore, unemployment is explained as being 'structural' and therefore there is a need for more reform of labour markets, which very often means accepting lower wage settlements, reform of pension funds and social security payments. The labour market is presented as something neutral governed by scientific laws and supply and demand and, as in the science of gravity, these natural laws cannot be changed. People have to observe these laws and accept the necessary reforms if they are to succeed. By contrast, the discourses of class, capitalism, exploitation resistances and struggle, are perceived to be obsolete or part of the language of class warfare and class envy. The new paradigm is defined by neo-liberal ideas of markets enterprise, competition and choice. In markets, there are no classes, but individuals with different talents, attributes and entitlements. In the world of markets there is no exploitation. Inequality is explained in terms of market inequality. The idea of family connections, histories and inheritance access, are denied. There is no room for collective struggles, but the self-reliance and self-help of individuals. Flexibility and employability emphasise the need of workers to become more flexible, which means their readiness to work longer hours, which undermines trade union resistance. Underclass and exclusion are preferred to the concept of class. The opposite of excluded is to become included. The policy of social inclusion must therefore focus on the nature of exclusion including access to employment, being a single parent and access to education. Social concerns become individualised issues.

> 'The effects of the new global vulgate are so powerful and pernicious that it is employed not only by partisans of neo-liberalism but by cultural producers and left-ist militants, that, for the most part still consider themselves progressives'. (P. Bourdieu, quoted from *World Social Forum*, 2001)

However, globalisation is not neutral and neither does it represent the end of history or the end of ideology. Present globalisation does not represent the triumph of market economies and the end of history, nor the end of politics. It does not exist as an event. It is a social construct being defined and shaped by specific economic interests and political decisions. There are vested interests giving shape and defining globalisation, which means that present forms of globalisation are neither inevitable nor immutable. UNCTAD (2002) estimates for total foreign investment in 2000 was approximately US$1.3 trillion, 80 per cent of which has been directed to the advanced economies. In the year 2000 for example, the USA received US$280 billion in FDI, the UK US$120 billion and Germany US$170 billion. By contrast, Africa, for example, received US$9 billion, while China has been the major beneficiary from FDI during the last decade. So while globalisation has been connected with the concept of the mobility of capital, it would seem that that capital mobility is still mainly confined to the Triad of Europe, Asia and the USA. In terms of world trade, only about 1 per cent of the GDP is exported from Africa, despite the fact that Africa has 10 per cent of the world's population.

The OECD countries continue to provide large subsidies to agriculture, which, in 2001, totalled some US$300 billion. The policy resulted in the over production of food and thus depressed prices, which in turn have displaced small farmers in the developing countries. UNCTAD (2000) estimated that two-thirds of the world's poor lived in rural areas. While world trade in manufactured goods increased by 5.8 per cent between 1985 and 2000, agriculture expanded by only 1.5 per cent during the same period. World trade in agriculture has actually declined for developing countries from 40 per cent of world trade in 1961 to 23 per cent in 2000. In the meantime, agricultural exports for the OECD area have increased at 3.5 per a year. UNCTAD (2000) concluded that the protection of agriculture was costing the developing countries about US$19.8 billion every year and that if developed countries phased out their subsidies, incomes *per capita* would increase by US$1 a day in South East Asia, US$6 in Africa and US$30 in Latin America. Keeping in mind that around 2.8 billion people are at present living on less than US$2 a day, a policy of reduced subsidies would make a major contribution to alleviate world poverty.

The question then arises why there seems to be the lack of political will to phase out subsidies in the advanced economies. In the EU, subsidies in the form of Common Agriculture Policy make up half the total of the whole EU budget of US$80 billion. There is a high political risk for the French and German Governments to agree major changes in the subsidy structure. In the USA, the subsidy to agriculture is about US$22 billion, two-thirds of which goes to the 10 largest companies. Subsidies in the OECD area have distorted agriculture in favour of intensive farming, chemicals and phosphates and animal feeds. In the world of globalised agriculture, markets are being constructed and shaped in a specific way. Small farmers in the developing countries are displaced by new the agri business directed to growing soybeans and intensive chicken farming, while native seeds are replaced by new hybrids, which small farmers cannot afford.

The political conflicts of interest are not just the developed economies of the North and the developing economies of the South. While it is true that the world's poor are in the developing countries, it is also true that in the advanced economies, there are also major problems of poverty. Studies of income inequalities confirm that both the USA and the UK have the highest levels of income inequalities in the advanced economies. Economic growth and prosperity since the mid-1980s have not benefited low income groups. There are a number of studies that now confirm the view that economic prosperity in the advanced economies has not resulted in the alleviation of poverty. In the USA, during the period 1979 to 1998, the lowest 20 per cent of income groups received increases of 0.4 per cent per annum, while the middle 20 per cent received 5.8 per cent and 22 per cent for the top 10 per cent. Equally in the developing countries an elite group of business interests, politicians, civil servants and military personnel have benefited from policies of de-regulation and liberalisation of trade. Those involved in the importing of goods and in financial services have done very well. Small farmers and workers in cities have seen their living standards decline.

The emphasis on the politics of globalisation is connected with the question of who benefits from the present forms of globalisation. In Port Allegre and the state of Rio Grande Do Sol, the councils have committed themselves to the concept of the participatory Budget involving local communities to decide spending priorities on health, education and agriculture. In 1999 some 199,000 people participated in the budget process. In 2000 over 280,000 people took part,

'We managed to give citizens a wake-up call and encourage them to take important matters of participation in their own hands. They not only indicate where public money is spent but also to make the money which is all of ours is going to the right place' (Solomon, 2001, p. 7).

The Zapatistas in Mexico have also shown that their form of resistance demanding autonomy and greater democracy can gain popular support. In Europe that has been an increase in industrial militancy since 2002, with more workers joining trade unions and what seems to be the beginnings of politicisation of the public space. The significance of these events cannot be exaggerated but they do represent the first signs of resistances to the prevailing paradigms of the new individualism, consumer society, greater privatism and the retreat from the public spaces. The protests against the war in Iraq also confirm that there is an increased willingness to be involved in the public spaces. It has been estimated that around 15 million people around the world have continued to protest against the war. New Groups, including school children, have become involved in the protest movement.

So what is the nature of present globalisation? Historically, countries have developed differently. Economies reflect different cultures, politics and institutions. While the UK industrial revolution reflected decentralised decision, economic development in Germany and Japan was more state directed. More recently, Germany developed corporatist structures to deal with economic management, Japan had MITI (Ministry of International Trade) while the UK and the USA have been more committed to a limited state and a more market liberal to economic policy making. However, rather than concentrating on differences it might be argued that the globalisation can be understood by asking how it is that countries having started so differently are increasingly looking so similar? This means that instead of assuming there is convergence and then looking for differences, that it would be better to contribute to the understanding of globalisation by starting from the view that points out the historical differences and then to start to look for similarities:

> 'Given that the seeds of a capitalist mode of production grew to maturity in very different gardens and evolved under the hand, as it were, of very different gardeners of very different state laws, constitutions and policies, would the forces of global structural change allow these differences to persist indefinitely. Or, alternatively, would the common logic of integrated world markets for more and more goods and services slowly but surely modify the old differences and bring national versions of capitalist production and exchange ever closer to a common patter? My bet was and is, on the latter'. (George, 1988, p. 182)

OUTLINE OF THE BOOK

Chapters 2, 3 and 4 seek to evaluate the dual concepts of citizenship and democracy and how citizenship and democracy need to be connected with economic globalisation. The first two Chapters deal with the concept of citizenship. In Chapter 2, the emphasis is on citizenship and points out that citizenship is a contestable concept and there are competing attempts at defining citizenship. In the aftermath of Enron, major US Corporations have committed themselves to the concept of Corporate Citizenship, arguing a case for greater openness to stakeholders and greater transparency. It shall be argued that there are five discourses on citizenship and that each of these discourses are being shaped and influenced by competing views of globalisation. These include 'public citizen' and the commitment to the ethics of participation and involvement. Public citizen is therefore concerned with transparency and accountability of Governments, but also the accountability of international organisations including the World Bank, the IMF and the WTO. These organisations can be made more transparent by committing themselves to the ethic of democracy, to open meetings and to greater surveillance of policy documents. It means increasing the capacity and expertise of poor countries to sustain trade negotiations at the WTO. It also means that the recent UN Global Compact needs to allow for verification, monitoring and evaluation. At present, the Compact is purely voluntary and signatories are asked to post on the UN website case studies of good practice. The emphasis is for signatories of the UN Compact to show their explicit commitments to freedom of association and trade union rights and impose on their subcontractors forms of good practice. The 'Independent Citizen' discourse derives from the language of market liberalism and the commitment to individualism and free markets. In the context of globalisation the independent citizen is served by the commitment of governments to free trade and economic growth. Companies should seek self-regulation. Politics is minimised. Governments are described as being corrupt. It is better for individuals to seek to private self-interest. The 'Entitled Citizen Discourse' is connected to the ideas of 'social citizen' and the role of health, education and social security policies in dealing with problems of income distribution and inequality. The argument here is that the commitment to growth alone does not result in greater social justice. There is a need for government to intervene to create social citizenship. Universal access to health and education allows individuals to explore their potential and where income is no longer the barrier to entry to health care or education provision. The 'Dutiful Communitarian Citizen' is located within the view of belonging and seeking identity through the nation state and community through tradition, institutions and authority. Citizenship is therefore about loyalty and about rights and obligations. In the context of globalisation this discourse reflects a 'conservative response' in the sense that economic globalisation is embraced while social globalisation including dealing with the challenges of immigration and universal discourses on human rights are described as being a form of intervention that undermine the sovereignty of the nation state. Finally, there is the discourse of consumer citizen and the view that citizenship is connected with consumer society and that globalisation allows for the development of a universal consumer culture.

In Chapter 3, the focus shifts to defining citizenship as resistance. Connecting citizenship with resistance makes the idea of citizenship an agency for social change and therefore shifts the focus for seeing citizenship as a set of clothing of political, social or economic rights. It is no longer a relationship between the individual and the state but rather the process of 'self-constituted' individual and the emphasis on personal identity. In the context of resistance therefore citizenship is connected with dialogue, the right to disagree and to be treated as different. In the context of the self-constituted individual, citizenship includes the recognition that differences are healthy, there is no attempt to create some false consensus but that the commitment to be awkward, to protest, to be aware of injustice, to live with change, to be vigilante, to discover and not accept the world as it is are essential elements of citizenship.

Citizenship is about resistance to oppressions, to make the connections with others, to become cosmopolitan to be everywhere and nowhere, not to be anchored by geographical space but to aim for global citizenship. Totalitarian regimes involved in slave labour and the denial of trade union rights are brought to account. Trans National Companies (TNCs) are asked to leave countries that violate human rights. Companies doing business in these countries are taken to court for aiding and abetting in the violation of human rights. There is no disavowal of responsibility. Companies ensure that sub-contractors observe codes of conduct, make a commitment to the Universal Declaration of Human Rights and the ILO Convention on workers rights.

Chapter 4 shifts the focus to ideas of democracy reflects on Sartori's (Sartori, 1987) thesis that democracy is both the 'is' of present realities of democracy and the 'ought' of the hopes and optimism of the potential of democracy. Discussions of democracy often reflect on the present limits of democracy but also provide hopes and optimism for democracy. The aim therefore is continually to create democracy in a context that is continually changing. Challenges to present democracy point to the need to deal with the continuing problems of oligarchy, plutocracy and the rule by the few. Greater transparency and accountability are the pillars of democracy. The present corrosion of the political process undermines democracy. The experiments in Brazil with Participatory Democratic Budgets show that people are willing to become involved if the process shows there is genuine involvement and that involvement means influence on the formulation of policy rather than being consulted about policy.

Chapters 5, 6, 7 and 8 deal with the nature of globalisation and examine the arguments as to whether present forms of globalisation are qualitatively different. The arguments presented here are that contemporary globalisation is creating a new individualism and focusses on the idea that people create their own individual biographies. Increasingly, issues such as unemployment, health care, old age pensions, etc. are defined as individual risks that require individual decisions rather than public issues which in turn require collectivist responses. In the context of the new globalisation the ideology of neo-liberalism is characterised by a decline in collective provision and a retreat from the public space. Recent studies of UK industrial militancy and days lost through industrial disputes show that the year 2000 recorded the lowest number of disputes since 1864. Paradoxically, income inequalities have increased for most of the OECD countries since the 1980s. Contrasts for the period 1950 to 1970 and 1980 to 2000 continue to confirm that economic growth was stronger for all countries in the aftermath of the Second World War, when compared with the late 1980s. In Latin American Countries and the Caribbean, the income per person grew by 75 per cent during the period 1960 to 1980, compared with a 7 per cent increase between 1980 and 2000. In Sub-Saharan Africa, the income per person grew by 34 per cent in the first period and has declined by 15 per cent since the 1980s. In the financial crisis of 1997, incomes in Thailand shrank by 10 per cent and in Indonesia by 13.7 per cent.

Chapter 7 seeks to make the connections between the causes and consequences of globalisation and asks who are the winners and who are the losers from present forms of globalisation? Income inequalities have widened since the 1980s, mainly because of changes in macro economic policy. De-regulation of labour markets, demands for flexibility and decline in trade union membership have resulted in falling wages. Insecurity in employment and the fear that companies will shift to other regions have resulted in lower wage demands. Furthermore, austerity budgets, reductions in public expenditure and high interest rates have also shifted the distribution of income in favour of higher incomes groups. Groups dependent on government for social security and state pensions have experienced falling incomes. Those with high levels of savings have experienced increases in income. Privatisation policy has benefited those who were able to buy shares in major companies at low prices. Financial de-regulation helps those with foreign currency holders.

Resistance takes different shapes and forms. Trade union history in Britain is different to that of France and Germany. Equally, social democratic parties in Sweden, the USA and Australia have different ideologies and different histories. Resistance develops within the specific histories, cultures and collective memories of communities. At present, resistances to globalism tend to be fragmented. Coalitions of trade unions, charity organisations, women's organisations, politicians, student groups, environmental and human rights groups reflect the different layers of globalisation. Modern technology creates the potentials for sharing information, for making connections of issues and to create the possibilities of cosmopolitan virtues and global citizenship.

An elite of financial interests, business, military experts, political leaders, bureaucracies, trade lawyers and experts at present defines contemporary globalisation. The global spaces need to be reclaimed which means that governance needs to be re-politicised. The retreat of the new individual to the quietism of home, work, family life and consumer society allows globalisation to be defined from the top. There is a need for a globalisation from the bottom that shows there are alternatives to the globalism of market liberalism and the Washington Consensus. The potential to develop alternatives requires spaces that provide for plural forms of resistance.

2. Democracy, citizenship and globalisation

INTRODUCTION

The following chapters seek to make connections between, on the one hand, the ideals and principles that underpin the commitments to democracy and citizenship and, on the other, the nature and shape of present forms of globalisation. One major criticism of globalisation at present is the absence of political accountability and transparency. The recently 'failed' World Trade Organization (WTO) talks in Cancun reflected the inability of developing countries to influence the WTO free trade agenda, which most developing countries argue, represent the interests of the EU and the USA.

One major example has been the continuing failure of the USA and Europe to make concessions on the subsidies to agriculture, which are seen as being to the detriment of the interests of small farmers in developing countries. The USA continues to provide a subsidy of US$4 billion to 25 000 cotton growers in the USA, while asking cotton growers in Africa to re-structure and diversify their industry. Two major globalising institutions including the International Monetary Fund (IMF) and the World Bank are controlled by the countries that make the major financial contributions. Stiglitz (2002a) pointed to the idea of the Washington Consensus to try and describe the shared values and ethics of the financial community including the IMF, the World Bank and the WTO and how they seek to impose a 'one size fits all policy' of globalisation on developing countries.

While the WTO claims to be a democratic institution, where each of the 146 counties have an equal vote, there is no attempt to evaluate the informal networks of trade lawyers, lobbyists and politicians that define and shape the intricate negotiations that take place in Geneva – and where developing countries are excluded in joining these networks because of their lack of trained personnel and the financial resources to locate people in Geneva. Present globalisation is criticised for not fulfilling the commitments to free trade and open markets, with governments in the more powerful economies providing subsidies to agriculture and manufacturing, while imposing high tariffs on imports from developing countries. While in previous globalisation epochs governments in the USA, the UK, Germany, France, Japan and South East Asia were ready to use tariffs subsidies and protectionist measures to protect and develop their infant industries, the emerging countries are put under pressure to liberalise their economies. Furthermore, countries in the advanced economies borrowed, stole or imported new technologies to help in their development. Under rules developed by specific interests in finance and pharmaceuticals developing countries have to observe intellectual property rights that even prohibit them from importing or developing generic drugs to combat diseases such as malaria and aids despite the high number of fatalities. Under GATS (General Agreement on Trade and Services), countries will be asked to liberalise and open up to competition government procurement, the provision of health and education services, communications and transport and also water and electricity.

The focus here is to re-visit core principles that underpin the commitments to citizenship and democracy and then to ask how these principles can be connected to the process of economic globalisation. The language of rights: universal human rights, social and economic rights, the rights of traditional and indigenous communities that see their cultures and means for economic sustainability undermined by globalisation and the rights of future generations to a healthy environment, give different layers of meanings to the commitments for democracy and citizenship.

The attacks on New York and Washington in September 2001 and the mobilisation for war in Afghanistan and Iraq have made the claims on democracy and citizenship that much more relevant. In times of war, there is often a desire to construct a collective will against an external threat, a tendency to erode dissenting voices and to increasingly justify the language of the 'us' and 'them'. Those who dissent and criticise become part of the 'them', accused of being unpatriotic and unreliable. Those who dissent are frozen out from expressing their opinions because of the fear of surveillance. In the immediate aftermath of 11 September 2001, Martin Wolff very quickly took the opportunity to make the connections between terrorism and the anti-globalisation movements:

> 'The time for paying more than passing attention to the anti-globalisers antics is over. Certainly those anti-globalisers who wish to be taken seriously will have to divorce themselves from the violent anarchists most of whom already blame this evil crime on US promotion of global capitalism. The protesters were always wrong in their opposition to trade liberalisation. Now is the time for policy makers worldwide to show they reject such dangerous obscurantism'. (Martin Wolff, *The Financial Times*, 14 September 2001)

The significance of that article was two-fold. First, there was the implicit attempt to connect protest with violence and therefore anti-globalisation protests with the potential terrorist violence. The public spaces had to be redefined, politicians and the public interest had to be made secure. Campaigners and protesters were put on the defensive as they came increasingly under pressure to divorce themselves from violence. One major consequence of September 11 was the increased limits on the 'public space' and provided for greater legitimacy of government to define surveillance and the imprisonment of suspects. The chilling effect has contributed to the further retreat into private lives, a shift from the 'public space' to increased 'quietism'.

The War in Iraq has compressed even further the spaces for dissent. Those who were anti-war have been marginalised, as it has become conflated with the arguments about the war on terrorism. The enemy within now includes the asylum seekers, Muslims and those with darker shades of skin. Recent surveys confirm increased discrimination and racism against Muslims. Relatives from Muslim countries trying to visit families in Britain have had their applications increasingly rejected by Immigration officers:

> 'The backlash from the war on terror on Britain's non-white population is growing. Applications to visit relatives in Britain from countries with large Muslim populations are twice as likely to be turned down than they were just over a year ago. The biggest rises in refusals were for applications from the Middle East and the Indian sub-continent. In Tehran, refusals jumped 188 per cent ... In Delhi refusals increased 105 per cent during the same period. Refusals of applications from families in Calcutta rose by 443 per cent and in Dhaka more than 60 per cent. Significantly refusals of applications from Nicosia, a gateway between Europe and the Muslim world rose by 1,300 per cent last year'. (R. Prasad 'Muslims need not apply', *The Guardian* 16 April 2003)

Within the American Infantry now serving in Iraq, Iraqis are described as 'ragheads'. September 11 has generated increased racism towards Arabs and Muslims – they are now to be treated with suspicion. The demand is for increased surveillance, for more power to the state and less accountability on human rights. In the war against terror, democracy and the public space become less important. This allows increased surveillance and creates fewer demands on government to be transparent and accountable.

By contrast, arguments for plurality, diversity of opinion and calls for caution against the powers of the nation state are increasingly perceived as luxuries when governments are sending young people into war. In the clamour, the possibility of an alternative view is defined as a criticism, a voice against, a danger and therefore someone who needs to be watched. The idea of citizenship, the need to be involved in the public space and the claim for greater transparency become less important when the priority of Government is the safety of citizens against an external threat.

The challenges of globalisation involve arguments about the re-distribution of income, dealing with new risks of environmental degradation, the use of forced labour, the exploitation of migrant workers and different forms of social exclusion. These elements are defined as being essential to the making of the global citizen. The universal provision of health, education and social security are connected with arguments for a sense of belonging confirming social, political and civil rights. Only when poverty, marginalisation and unemployment overspill from the private arena of the home into public arenas and become recognised collective experiences of a community, that these privatised issues become demands and claims on the public space, on government and democracy. People elect government to create climates of accountability and transparency, which often means not allowing economic power to influence the political space and therefore blur the relationships between business interests and government.

DEMOCRACY AND CITIZENSHIP

Democracy can be described as being contestable terrain occupied by competing definitions:

> 'Anyone attempting to give a defensible definition of democracy has to address a number of problems. Once is the sheer number and diversity of meanings attached to the term over the last half century or so, of which the following is but a small selection: rule of the people, rule of the people's representatives, rule of the people's party, majority rule, dictatorship of the proletariat, maximum political participation, elite competition for the popular vote, multi-partyism, political and social pluralism, equal citizens rights, civil and political liberties, a free society, a civil society a free market economy, whatever we do in the UK (or USA or wherever) the 'end of history', all things bright and beautiful'. (Beetham, 1999, p. 1)

Elections and the secret ballot are not sufficient to guarantee democracy. The media and the presence of multinational corporations play a significant role in shaping opinions. It is estimated that the top 100 donors in the USA had donated over US$1 billion between 1989 and 2002, to the two major political parties. Elections generate income for media owners with political parties issue campaigns buying airtime and advertising to get their messages across. Interest groups with access to financial resources advertise their concerns in their attempts to influence public perceptions. During the UK election campaign of May 2001, both the Labour Party and the Conservative Party spent some £25 million over a 4-week period. Likewise in the Presidential elections of November 2000, Republicans and Democrats received some US$400 million in campaign contributions from business and individual donors. In the congressional elections of 2002, congressmen spent some US$900 000, while their challengers, by contrast, raised about US$198 000. In the senate elections, the average spent by an incumbent senator was US$6 million in contrast to the challenger, who spent about US$1 million dollars. During the 2002 cycle elections, 98 per cent of congressmen were re-elected, while 85 per cent of senators also held their seats. The Bipartisan Campaign Reform Act (BCRA) of 2001 initiated by Senators McCain (Republican) and Feingold (Democrat) represented an attempt to stop federal politicians and office holders from soliciting soft money from large donors and also to stop the financing of 'ad campaigns':

'resentment about the unfair influence of money in politics is simmering just below the surface of American society. So far, by and large, that resentment has contributed to disaffection, cynicism, disenchantment and a lack of voting. But three times in the 1990s, conservative demagogues have used it to spark their campaigns – Ross Perot in 1992, Jesse Ventura in 1998 and McCain this year. Liberal and left wing leaders – including Ralph Nader in his presidential campaign – have so far been unable to use it to similar advantage. But there's no telling what might happen in the event of a serious economic or political crisis. With or without McCain-Feingold, a corrupt and corrupting system will continue apace'. (*Public Citizen*, June 2001)

Financial contributions to political parties and individuals are essential to sustain successful election campaigns. The problem is that those who make the financial contribution also seek to influence policy making. Soft money is used to advertise single-issue campaigns that are not specifically tied to political parties, yet these campaigns have a major impact on the policy process. So democracy is now tied with campaign financing, the financing of elections and political parties. Corruption of the public spaces leads to disillusionment with the political process and also contributes to the decay of democracy.

Struggles for Democracy

The histories of citizenship, democracy and economic change are histories of struggles and resistances against, oligarchy, the Old Corruption of the state, the church and landed gentry. Struggles for democracy from the Peasants Revolt of 1381 to the Chartists in the 1840s took shape in different contexts and met different resistances. The Peasants Revolt came about among other upheavals including the Black Death, shortages of labour, the challenges to feudal society and the landed aristocracy. The Chartists Movement sought alliances with industrialists and the radical elements in the Tory and Whig Parties in a political context of Parliament and established political parties. Equally the history of citizenship is of claims on governments, denials and resistances. The late EP Thompson (1976) the English historian of early working class struggles to establish rights wrote:

'Whenever the pressure of the rulers were relaxed men came from the petty workshops or the weavers' hamlets and asserted their claims. They were told that they
had no rights but they knew that they were born free. The Yeomanry rode down their
meeting and the right of public meetings was gained. The pamphleteers were gaoled
and from gaols they edited pamphlets. The trade unionists were imprisoned and they
were attended to prison by processions with bands and union banners'. (Thompson,
1976, p. 914)

History is made of a series of claims and counter arguments for more accountable government, elections, a wide franchise, secret ballots, political equality
all of which represent both the is and the ought of democracy. Struggles for a
wider franchise represented both the claim for the equal right to vote but also
the optimism associated with the ideals of democracy and the potential to
bring about social change. How democracy operates and how it should operate often becomes blurred. Securing a wide franchise in 1884 was not the end
of the struggle, but the beginning of a campaign for women to seek the equal
right to vote. The birth of the Labour Party eventually resulted in Labour
Governments, with hopes of building a New Jerusalem, but also resulted in
broken promises, disenchantments and feelings of betrayal. Lessons are
learned, while changing contexts create new challenges, new elites and new
forms of resistance. Demands for freedom of information, the strengthening of
Parliament, greater transparency and the attempt to regain the public spaces,
confirm and reflect challenges and struggles in defining and re-defining
democracy:

'Men and women seek to be empowered against the daily threats and risks that their
natural and social world imposes on them. Against the arbitrariness of the slings and
arrows of outrageous fortune, they wish to establish the regularities of the rule of
law . . . Citizenship or the power to make the laws under which we live can really
only exist where all individuals have equal decision-making power. This can be
expressed most clearly through each person having a vote of equal value'.
(Davidson, 2000, p. 110)

The struggles for democracy are defined by the two principles of popular
control and political equality, that is, of people claiming the right to elect the
government that make decisions that effect and impact their lives. A further
common theme is the optimism of the possibility of change, transparency
and accountability of politicians and decision makers, securing individual
rights and collectivist resistances that put limit on the influences of global
corporations:

'If we examine the main theorizing about democracy from the ancient Greeks
onwards, if we pay attention to what those claiming to struggle for democracy have
been struggling for, in particular if we notice what the opponents of democracy
throughout the ages have objected to about it, then a relatively clear and consistent

set of ideas emerges. Democracy is a political concept, concerning the collectively binding decisions about the rules and policies of a group, association or society. It claims that such decision-making should be and it is realised to the extent that such decision making actually is, subject to the control of all members of the collectivity considered as equals'. (Beetham, 1999, p. 154)

In present democracies, it is the political elite that occupy the political stage, while populations are asked to be the quiet audience in the auditorium. It is this political elite that defines and shapes globalisation. Political differences are reduced to incremental change, of additional spending or a reduction in taxation and marginal reform in health or education provision. The logic of the globalised economy is taken as given, with governments increasingly encouraging a language of passivity and inevitability of embracing the market as the only possible economic agenda to agree to less intervention, less rigidities and less regulation.

Public policy decisions and non-decisions make a difference to people's quality of life. Early struggles to limit the numbers of hours people worked, child labour, sanitation, public health and, much later, pensions, unemployment insurance, education and healthcare provision all represented outcomes of struggles and resistances. Despite visions of the new economy of freelancers, web-page designers and ownership of dot.com companies, for the foreseeable future the majority of people will continue to depend on wages and paid employment. In addition, modern economies are still vulnerable to economic cycles of growth and recessions and will need the state to intervene in the regulation of the conditions of work, pensions and unemployment. Furthermore, the legitimacy of government and democracy depends on the notion that governments can bring about changes in people's lived experiences. The argument that the state is purely a handmaiden, a night watchman, is defined by a liberal ideology that favours those with power and influence who seek minimal state intervention. For most of the time, the majority looks to the elected government for protection against the unfettered market. Democracy still does have meaning within the boundaries of the nation state. Frequent elections, a wide franchise and a secret ballot make it possible to change a government and provides the means for the accountability of the day-to-day policy making process.

Democracy and Anti Politics

Contemporary social, economic and political landscapes provide growing evidence of increased fragmentation and diversities of interests. This is not to imply that there existed some previous golden age. History is a catalogue of conflicting interests, fragmentation and change. Agrarian communities were layered between different interests as much as industrial communities. In villages, farmers, craftsmen, the local clergy and doctors had different interests to farm labourers. Equally, in steel making communities, corner shops, local small businesses and the self-employed shared very little with the experiences of plant closures and redundant steel workers. When miners, steel workers and textile workers lost their jobs, many local industries and business survived.

NEW FRAGMENTATIONS AND NEW POLITICS

Present democracy is equated with increased individualism, while the age of Modernity is associated with Industrial communities defined by the rhymes and rhythms of work with shared collectivist experiences that enabled the developments in social provision, by contrast, Postmodernity is associated with the new individualism. Life is described as a do-it-yourself (DIY) biography. The 'cult of personality and the celebrity is defined by the new rich including the new aristocracy of film stars, football players, golfers and tennis players seeking rewards that most people can only dream of. According to the Congressional Budget Office Report (May 2001), incomes for the top 1 per cent of earners increased by US$414,000 during the period 1979–1997, while for the bottom 20 per cent, incomes actually fell by US$100. CEOs claiming to be part of the cult of celebrity seek rewards for their star quality, while politicians and higher civil servants also aim to be included in the circle of the new rich. The race is for the promised world of the famous, writing a sensational biography, memoirs, becoming a star, being in the public eye seeking sponsors and advertising. The cult of the celebrity legitimises who occupies the public spaces. The celebrity needs to be in the news to ensure popularity because being in the public eye signals the price of being famous and in the public space. The cult of the celebrity creates a new industry of numerous magazines, television shows, filmmakers, art critics, celebrity analysts and celebrity promoters. The new aristocracy seeks to make money, to feel safe from the hoards that live in the city and are left behind. The new rich live behind steel gates, new surveillance technology and safety buffer zones of forests and woodlands that surround their estates. The condition of the global stage is made up of strife and conflict on council estates in landscapes of hopelessness, of global protesters of famine and child labour. For many, in between these worlds very little changes, as they seek to live with secure employment in a world that is less secure and they still look to elected government to deal with corruption and to provide a framework of social provision.

In this fragmented context, politics becomes unstable. Politicians find themselves having to appeal to different audiences where the concept of common wealth is not present. The Metropolitan elite has already embraced the new globalisation, living with uncertainty and new risks. They seek loose political ties because of their cosmopolitan experiences. Migrants and asylum seekers are not a problem, they are part of the globalised world. By contrast, the young unemployed, the new disenfranchised who can read about the incomes of the new stars, perceive only collusion by a political elite that no longer reflects their needs. Politicians in the American South make claims that the Confederate flag is a symbol of history and tradition, while Afro-Americans judge that same flag as a symbol of slavery and oppression. In France, the right to be different is argued for by those on the politics of the left and right, while segregation and discrimination are given great legitimacy. Romas in the Czech republic are classed as black and Gypsies lose their rights in Slovakia. Politics increasingly becomes neutral and devoid of ideologies and principles since the political agenda for change becomes narrower and the options much more influenced by connections with wider international institutions rather than the needs of the local.

Postmodernity, as mood points to a world that rejects the big explanation and instead puts into place the analysis of discourses as the means of understanding power relations. The analysis of discourses is layered (archaeology) and also points to ownership and dominance (genealogy). Discourses need to be de-constructed to provide an understanding of hidden previous hypocrisies. The concepts of science, truth and reason are replaced by the world of vocabularies. Rorty (1989) argues that in a world of competing perspectives, liberal democracy can be defended on pragmatic grounds in that it represents the more attractive vocabulary:

> 'What bind societies together are common vocabularies and common hopes . . . the principle function of the vocabularies is to tell stories about future outcomes which compensate for present sacrifices. To retain social hope members of such a society need to be able to tell themselves a story about how things might get better and to see no insuperable obstacles to this story's coming true'. (Rorty, 1989, p. 86)

Liberal democracy with the commitment of not causing harm and freedom of fear provides the best framework for safeguarding the individual. Democracy is about the 'is' and how it works in practice rather than democracy as the 'ought' which pins too many optimist hopes and which is due to fail because the term becomes overburdened. Churchill praised democracy because he argued it was the best between all other evils.

Thin Democracy – Cool Citizenship

Turner (2000) in a recent analysis of citizenship, democracy and postmodernity, came to the conclusion that the best hoped for political strategy was the

emergence of cosmopolitan virtues. Turner pointed out that this required both
a 'thin loyalty' to the democratic process as well as a 'cool commitment' to
citizenship. This has to be compared with the classical arguments that democracy and citizenship require a 'thick' commitment to the democratic process
and a 'hot' commitment to solidarity. Turner's view is that in the context of
greater diversity and fragmentation, the need is to make a commitment to the
postmodern ethics of greater individualism and therefore the need for greater
distance between the individual and the state:

> 'Cosmopolitanism can be justified morally because hot loyalties and thick solidar-
> ity are more likely to be points of conflict and violence in postmodern ethically
> diverse labour markets. Indifference and distance become personal strategies in a
> risk society where ambiguity and uncertainty reign. In a more fluid world, the ironic
> citizen needs to learn how to move on, how to adjust and to adapt to a world of
> cultural contingency'. (Turner, 2000, p. 30)

The implication of Turner's approach is the recognition of the limits of democracy and citizenship. Citizenship resonated in an era of nationalism when the
state conferred citizenship in relation to national identity, work, the defence of
the nation state and the family. It was inclusive, but also exclusive of those
who were defined as not belonging to the national community. In accepting
that we live in a postmodern mood, the need is to recognise greater diversity
of cultures; the break up of the family, the end of jobs for life and industrial
communities. Industrial communities of shared experiences provided the
context for thick democracy and hot commitments to solidarity. Changes in
employment and the break with traditional ties of manufacturing create the
context for a looser commitment to democracy and community. In the age of
postmodernity, people live with multiple identities in multiple communities.
The new individualised workers of the new economy show no commitment to
the politics of the cities in which they work. The individual retreats to the
suburbs. There is a disavowal of responsibility to the public space and city
politics. The commitment is to thin democracy and the loyalty to solidarity is
cool. It is those behind in decaying houses, including the low paid and the
unemployed, that seek to make claims for thick democracy and hot solidarity.

Turner's (2000) view of postmodernity and cosmopolitan virtues justifies
the idea of the new individualism and the retreat from the public spaces.
However, the thin loyalty to democracy and the cool commitment to citizenship
are also compatible with the neo-liberal perspectives that too much politics are
dangerous and their argument for a more limited government. New liberalism
has always pointed to the justice of living with the market when contrasted with
the injustices of politics. Politics according to a liberal perspective have always
been described as arbitrary; that it serves those with a loud voice and those who
know their way around the corridors of government. However, retreat does not

mean that those who know their corridors of government will also retreat, because politics, however limited, are here to stay. Governments will always have financial resources to dispense in the form of subsidies, but government is also increasingly important in acting as advocate and as a voice on the world stage.

While postmodern advocates and neo-liberals urge anti politics, the political space is increasingly occupied by professional lobbyists and corporate lawyers and accountants who advise government on policy and on legislation. The emerging elites provide advice to governments on privatisation policy, on liberalisation of financial markets and intellectual property rights. Parliaments are unable to bring ministers and executives to account. Privatisation policies and contracts are classified as confidential. Ministers and public sector officials resist demands for openness and scrutiny of public policy advice and discussions arguing the need of anonymity.

The retreat into private lives allows others to occupy the public spaces with less resistance and less protest. Policies are made, which are then difficult to unmake. The privatised individual finds a deteriorating rail network of late and cancelled trains, of traffic jams on roads and increased pollution, which endangers children's health and the individual asks why has the quality of life been allowed to deteriorate, without asking how becoming private and not becoming involved also contributed to the policy outcome. In reality, the cosmopolitan virtues of thin loyalty to the state and cool commitment to community are strategies that can only be afforded by the few who can be chauffeured in limousines and who can afford to live within walled estates and electronic gates. The demand for less government is a privilege of the few, while for the many public policies continually impact their quality of life.

Therefore, in the global world, there is a greater need for more transparency and openness in policy making and not less. Democracy provides the only means for political equality and the spaces for optimism to bring about policy change. There will always be individuals and interest groups who have easier and more frequent access to the policy process. Owners of newspapers are perceived as being the movers of opinion and therefore politicians seek to ensure that they are there. Corporate lawyers, trade and financial advisers working on behalf of multinational corporations together with professional lobbyists have ready access to the political process. Contributors and donors to politicians and political parties have easier access to policy makers.

The concept of globalisation emphasises the new convergence, the global political economy straitjacket of the Washington Consensus. Globalisation is defined by a policy framework of increased competition, capital mobility, liberalisation of trade, financial markets and privatisation, all seeking to alter and reshape the relationships between capital, employment and the role of government. The policy framework of neo-liberalism makes financial capital more mobile and no longer tied to the nation state. Those who depend on wages and employment will always be less mobile and more dependent on the nation state. Increased competition has put pressures on government to review and reform their welfare states with the primary aim of reducing non-labour costs. The Swedish distribution model has also had to come to terms with the limits of re-distribution and to reduce commitments on high pensions costs and subsidies to state own industries. The concept of wage equality is under the pressure of market forces, with employers seeking greater wage flexibility to reflect the demands of changing labour markets. Sweden has the highest spending level within the OECD, comprising some 60 per cent of GDP. Social expenditure makes up 24 per cent of total consumption, while 37 per cent of the workforce are employed in the public sector. This shift towards public sheltered employment has distorted wage settlements, which in turn have made the Swedish economy less competitive.

Globalisation has been equated with increased homogeneity of expectations. Cultural differences are undermined by the worlds of McDonalds, Starbucks Coffee, Fox TV, all of which are packaged within an American perception of living. Globalisation is defined in terms of the Americanisation of culture. The liberalisation of trade provides the means for American multinationals to secure new markets that put pressure on coffee growers to cut down forests and increase their coffee outputs and by cattle that make the beef burger. According to the globalisation argument, the pressure is on British and US economic liberal reforms of increased de-regulation of labour markets, great flexibility and lower tax burdens. Recent reforms in Germany have aimed to reduce the government's commitments on state pensions, while reducing the tax rate on individuals and business.

GLOBALISATION AND DEMOCRACY

While accepting some of the argument on the nature of globalisation, there is equally a strong argument that pertains governments can still make a difference. It is an argument that rejects the new convergence and the capital logic of globalisation. As Beck has recently suggested, there is at present a conflation between the processes of globality, globalisation and globalism. Discussion on globalisation has tended to refer to the new ideology of globalism as the ideology associated with market liberalism:

'Globalism reduces the new complexity of globality and globalisation to a single economic dimension which is itself conceived in linear fashion as a constant expansion of dependence on the world market. All other dimensions (ecological globalisation, cultural globalisation political polycentrism, the emergence of transnational spaces are treated, if at all, only within the assumption of the dominance of economic globalisation. World society is thus truncated and falsified as world market society. In this sense neo-liberal globalism is a form of one dimensional thinking and acting, a mono causal economist view of the world'. (Beck, 2000, p. 118)

World trade has been expanding for over 400 years. International trade expanded between 1870 and 1914. The invention of the telegraph in 1906 defined globalisation. The First World War with demands for greater protectionism interrupted the globalisation process. There has always been capital mobility. During the 1870s, British capital was invested in the making of the railways in South America and in India. In the early 1900s, over six million people migrated from Europe to the USA. The possibility that economic power will overspill into political influence was recognised by Brandleis and Woodrow Wilson during the Presidential campaigns in the early 1900s (Sandel, 1998) when they both argued that the principle of the republic was being undermined by the spread of employment and more people become dependent on wages:

'From the standpoint of the republican tradition, the demise of the political economy of citizenship constituted a concession, a deflation of American ideals, a loss of liberty. Republican political theory teaches that to be free is to share in governing a political community that controls its own fate. Self government in this sense requires political communities that control their destinies and citizens who identify sufficiently with those communities to think and act with a view of the common good'. (Sandel, 1998, p. 274).

Woodrow Wilson campaigning for the presidency in 1912 declared:

'There is a sense in which in our day the individual has been submerged . . . Most men now work not for themselves or in partnership with others but as employees of big corporations. Under such conditions the individual is swallowed up by large corporations, caught in a great confused nexus of all sorts of complicated circumstances helpless in the face of vast structure of power . . . the everyday relationships of men are largely with impersonal concerns with organisations not with other individual men'. (Woodrow Wilson as quoted in Sandel, 1998, p. 204)

Liberalism and the concept of the neutral state abandon the notion of the political economy of citizenship. The arguments against the bigness of business and their influence on government are downgraded in favour of those who emphasise efficiency and consumer welfare. Concerns about political and economic democracy become the concerns about economic growth, employment and distribution of incomes. The shift towards consumer citizenship represents a break from the republican concept of active citizenship. Keynes economics and social policy are perceived as processes that nationalise government. The economic shifts towards large corporations leads to big government. The process of economic globalisation demands the shift towards the global citizen.

The social dimension of globalisation is concerned with the potential transfer of resources. Social policy allows for the provision of health care and access to education, to social security and pensions. The agenda of poverty reduction and pro-poor policy reforms seeks to mitigate the outcomes of a globalisation that is defined by neo-liberal principles. Those with wealth and property demand laws that restrict capital gains taxes to allow for their children greater possibilities of inheritance. The propertyless demand higher taxes to lessen continued inequalities in between and within generations. The interests of shareholders are different from those of the chief executives as they are different to those of managers and the workforce. Recent comparative studies have confirmed that CEOs in the UK are receiving the highest remuneration after the USA. They are paid about £590 000 per annum, which is about £100 000 more than their German and French counterparts. The recent payments to the CEOs of Railtrack and Marks & Spencer indicate there is no connection between performance and pay. In the meantime, the UK labour force has experienced declining wages as a share of national incomes. While executive pay has increased by 69 per cent, wages have increased by 12 per cent during the last decade. The workforce suffers from the threat effect of unemployment and increased competition in the context of global markets. The role of government is to ensure that these numerous interests and transactions are congruent with macroeconomic objectives.

Implicitly or explicitly, governments have a policy on incomes and wages, since these are likely to threaten inflation. Workers collective resistance through strikes is likely to result in a squeeze of profits in shifting the balance to labour and away from capital, which in turn is likely to result in lower investment and eventual job loses. Shareholders who see their dividends threatened are likely to sell shares in economies troubled by industrial militancy. Strikes and trade union militancy confirm the workings of democracy. Trade unions represent opposition. The right to belong to a trade union, the right to strike and trade union recognition are part of the meaning of citizenship. Government legislation on industrial relations can extend or obstruct the legitimacy of trade unions.

Social policy has the potential of re-distributing income. Public provision of health care, education and social security allow contributors to keep more of their disposable income. Collective provision is always cheaper than private insurance. Trade unions are directly influenced in the making of social wages since their members' families directly benefit in the provision of health care and education. Furthermore, there is a connection between pensions and trade union interest, since trade union members eventually become pensioners. Children of trade unionists go to school and university – their families use public health. Finally, trade union members are involved as workers in the provision of social policy as teachers, doctors, nurses and the police.

The social dimension embodies a number of government functions and programmes that allow for the re-distribution of resources between different groups and interests. Public provision in health care allow for the possibility for those who need health care to be provided with the best services irrespective of their incomes. Social security represents the pensions budget unemployment and social benefits.

CONCLUSIONS

The attempt to review and re-analyse the linkages between democracy, citizenship and globalisation are increasingly becoming of major concern. In 2001, the UK had one of the lowest electoral turnouts since 1885, when only 60 per cent of electors bothered to vote. The second Blair Government gained just over 10 million votes but also won an electoral landslide with 167-seat majority. This result has to be compared with the vote of 11 million achieved by the previous leader, Neill Kinnock in 1992, when Labour actually lost that election. Throughout Europe there continues to be a steady decline in electoral turnouts. Since the early 1950s, there has been a decline of 10 per cent of voters actually voting in elections. Turnouts tend be especially low among the younger age groups between the ages of 18 to 24, while the highest turnouts tend to be within the groups of age 60 plus. In the USA, the turnout for the presidential election in November 2000 was below 50 per cent. The majority of Americans mainly the young and black do not even bother to register to vote.

Democracy seems to be in decay. There is general agreement that the role of Parliaments is no longer the place where the executive is made accountable and transparent. The discipline of party politics ensures that there is little dissent. Members of Parliament have become the numbers that are marshalled through the lobbies to give passage to the Government's programme. Government is increasingly conducted through the media and policy is outlined at press briefings. Parliament is increasingly by-passed, as Ministers of State aim to capture the favourable media headlines. Policy becomes image rather than substance. There is a disavowal of responsibility, with politicians seeking to take credit for policy success but looking for fault elsewhere for policy failings.

Hertz (2001) has recently described the nature of the new globalised economy as a silent take-over. In the context of globalisation, the nation-state becomes less relevant as governments seek to adhere to the logic of the global straitjacket. In the silent take-over it is the new corporations that are the centres of decision-making. According to UDP (UDP 2001) there are some 360 billionaires who between them own some 60 per cent of the world wealth.

Some multinationals have wealth, which is greater than the GDP of whole countries:

> 'The hundred largest multinational corporations now control about 20 per cent of global foreign assets – fifty-one of the hundred biggest economies in the world are now corporations only forty nine are nation state. The Sales of General Motors and Ford are greater than the GDP of the hole of sub-Saharan Africa, the assets of IBM, BP and General Electric outstrip the economic capabilities of most small nations and Wal-Mart the US supermarket retailer has higher revenue than most Central and Eastern European states including Poland the Czech Republic Ukraine, Hungary Romania and Slovakia'. (Hertz, 2001, p. 7)

These large corporations have direct access to governments. The financial contributions to political parties, the hiring of professional lobbyists, their strategic locations in the national economy and the number of people they employ give multinational corporations power and influence. In the Enron case, it has now been shown that the corporation contributed US$6 billion to both US major political parties. Enron executives became advisers to the Bush Administration on Energy policy. Governments learn to listen to the concerns of these corporations and eventually become their policy advocates in World Trade negotiations. The concern of the oil and energy producers are now involved in the policy-making process in the George W. Bush' Government. Their influence provided the President with the policy agenda to resist the Kyoto protocol on climate change and have also provided the policy priority of drilling for oil in Alaska, despite concerns about biodiversity and oil spillages that could undermine the local ecosystem. Agriculture is increasingly dominated by an agribusiness, including the chemical industry, laboratories involved in experimenting with new seeds and patents, the energy industry and animal feeds. These industries lobby governments for subsidies to agriculture that at present amount to over US$300 billion in the OECD area and which, in turn, are displacing small farmers in the developing countries.

> 'This is the world of the Silent Takeover, the world at the dawn of the new millennium. Government hands are tied and we are increasingly dependent on corporations. Business is in the driving seat, corporations determine the rules of the game and governments have become referees enforcing rules laid down by others'. (Hertz, 2001, p. 7)

The retreat from democracy has implications for the claim of citizenship. Citizenship represents a benchmark of civil, political and social rights that confirm the existence of the individual, that is the person with dreams, hopes and aspirations that very often need the intervention and regulation of the state. Citizenship however, is not conferred through the state as a gift, but it is often an arena of struggle. The workplace is still a dangerous place where people lose their lives and work in hazardous conditions with new materials. Consumers are exploited by fixed pricing systems, they are mis-sold pensions, lose their homes, are still vulnerable to lose their jobs, become sick, get old and need caring. Non-decisions about such issues are still decisions. Regulation is perceived to be a cost to the market, it represents yet another rigidity, it imposes a cost, it increases the costs of labour. Countries and companies need to compete and the pressure is to reduce labour costs. Companies are in the business of searching lower labour costs de-centralising and sub-contracting production. Dangerous work is sub-contracted to the periphery to the developing economies with low labour standards. In the meantime, poor countries welcome the foreign direct investment because it represents jobs and incomes. Stitched footballs and running shoes made by forced child labour are taken for granted. Multinational corporations disavow responsibility, pointing out that the production has been contracted out and that is the sub-contractors who establish the labour standard, which means that it is the indigenous business community that exploits its labour force. Child slave labour in factories and coffee plantations are exploited by local overseers – the modern version of the factor and taxman, who ensured that the high-landers paid their rents, irrespective of their level of poverty.

3. Globalisation and models of citizenship

INTRODUCTION

The concern of this chapter is the nature of the relationship between globalisation and claims for citizenship. As suggested earlier, present forms of globalisation are being shaped and defined by rules and regulations outlined by international agencies, including the IMF and the World Bank. Global rules reflect deals and bargains between the more powerful economic blocs such as the EU, the USA and Japan. National Governments are increasingly becoming the lobbyists, expressing business and financial interests. This approach to globalisation creates a specific discourse of citizenship. Citizenship is equated with consumer citizenship. Globalisation is presented as competitive markets and increased consumer choice. Citizenship in this sense is guaranteed in the marketplace. This chapter points to a number of competing discourses of citizenship. Since there are competing discourses of citizenship, there are also alternatives about the shape of globalisation.

Sen (1999) has pointed out: 'there are no famines in a democracy', because he argues democracy provides the means to bring about a change of government and therefore make political elites accountable. Famine, disease and social deprivation represent policy choices and policy priorities of how to distribute resources. Political elites in non-democracies seek to reinforce existing social, economic and political structures By contrast, democracy enforces accountability and provides populations the opportunity to bring about a change of government and changes in policy priorities:

> 'no substantial famine has ever occurred in any independent and democratic country with a relatively free press. Famines are easy to prevent if there is a serious effort to do so and a democratic government, facing elections and criticisms from opposition parties and independent newspapers, cannot help but make such an effort. Not surprisingly, while India continued to have famines under British rule right up to independence (the last famine, which I witnessed as a child, was in 1943, four years before independence), they disappeared suddenly with the establishment of a multiparty democracy and a free press'. (Sen, 1999, p. 7)

Hobsbawm (1995) has described the twentieth century as 'The Age of Extremes', while Bauman (1995) has expressed it as the 'Century of the Camps'. The twentieth century and the beginnings of the new millennium continue to confirm the fragility of human life, of the arbitrary use and abuse of power, imprisonments without trail, etc. and it continues to reinforce the relevance of democracy, citizenship, equality and human rights. In the absence of democracy, political elites do not come under pressure to bring about policy change:

> 'What exactly is democracy? We must not identify democracy with majority rule. Democracy has complex demands, which certainly include voting and respect for election results, but it also requires the protection of liberties and freedoms, respect for legal entitlements and the guaranteeing of free discussion and uncensored distribution of news and fair comment . . . Democracy is a demanding system and not just a mechanical condition (like majority rule) taken in isolation. Viewed in this light, the merits of democracy and its claim as a universal value can be related to certain distinct virtues that go with its unfettered practice. Indeed, we can distinguish three different ways in which democracy enriches the lives of the citizens. First, political freedom is a part of human freedom in general and exercising civil and political rights is a crucial part of good lives of individuals as social beings. Political and social participation has intrinsic value for human life and well-being. To be prevented from participation in the political life of the community is a major deprivation'. (Sen, 1999, p. 4)

In an attempt to construct a 'politics of citizenship' Marshall (1992) argued the case that ideas of citizenship were associated with the commitment to ideas of belonging and of being a member of a community. It was the combination of civil, political and social rights that defined citizenship. However, Marshall also recognised that formal and procedural political and civil rights were not sufficient in themselves to the making of citizenship. It was also the commitments of the right of access to the provision of health, education and social security that made social citizenship. The sense of belonging was created through the process of minimising the influence of income as the barrier to access to health and education provision. People had the right to explore their potential, rather than income defining their horizons. Marshall accepted that claims for citizenship and the class system were in conflict and that the claims for social citizenship aimed to modify the whole pattern of social inequality. Implicitly, Marshall recognised that claims for citizenship reflected class struggles on issues of resources and re-distribution of income:

> 'there is a general enrichment of the concrete substance of civilised life, a general reduction of risk and insecurity, an equalization between the more and the less fortunate at all levels . . . Equalisation is not so much between classes as between individuals within a population which is now treated for this purpose as though it were one class. Equality of status is more important than equality of income'. (Marshall, 1992, pp. 102–103)

So, despite major limitations, the commitments to democracy and ideas of citizenship do provide the spaces and the necessary language for universal claims of political equality and freedom. Both Marshall and Sen have made connections between democracy and social citizenship. Civil, political and social rights are inextricably linked. In the context of Marshall's citizenship, the commitment to social provision has to be founded on universal principles with commitments to a universal health service founded on need and universal education founded on ideas of meritocracy. Equally, in dealing with problems of poverty and income, the focus shifts from ideas of poverty, based on minimum subsistence, to ideas of relative poverty, citizenship and participation. The social citizenship of Marshall is inherently connected to ideas of universal rights but also of membership of a community, a sense of belonging, unity and solidarity between individuals.

In its statement of intent, the International Labour Organisation (ILO) has explicitly endorsed the ideas of connecting policies on basic needs, relative poverty, belonging and citizenship:

> 'The satisfaction of basic needs means meeting the minimum requirements of a family for personal consumption: food, shelter, clothing: it implies access to essential services, such as drinking water, sanitation, transport, health and education . . . It should further imply the satisfaction of needs of a more qualitative nature, a healthy, humane and satisfying environment and political participation in the making of decisions'. (ILO, 1976, p. 7)

Furthermore, recognising the differences of development between countries including differences of culture, politics and social expectations, the ILO also declared that:

> 'Basic needs are therefore in a large part, a relative concept, but there are also certain minimum levels of personal consumption and access to social services which should be universally regarded as essential to human life'. (ILO, 1976, p. 7)

Critics have pointed out that Marshall's ideas of citizenship are founded on the narrow assumptions of homogeneity of community, of likeness, of common identity and stability, which in turn have the potential to exclude the stranger, the migrant and the other. Dahrendorf (1988) argues that citizenship has to reflect difference and equality of treatment:

> 'People want to know where they belong and they want to belong to familiar and homogeneous groups, not to a Czech and Slovak Federal Republic, but to the Slovak and perhaps to the Hungarian ethnic minority within it . . . The true test of the strength of citizenship rights is heterogeneity. Common respect for basic entitlements among people who are different in origin, culture and creed proves that

combination of identity and variety which lies at the heart of civil and civilised societies'. (Dahrendorf, 1988, pp.16–17)

Marshall has therefore been criticised for outlining a model on citizenship which is 'top down' that puts too much emphasis on the role of the state in the provision of rights rather than the 'bottom up' which puts the focus on struggles and resistance. According to this latter approach, citizenship reinforces the idea of process where citizenship is being continuously contested and redefined (Mann, 1987; Hindess, 1993). This is the model of citizenship as resistance where struggles for citizenship involve contradictory processes of inclusion and exclusion; where some might gain rights and become the 'in group' and, others become the disadvantaged and 'out group'. Since the Velvet Revolution in 1990, the process of exclusion has accelerated especially in Eastern Europe. The vacuum left with the demise of the Soviet Union has resulted in newly elected governments constructing constitutions, which have directly influenced the lives of large numbers of peoples who overnight lost their citizenship rights and became defined as the 'other'. Gypsies have lost their citizenship rights in the Czech Republic. Czechs are referred to as 'white' and gypsies as 'black' 'legitimating' a new racism and discrimination in housing, employment and the rights of residence. Gypsies are told that are not Czech that they are Slovaks and should return to Slovakia. In the meantime, Russians have lost their rights to vote in Estonia and Hungarian minorities are increasingly marginalised in Slovakia.

Soysal (1994) has suggested that struggles for citizenship have become postnational, have shifted the concerns from state-hood to person-hood. Citizenship is now increasingly focused on the universal rights of the individual and the recognition of the politics of difference. The meaning of citizenship has increasingly become a universalised narrative, where the claims of citizenship are no longer legitimated within the confines of the nation-state, but are given leverage in international codes and laws including the EU Declaration on Human Rights and the European Courts of Justice. This universal discourse makes it possible for those who are excluded to claim their rights as citizens outside the confines of the nation state. However, in contrast to the optimism of Soysal, recent studies of migrants in Holland and Germany (Bussemaker, 1999) would suggest otherwise. Most constitutions in Europe are a hybrid of discourses. For most foreigners, the avenue to citizenship is through a process of naturalisation. For instance in Holland, it takes 5 years of residence, together with proved ability to communicate in basic Dutch, for a migrant to become a citizen. In Germany, children of Turkish parents do not have the right to German citizenship, they have to apply for naturalisation, unlike the children of German parents, who have the ascribed right to German citizenship. By contrast, in France, all children born in France have the right to French citizenship.

'Two Turkish brothers, one being born in Germany the other in France. The later gains EU and French citizenship after coming of age, but the brother born in Germany is still subject to general naturalisation principles and remains a non EU citizen. If the French-born Turk was to work and reside in Germany he would vote in municipal as well as EP elections. Whereas the German-born brother who had lived and worked all his life would be exempt such rights. Both are Turk, both born in EU member states, but only one is a Citizen of the Union'. (Hansen, 1999, p. 22)

The outsider, the stranger, the other, is forced into the position of the 'parvenu' who seeks to be assimilated and accepted within the discourse of integration. This discourse is based on ideas of homogeneity and the imagined community of what it is to be English, Dutch or German. The outsider has to accept the culture of that homogenous community showing an allegiance to that imagined community and therefore has to deny connections with other possible identities. The process of defining citizen is not questioned by those who are 'included' as citizens through what is perceived a natural process in contrast to those who are excluded and marginalised and who see the definition as arbitrary, discriminatory and oppressive.

'We must therefore be suspicious of ideologies of solidarity, precisely because they are so attractive to those who find liberalism emotionally unsatisfying and who have gone on in our century to create oppressive and cruel regimes of unparalleled horror. To seek emotional and personal development in the bosom of a community or in romantic self-expression is a choice open to citizens in liberal societies'. (Schklar, 1989, p. 36)

A brief reflection on my personal biography may help to illustrate the pressures on the stranger. My mother came to England in 1951. She put a photo of the Queen in her front room to show her English neighbours that she was a royalist like them, firmly believing that this would make it easier for her to be accepted. She believed that in Britain, people had a photo of the queen in their front rooms. The story is telling for two reasons. First, that my mother was trying desperately to be accepted by the insider community and, second was the assumption that there was such a thing as a homogenous English identity, which she had to identify with, while at the same time surrendering her own identity. She felt she had to surrender her past. She stopped talking to my brothers and sisters in our native language. We felt under pressure to become English. She did everything that David Blunkett the present UK Home Secretary is asking today of migrant communities in Britain. She did not think it was possible that there might have been people without a photo of the queen in their homes or the possibility that some people were actually indifferent to the monarchy. Despite her 'passing' the English test she still continued to feel marginalised and excluded.

The stranger is put in a position of disadvantage, afraid to articulate dissent. The UK Anti Terrorist Act of 2002 actually allows the Home Secretary to deport people who hold dual citizenship if they are perceived to be a danger to the state for inciting hatred and racism. Mr Blunkett's vision of citizen is the parvenu – the migrant who needs to be assimilated and accepted not in his/her own right, but on conditions set by the Home Office.

The 'pariah' does not seek to be assimilated but instead asks to be accepted in his/her own right; respected and valued for being different and demands the right to dissent and to be awkward. In this context, citizenship becomes a form of resistance, that a sense of belonging cannot be artificially constructed in a language that gives priority to homogeneity and therefore by implication, undermines the right to be different, the right to dissent, to disagree and to resist.

DEFINING CITIZENSHIP

The following sections seek to go beyond Marshall's vision of citizenship. It shall be argued that while the right to vote is a pillar of citizenship; claims for increased participation, involvement, transparency and accountability are becoming more central in shaping citizenship. The late Martin Luther King in his attempt to give vision to the Civil Rights Movements in the USA during the mid-1960s argued about the need:

'to make real the promise of democracy – to bring our nation back to those great wells of democracy which were dug deep by the Founding Father'. (Boyte, 1993)

King was aware that his claims for citizenship were more than concerns about the de-segregation of buses and universities and the right to vote. Citizenship for Afro Americans had to focus on 'economic' and 'social' access that meant equal employment rights, the ability to earn a living and to move out poverty and the urgent need for people to be involved in day-to-day politics. King pointed out that he was reclaiming the vision of Thomas Jefferson that citizenship was:

'where everyman is participator in the government of affairs, not only at an election one day in the year but everyday . . . he will let the heart be torn of his body sooner than his power be wrested from him by a Caesar or a Bonaparte.' (Thomas Jefferson, as quoted in Boyte, 1993, p. 3)

Citizenship is not a static concept, but reflects changing hopes and aspirations. Citizenship is continually being created and re-created, a process that reflects continuing challenges and changes. Citizenship is not sufficient without access to social and economic resources. The right to a secure income including pensions, unemployment insurance, sickness benefits, access to health and education are of equal importance in the making of citizenship as the right to vote. Anti-politics and indifference to politics are both connected to economic and social contexts. Those who feel 'economically dispossessed' are also more likely to be disinterested in the public spaces. Bauman (2000) has defended the case for a citizen's income as essential to overcoming the climate of anti-politics, apathy, isolation and quietism:

> 'The decisive argument in favour of the unconditional social guarantee of a basic livelihood can be found not in the moral duty towards the handicapped and destitute, not in philosophical renditions of equity or justice and not in the benefits for the quality life in common but in its political significance or its importance for the polity, its crucial role in the restoration of the lost private/public space and in filling the now empty private/public space. In other words in its being a condition sine qua non of the birth of fully fledged citizenship and republic, both being conceivable solely in the company of self-confident people, people free from existential fear – secure people'. (Bauman, 2000, p. 183)

The present condition of anti politics, of quietism and retreat from the public space reflects a series of economic and social insecurities including high levels of unemployment, access to public provision and also the inability to provide a coherent form of resistance to contemporary economic globalisation. The retreat from the public space confirms powerlessness, a feeling that it makes no difference who is the government. Stories of world poverty emphasise insecurity in the knowledge that jobs are insecure. Insecurity makes individuals look inwards towards the safety of domestic life and the community seeking to exclude the stranger and the migrant who become the focus of that insecurity.

Citizenship as resistance represents the alternative to the retreat from public space. Economic globalisation provides the opportunity for globalised resistance but that resistance is at present fragmented and rather ephemeral. However, it is never 'the end of history'. The language of citizenship still provides the potential universal language of resistance. Protests against water privatisation in Ghana, electricity privatisation in Mexico, anti-market liberal policies in India and Argentina and the unity of trade union action against Benetton across borders in Mozambique and South Africa reinforce the possibilities of linking industrial, environmental and human rights coalitions.

Citizenship is of direct relevance to people's lives because it represents the benchmark of personal freedom, dignity, hope, freedom from fear and personal autonomy. Sartori (1987) asked 'that if one wanted to know what freedom meant then one would simply ask those who do not have it'. The commitment to citizenship implies the willingness to explore ways that deal with a series of contradictions and dilemmas. The commitment to universal human rights is a pillar in the definition of citizen. Human Rights include the claim that the individual is an end and not a means to an end. The recognition of the constituted individual able to make choices also means having access to political, economic and social resources. Commitment to citizenship also therefore means commitment to issues of access to resources. Commitment to political rights also embraces economic and social rights.

In addition, the meaning of citizenship has to involve the recognition of universal rights as well as the right to be different. People with disabilities are as equal as those who are defined as being normal. In multiracial communities, there has to be mutual respect and tolerance for people to live as Christian, Jew, Hindu or Muslim. Brazil has often been regarded as an example of the possibility of accepting the right of difference as a positive value:

'We Brazilians, due to our historical experience, are a people of mixed descent, a 'mestico' people, composed initially of Portuguese, Indians and an enormous African contribution. Today the Brazilian population also includes more than 20 million citizens of Italian descent, more than 10 million of German descent, 7 or 8 million of Arab descent, about 1.5 million of Japanese descent and several million of Ukrainian, Polish or Spanish descent. We are truly a mestico people, although not the only one. Many nations are composed in this way. But there is one value of ours that I would like to highlight – namely, that we like being mesticos (though here again, we are not the only people for whom this is true). Not only do we have a huge 'melting pot', as it is called in the United States, but we have the true 'melting pot' in Brazil, because here we say that being such a mixed people is a positive value. We have learned that this diversity is an element that enriches our experience as a people and a nation'. (Cardoso, 2001, p. 14)

Citizenship has to be more than homogeneity. It has to reflect plurality and diversity and the right to express difference and dissent. When George W. Bush claimed in his address to congress in the aftermath of the terrorist attacks that people had to choose between being for or against America, this view in a way reflected the lack of willingness to accept dissent since voices of opposition were likely to be defined as being anti-America. It is a process that results in a chilling effect on those who might want to disagree, but become afraid of disagreeing because of the potential of surveillance.

The Language of Citizenship

The concept of citizenship is a contestable concept (Connolly, 1983) in the real sense that it is a space, which is at present occupied by a number of competing discourses. The building of consensus can no longer be achieved through the ascendance of one paradigm. The recognition of multiple discourses confirms pluralism. Deconstruction and excavation of discourses allows for issues of power and dominance previously hidden to be exposed and made transparent:

> 'To say that a particular network of concepts is contestable is to say that the standards and criteria of judgement it expresses are open to contestation. To say that such a network is essentially contestable is to contend that the universal criteria of reason, as we can now understand them, do not suffice to settle these contests definitively'. (Connolly, 1983, p. 225)

Language has always been essential in putting limits on the hopes of democracy and citizenship. In the early stages of writing the American Constitution there was a recognition that the will of the people had to be defined within the limits of individual property rights. According to Nedelsky (1990), the Founding Fathers were already well aware of the need to put limits on the notion of power to the people. Claims on and expectations of the democratic process had to be balanced with the rights of the individual and to property. The worry was that the democratic process would lead to claims for reforms of property ownership. Democracy was to be defined as protecting rights and putting limits on the state. The pre-occupation of the citizen was to increase personal wealth within a framework of law that allowed the citizen to prosper. Citizen was defined as the right to vote during elections. Voters were to be the quiet audience. For large parts of their lives citizens were to be private citizens:

> 'The Constitution was designed not to foster but to confine and undermine political participation. The highly mediated system was designed to turn the attention of the people to the pursuit of their private interests rather than to politics. Prosperity not participation would bind citizens to the government. The protection of vested rights from encroachments of democratic legislatures was the central issue on which courts asserted their power to protect individual rights from democratic attack. The court became the guarantor and mediator on the basic tension of the system – a tension which held property rights as the center'. (Nedelsky, 1990, p. 247)

The Public Citizen

The interpretation of public citizen combines the concepts of deliberative, thick democracy and the democratic culture. The model of the Public Citizen makes the public space central because it is essential in defining personal freedom. The commitment to the public space reflects the commitment to: listen to the 'other'; to accept the presence and the existence of and differences and therefore, to accept the ethics of dialogue, compromise, honesty, sincerity and transparency. The recognition of the 'Other' accepts that consensus cannot be taken as assumed. The other cannot be reduced to sameness, but rather confirms *l'autrui of Levinas* (Bernstein, 1991) an ethos for questioning and challenging the processes of colonization and the imperialism that seeks to reduce the other to the same.

For Voet (1998), participation is the cornerstone of citizenship:

> 'A full citizen in its most complete sense is someone who participates in legislation or decision-making in public affairs. It concerns participation through which one reflects upon the desirable new character of society and through which one rejuvenates society by cooperating with other people. It is participation whereby one discusses common affairs with others, reflects upon the common good, learns to bear responsibility to judge and to decide'. (Voet, 1998, p. 137)

The Public Citizen discourse is concerned with the ability of individuals to give shape to societal change as opposed to being the passive watchers of events and accepting that events happen to them. Citizen is defined by the ability to give shape to events and to define the priorities. It entails the continuing involvement in public discussion; reflecting, judging, living with experience and being able to make changes collectively in contrast to living with the public space that is defined by an elite of politicians, business military and bureaucracy, of the rule of nobody and the experts.

Critics of present globalisation point to the lack of global political accountability and to a political landscape where public spaces are corrupted by a plutocracy of political elites, business interests, the financial community trade lawyers, professional lobbyists and individuals donors to politicians and political parties. The silent takeover (Hertz, 2001) of public space leaves the majority as the quiet audience sitting passively in the darkness of the auditorium watching the political actors on the stage (Sennet, 1979). The audience is encouraged to be passive. By contrast, the public citizen discourse seeks to widen the meaning of the public space, to include workplace democracy to wider social rights in terms of access to areas of public provision and to make the privacy of the family the concern of the public space.

The concept of the public citizen corresponds with the commitment to the idea of 'deliberative democracy'. Bobbio (1987) pointed to the six broken promises of liberal democracy to explain the disillusionment with public space. According to the author, the six broken promises included the persistence of oligarchy, the limited spaces for democracy, the uneducated citizen and the stalemate of pluralism. All these factors have contributed to a functional rather than a deliberative:

> 'communication – argument challenge, demonstration, symbolization and bargaining – is as central to democracy as voting. Deliberation induces individuals to give due consideration to their judgements, so that they know what they

want, understand what they want and can justify their judgements to others . . .
Theories of deliberative democracy emphasize this ideal complementarity of deliberative judgement and power'. (Warren, 2002, p. 173)

Dialogue is the process that allows for the respect of the other and for the
acceptance of plurality. Conflicts have to be resolved through dialogue and
through spaces, which allow for trust, compassion, compromise tolerance and
safety. The Good Friday Agreement in Northern Ireland, the Committee on
Bloody Sunday and the Peace and Reconciliation Committees in South Africa
and more recently Rwanda, represent examples of the potential of dialogue to
deal with historic ruptures. By contrast, the politics of liberal democracy
encourages estrangement, difference and polarisation.

In the middle of the English Civil War, during the Putney debates, Colonel
Rainborough argued that the hope of the Civil War was to make the commitment to political equality:

'for really I think that the poorest he that is in England hath a life to live, as the
greatest he'. (quoted in Kateb, 1989, p. 191)

Arguing the case that in the aftermath of the civil war those who had fought
for Parliament now had a right to political equality, Rainborough was arguing
the case for a democracy of equality and freedom, but furthermore also recognised that the poorest had a right to a life as much as the rich, which also
pointed to the view that political equality also required the possibility for the
redistribution of economic resources:

'In the view that I am proposing here one may distinguish two aspects of freedom:
first what I would call freedom as capacity and second, freedom as the exercise of
this capacity in the form of self-development'. (Gould, 1990, p. 45)

In the context of political practice, resistance involves the here and now and
what can be called the 'politics of the street'. An example of the politics of the
street is the attempt to deal with racism and racial harassment and how Asian
and Afro-Caribbean youth in Britain seek to dissolve their separate identities
and turn the racist term 'black' into a positive identity of resistance and the
making of the black Diaspora (Boyarin and Boyarin, 1993; Gilroy, 1987,
1993; Clifford, 1997). The black Diaspora becomes a form of resistance when
the migrant is no longer isolated as an individual but becomes part of the black
community and seeks to be become citizen through resistance.

'Diaspora discourse articulates or bends together both roots and routes to construct
what Gilroy (1987) describes as an alternative public sphere. The language of
Diaspora is increasingly invoked by displaced peoples who feel (maintain, revive,
invent) a connection with a prior home'. (Clifford, 1997, p. 256)

Anti-Semitism in Europe was historically linked with the suspicion of the cosmopolitan Jew, who was often described as lacking roots, a sense of community and therefore loyalty to the state. The cosmopolitan Jew was not to be trusted by the citizens and was excluded and defined as the 'other'. As a form of resistance and safety, the Jews demanded the protection of their ghetto and the making of the Jewish Diaspora during anti-Semitic riots, especially during Easter celebrations. The ghetto became the place of safety, the place of defining Jewish separateness and Jewish Diaspora.

The Independent Citizen

The interpretation of the Independent Citizen is located within the discourse of classical market liberalism and the commitment to competition and the market economy. Within this discourse, the emphasis is on rational individualism. The rational individuals continually make decisions aimed to maximise their opulence – decisions based on natural competence (individuals pursue happiness whilst avoiding pain) and technical competence or the ability to acquire and accumulate information. The individual makes decisions based on knowledge and information, aware of opportunity costs; of having to make decisions between different priorities; of a willingness to pay a price for a given good. The independent citizen prefers to live with the injustice of the impersonal forces of the market rather than the injustices of the political process. The injustice of the political process is founded on arbitrary decisions made by politicians who seek the favours of specific interests groups and where decisions tend to disadvantage the individual who does not belong to the pressure group, which has muscle or has the ability of voice and exit.

The injustice of the market is the result of the price mechanism. In the market, people are not discriminated against because of colour or gender difference. The barrier to the market is price and if individuals are either unable or unwilling to meet the price, then they are excluded from a specific market, but they always have choice to enter other markets.

The independent citizen is an end and not a means to an end. The individual is entitled to keep the rewards because these reflect personal endowments, attributes and talents. Politicians use people as means to an end – as instruments to create their vision of the good society. Market Liberals have no vision of the good society – individuals decide for themselves. There is no attempt to moralise what is the good society. The Independent Citizen decides what is in her best interest.

'The moral side constraints upon what we may do, I claim, reflect the fact of our separate existence. They reflect the fact that no moral balancing act can take place among us; there is no moral outweighing of one of our lives by others so as to lead to a greater overall social good. There is no justified sacrifice of some of us for others. The root idea, namely that there are different individuals with separate lives and so no one may be sacrificed for others. . . it also I believe, leads to a libertarian side constraint that prohibits aggressions against another'. (Nozick, 1984, p. 106)

While the discourse of the public citizen seeks to make central the importance of public space, by contrast, the independent citizen seeks to squeeze and put limits on the public space. The independent citizen discourse is about redefining the public-private divide. The independent citizen discourse is about less government, less intervention and more reliance on individual self help, markets and competition.

The independent citizen is respected for making decisions as a rational individual. All decisions are rational and of equal value, individual life projects have to be respected, people have to be given the autonomy and the choice to fulfil their projects.

In the context of globalisation the commitment to privatization and liberalization policies confirm the commitment to the ideas of the independent citizen. Third World poverty is increasingly attributed to corrupt governments. The IMF and World Bank commitments to ensure compliance with anti poverty strategies that seek to reduce public expenditure and the role of government confirm the view that it is better for people in Third World countries to embrace privatisation as the way to securing the idea of citizenship.

The Entitled Citizen

The emphasis of the entitled citizen is the commitment to the social dimension of citizenship. Within a Marshall approach to citizenship the meaning of membership indicates the sharing of lived experiences. The concept of lived experience makes the meaning of citizenship more than just the commitment to formal and procedural rules. Citizenship is more than having a passport or the passing of the citizen test. Individuals may have a legal claim on citizenship, but unless they have access to the courts and the justice system, then that definition of citizenship remains formal. Citizenship requires a series of policies, which ensure that irrespective of income, individuals can substantiate their rights to citizenship. Policy commitments to equal pay, equal opportunities and anti discrimination all need processes of access where individuals who feel injured can have their case adjudicated with minimum costs and with minimum delay.

The ideas of membership and belonging involve social membership, which means access to a multiplicity of experiences that shape daily life. Membership of community involves shared experiences in access to health and education services, of shared environments, which deliver health care and education services. Belonging suggests that access should not be based on income, but on need. Universal access to public health and education ensure that income is not a barrier to entry. Furthermore, with public services directed at meeting individual need, it makes it possible for individuals to become self actualised and fulfil their life projects. In this sense, the commitment to the 'entitled citizen' is seen as essential if the public and independent citizen is to be achieved. Commitments to life projects, choice and autonomy cannot be delivered in a context of income equality and in a context of gender and race discrimination.

The discourse of the entitled citizen is at present being questioned by discourses, which point to various crises of social citizenship. The entitled citizen is at present being undermined by the language of fiscal crisis which points out that the entitled citizen puts too many claims on the state and that the state cannot meet these expectations and entitlements. There is an increased reluctance by people to finance the welfare state. The commitment to the entitled citizen has created a number of unintentional consequences including problems of moral hazard and dependency. The attempt to replace the network of families, friendships communities and neighbourhood through state financed services has created a vacuum where people feel that the duty starts and finishes with the taxes they pay and there is no obligation to care for others since this is the responsibility of professionals and bureaucracies The problem is that, despite major increases in expenditure, governments cannot replace the plurality of informal networks of civil society.

The Communitarian Citizen

In contrast to the individualism emphasised in the independent citizen model, the 'communitarian citizen' is firmly located in a social context, embedded in a community, deriving identity from the story of the community. Rather than being unencumbered, the individual identifies with responsibility, attachments, friendships and commitments. It is attachment, which gives the individual identity. Issues of freedom, liberty and individualism are meaningless when discussed in the abstract and it is only through context that such concepts gain meaning and are given value. We experience freedom and liberty in the context of community (Taylor, 1979; MacIntyre, 1981).

'We all approach our own circumstances as bearers of a particular social identity. I am someone's son or daughter, someone else's cousin or uncle; I am a citizen of this or that city, a member of this or that guild or profession; I belong to this clan, that tribe, the nation. I can only answer the question 'what am I to do?' if I can answer the prior question 'Of what story or stories do I find myself a part?' the story of my life is always embedded in the story of those communities from which I derive my identity'. (Macintyre, 1981, p. 205)

The communitarian citizen lives in a context, which is characterised by rights and obligations. Community confers rights on the individual but also assumes that the individual is also responsible for sustaining and maintaining community.

Community is the anchor; it provides certainty, regularity and rhythm, in a community, people know their place and they know what is expected of them and equally what to expect of others. Community is about rights and obligations. The community defines the individual. Life is stable and predictable and it is the stability, the durability and continuity of rhyme and rhythm that give people a sense of belonging, identity and citizenship.

The communitarian discourse provides an implicit criticism of the independent citizen. The independent citizen is described as unencumbered, making rational atomised decisions in the context of the market and has no attachment or responsibility. The market creates the ethic of competitive individualism, possessive individualism, of personal striving without taking into consideration the impact this has on community. In the context of the market, there is no commitment to solidarity. The drive towards the market creates the emptiness of city centres and of public places, which become increasingly unsafe. The communitarian citizen is located in the context of collective memories and of shared histories. Community is inclusive, where the 'in group' is made up of those who share in the story or narrative. The community is exclusive; it builds on tradition, institutions and authority.

The Consumer Citizen

According to a postmodern perspective, the discourses just outlined are defined as having been constructed within the language of modernity. Within modernity there is the implicit assumption of a shared language; of accepted universal concepts and of spaces for argumentation. By contrast, post modernity points to fragmentation, disintegration, diversity and competing discourses. Within a postmodern, discourse the consumer citizen is no longer attached to community, tradition, authority or institutions. The consumer citizen lives in a post-traditional, post-scarcity society where life politics replaces the emancipatory politics of modernity.

The consumer citizen lives in a world of continuing changes in wants and desires. There are no fixed essentialisms, no fundamentals, but continuing evaluation and self-reflection. The consumer citizen is the citizen of temporary and voluntary contract, of temporary attachment (Giddens, 1993). The consumer citizen seeks to deal with the problems of living in a society of strangers where there is no community, but where the challenge is to live with uncertainty and fear (Bauman, 1995). The consumer citizen perspective is implicitly critical of the assumptions that construct communitarian citizen.

Communitarianism is perceived as the attempt to re-occupy the vacuum of uncertainty and the emerging pluralism with pre-modern notions of community; anchors of family, neighbourhood and authority. Having glimpsed the possibilities of escaping the hypocrisy of modernity, of having brought into the light forms of domination, which were hidden, in the language of modernity, the consumer citizen seeks to live in the context of uncertainty.

Consumer society is therefore a criticism of collective memories and the imagined community. Modernity produced exclusion, separation and dominance. The public citizen discourse is founded on the assumption that in the context of public space there still is the possibility for dialogue and deliberative democracy (White, 1995). The contribution of Foucault, Derrida and other postmodern writers (Bernstein, 1991) has been the emphasis on the need to deconstruct the language of false consensus.

Within the context of postmodernity, there is no appeal to universal language, but an acceptance of fragmentation and the plurality of competing discourse, each feasible and coherent. The consumer citizen discourse displaces the politics of emancipation with life politics. There is no longer an emancipatory category that is likely to deliver the promised land of the classless society. There is no New Jerusalem but the world is as it is, a series of contradictions of both optimism and pessimism; of wonder and tragedy; of hope and despair; of fear and security and of certainty and uncertainty. In the absence of an emancipatory category, politics becomes a politics of issues, of pressure group politics and of neo-tribalism, with each tribe having its own language.

Within the context of issue politics, life politics emerges as the politics of lifestyles of emphasis on difference, on the discovery of personal identity as opposed to the politics of life chances and opportunity. The consumer citizen retreats from the public sphere as presently constituted. Politics is increasingly perceived to be irrelevant. The strategy of retreat into increasingly privatised lives confirms the degree to which political discourse becomes a non-issue. Politics, elections and parliaments reflect the self-serving interests of political elites.

The consumer citizen lives in a world of knowledge and information, where knowledge increasingly leads to uncertainty and fear. Information provided by experts is inherently conflictual, research findings are temporary and the decisions the citizen makes become increasingly individualised. Unemployment is no longer a social issue, but a personal experience – people are increasingly learning to live with the market, a context which they cannot shape, so rather than shaping the market they come to accept the need to live with markets. Employability and flexibility is the new language of post modernity. Unemployment in this sense becomes a personalised experience of acquiring skills and knowledge, of human capital investment, where investment is an individual decision.

In a consumer society, consumption defines identity and citizenship. The clothes we wear, the car we drive, our leisure pursuits and the football team we support give us identity. Consumer society lives on the emotions of signs. This is the age of the super highway of images when we experience climbing Everest without leaving the armchair. This is the age when we continually see images of starvation, of atrocity on TV screens and we continue to get on with the routines of our daily life. In this sense therefore, we are becoming global citizens. We are sharing emotions on the global level, yet being the global citizen proves to be too much.

The consumer citizen retreats into private, because the private is more secure, while the public is less secure. The public space is filled with the noise of tribal languages – the tribal languages of Protestants and Catholics, of Serbs, Croats and Czechs. There is little room for negotiation or compromise, no room for compassion or for listening to the other. Consumer citizen is the response to the limits of the entitled citizen. The lived experience of those dependent on social security is that of dependency shaped by the language of prejudice, of politicians creating images of the deserving and the undeserving poor and of public bureaucracies dispensing benefits. A welfare system financed through taxation makes some people dependent on others. The welfare state replaces private patriarchy with state patriarchy. The life politics of the consumer citizen seeks to replace welfare dependency with a generative approach to welfare where individuals are valued when intervention is justified if it empowers and enables individuals to secure their autonomy and choice.

THE LIMITATIONS IN DEFINING CITIZENSHIP

Dimensions of Citizenship

The concept of citizenship is contestable. The number of discourses on the meaning of citizenship re-affirms the lack of agreement as to what constitutes citizenship. This contestability results in academic impasse, because the concept is treated as something static. The concept has to be firmly located in people's daily lives and that there has to be a continuous engagement with the term to give it meaning and make it relevant to the here and now. Citizenship continuously reflects changes in expectations and hopes. The concept of citizenship has to be re-created and re-defined.

Universal Human Rights Discourse

The first major concern of citizenship must revolve around the issue of human rights. The preservation of individual human rights constitutes safety, freedom from fear and the arbitrary loss of civil liberties. The problem of human rights is that such rights are now very often abused within the boundaries of nation states. The democratic process is no longer a guarantor of human rights for minority groups. Human rights have to be protected at the global level through international agreements and a universal human rights discourse. In the global economy, forced child labour, slavery and sweatshops reflect human rights abuses.

The concept of universal citizenship provides a discourse of rights. The Nuremberg trials in the aftermath of the holocaust took for granted what was meant by decent human behaviour. The judges did not accept as appropriate defence the argument that those accused had received orders from above. Individuals are not automatons, they have their own minds and they know what is right and what is wrong. Individuals make choices and are therefore accountable for the choices they make. There is therefore the assumption that people have independent minds, that they take responsibility for their actions and that there is a shared universal morality of what is right and wrong.

The concept of universality appeals for the need to create inalienable rights – rights that cannot be undermined. Universal rights provide security and stability. The citizen can appeal to individual courts of justice that have to be kept insulated from political interference. By contrast, the emphasis on context results in a commitment to relativism where rights become relative and changed. The emphasis is on the understanding of the context. Afghan fighters have been imprisoned without access to lawyers, an action that has been justified in the context of terrorism. The prisoners have being defined as non-combatants and therefore have no status either as criminals or as prisoners of war, yet the military tribunals might find them guilty. Being held in Cuba ensures that the prisoners have no claims on US human rights.

Universalism has to be combined with the right to be treated as being different. Within modern nation states there are now substantial ethnic minority groups who derive their dignity from their communities. The right to worship and to be educated in separate Muslim Jewish Catholic or girls schools confirm a new morality of pluralism, toleration and freedom (Parekh, 1995). Pluralism in the context of a multicultural and multiracial society means a diffusion of power, a break with the dominance of an 'in group' and a willingness to decentralise power.

Feminism has also emphasised the dimension of difference. Women have been described as being qualitatively different to men; that their priorities, their values and attitudes are different and that they should be treated as different, if they are to achieve more equality, more autonomy and choice in securing their life projects (Eistenstein, 1989). Some feminists are doubtful as to the relevance of citizenship, arguing instead that the concept is a male construct only relevant to issues of the state and the individual in the public spaces.

Women tend to occupy other spaces including the spaces of domestic and family life and caring for others. These spaces are made invisible in debates on citizenship. Women have been excluded from citizenship often because citizenship is associated with the public sphere.

Citizenship is often defined in terms of the individual, which critics argue confines the debate to Western liberal democracies. Such criticisms include communitarian perspectives, which point out that liberal individualism is associated with atomisation; the asocial individual and the notion of the unencumbered self. Communitarians argue that individuals make sense of life through their networks and experiences of belonging and commitments.

The issue of individualism is difficult to resolve in the sense that it creates the circular argument of whether the individual actually exists or whether the individual is a social construct. The concept of citizen starts from the existence of the individual with rights. Rights are easier to bestow on an individual than on a community, since communities do not experience losses of rights. Liberalism assumes that it is individuals who make communities, rather than communities who make individuals.

A final issue is the relationship of race and citizenship. Any attempt to define citizenship leads to forms of exclusion and it is usually people who are defined as not being part of the endogenous population who are defined as non-citizens. Besides the issues of exclusion however, there is the issue of racism, in terms of how certain groups become 'accepted' by the indigenous population. The argument here is that even if a migrant holds a passport, which confirms procedural citizenship, there are still experiences of racism and discrimination in day-to-day life. Arendt (1951) has argued that there are two strategies that migrants seek to adopt in seeking acceptance by the majority. One strategy is that of the *parvenu*, who is continuously seeking acceptance and recognition and adopts the majority culture. The problem is that the parvenu will still continue to experience marginalisation and exclusion – the migrant continues to be a stranger. The parvenu vomits her past and her other identities in the course of becoming accepted. The second strategy is that of accepting the role of being the *pariah* – the idea that the pariah accepts the consequence of being the other and being different. The pariah asks that society has to treat the 'other' as a person who is separate and unique and that acceptance has to take place in a context of plurality and difference.

The issues of universal individualism and the rights to be different are major challenges for contemporary liberal democracies. Increasingly, liberal democracies are becoming societies made of strangers rather than communities. The challenge is the extent to which liberal democracies can cope with the context of strangers. In dealing with fear and uncertainty, the state increasingly adopts strategies that seek to re-affirm the commitment to an imagined community sharing a collective history and collective memories. Institutions, traditions and authority become the anchors of stability in the context of fear and uncertainty. The problem is that any attempt to construct 'imagined community', as defined by the state, is likely to be inclusive of those who see themselves as sharing in the collective memories of that community, in contrast to those who are defined as the outsiders. The making of culture, memorial parks, statues and commemorative events, become a celebration for some and symbols of oppression for others.

The Recognition of Difference

The commitment to universal human rights is compatible with the commitment of the right to be different. The right to be gay or lesbian and the right to be Muslim are connected with commitment to the recognition of difference of living within a plurality of paradigms. The commitment to human rights guarantees the rights of the individual. The person with physical disability or learning difficulties has to be treated differently, only in the context that difference is a commitment to the rights of the individual.

The recognition of communities, of the need to recognise difference between communities and to give communities autonomy, tends to confirm separatism and segregation. The attempt to create ethnic enclaves in the former Yugoslavia might be a short-term answer to bring about peace and stability, but in the longer term, the commitment must be to re-create the state of Bosnia Herzegovina committed to ethnic pluralism and human rights. According to Obrad Savic, editor of the *Belgrade Circle*:

'Let people know another Serbia and Croatia exist, Bosnia is the key. If democracy fails there, it fails everywhere. We lost the future. We lost the hope, Utopia, everything. We live in the past – a collective process of regression, a sort of schizophrenia. It's not postmodern, it's pre-modern: a loss of social rationality. We live in the past and lose the future. Nationalism is an ideology of the past. We glorify only those Serbs and Croat thinkers who celebrate the dead – we are cultural necrophiles . . . I have a dream of millions of Yugoslavs all crying together aloud as a sort of primal scream'. (*New Statesman and Society*, 3 November 1995, p. 23)

The right to be different within the context of the modern state is only of limited relevance, since the modern state is a territorial state and individuals, groups and communities are located within the territory of the modern state. According to Parekh (1995):

'The modern state privileges the territorial identity. Its members do, of course, have multiple identities, affiliations and allegiances, but the territorial identity is overarching and dominant . . . Unlike its earlier counterparts, it territorialises and totalises human relations and activities and gives them a wholly new dimension'. (Parekh, 1995, p. 28)

Policies of assimilation, integration and multiculturalism have to be understood in the context of the modern state. Most modern states are constituted of pluralities of identities, of communities and ethnic minorities. The nature of legislation has often been constructed within the framework of sustaining a majority paradigm that does not question the nature of dominance and oppression, and does not seek to be reflexive and critical. Modern European states have tended to be nationalistic, emphasising homogeneity, commonality, where the individual is deeply situated within the imagined community as constituted by the state. The nationalistic nation state of Europe creates a policy framework, which hides and disavows oppression of those who do not belong to the imagined community. Collective memories and living with the past imprisons individuals in the past and creates an obstacle to optimism and the ability to be different.

> 'The dangers of nationalism are all too well known to need elaboration. It is exclusive and chauvinistic . . . it is suspicious of differences between individuals and groups and postulates a non-existent national soul or spirit,. privileges national identity, denies the role of mediating agencies, has a collectivist thrust fears outsiders and rules out intercultural borrowing'. (Parekh, 1995, p. 48)

Public and Social Contexts

The commitment to human rights needs an environment of transparency. The confirmation of human rights in a written constitution is not sufficient, since human rights need to be protected in an environment of political accountability, democratic culture and public participation. This commitment requires a form of governance that is decentralised and governance that encourages a 'thick' democracy. The public space needs to be made safe. Multinational corporations have to be separated from government, which means that the way politics is financed has to be come more transparent.

Aspects of Marshall's social argument are still relevant to the challenges of consumer society capitalism. Denial of access to health care, education and social security are still major barriers to citizenship. Civil liberties and human rights need to be combined with social rights. Since the mid-1970s, Keynesian economic ideas have been abandoned as a macroeconomic framework. The conduct of economic policy during the past 20 years has been about the control of inflation, the money supply and reducing the public sector deficit. The ascending paradigm has been associated with market liberal ideas of de-regulation and privatisation, which in turn has contributed to increased income inequalities. The break with full employment has made trade union resistance more difficult. Continuing high levels of unemployment in Europe have created insecurity. Most European countries have now experienced long-term unemployment. Unemployment has persisted in

Germany throughout the last two decades. Unemployment in Europe has remained stagnant at around 9 per cent of the working population. In the meantime, the United Nations estimates that there are 140 million people worldwide who are unemployed.

The abandonment of the Beveridge/Keynesian paradigm did have major implications for the social citizen of Marshall. Market Liberalism has resulted in widening income differentials and inequality. The welfare state no longer creates citizenship, but dependency targeted at specific income groups. The welfare state looks more and more like a place of deterrence and a place to stay away from. Reducing taxes has meant that the tax base for funding the welfare state has been eroded, which, in turn, means that future governments will have to depend on growth to fund additional expenditures, while at the same time, they will be under equal pressure to deliver tax reductions, so that people can feel they are sharing in prosperity.

'If we can, we buy ourselves individually out of the underprovided, shabby schools, the overcrowded, undernourished hospitals, the miserly state old-age pension . . . The more we do so, the more reasons we have for doing it, as the schools grow shabbier, the hospital queues longer and old-age provisions more miserly still' (Bauman, 1995, p. 272).

CONCLUSIONS: THE GLOBAL CITIZEN

'The collective power of people to shape the future is greater now than ever before and, the need to exercise it is more compelling. Mobilising that power to make life in the twenty-first century more democratic, more secure and more sustainable is the foremost challenge of this generation. The world needs a new vision that can galvanise people everywhere to achieve higher levels of cooperation in areas of common concern and shared destiny'. (The Commission on Global Governance, Our Global Neighbourhood, 1995, p. 1)

The globalised economy requires a commitment to widening political account-ability where people feel that they are part of the universe, involved in decisions which effects their lives, their environment and the world to be left to future generations. It is within this context that civil society, civic virtue and citizenship has to be redefined. Citizenship has to be developed in a post enlightenment context or as Bridges (1994) has suggested a postmodern civic culture, which still needs to be coined.

'The new vocabulary of citizenship will be shaped by concepts of moral liberal ideals that emphasise their cultural particularism and their partial nature . . . This requires a re-thinking of virtually every aspect of liberal democratic citizenship'. (Bridges, 1994, p. 114)

The new citizenship has to combine a commitment to universal human rights with the right to be different. Rorty (1989) has tended to provide a pragmatic defence of liberal democracy, arguing that liberal democracy continues to be our best hope, despite its limitations. By contrast, Lyotard (Bridges, 1994) has tended to argue that liberal democracy is a form of government, which replaces monarchy as a form of government but that the form of power in liberal democracy continues to be despotic. There is therefore a need to reclaim public space for a democratic culture. The democracy of the public space still offers the best hope for dialogue and compromise.

4. The relevance of democracy

INTRODUCTION

According to the *New York Times* editorial of 2 April 2003, the War on Iraq was equated with America exporting its republican values and revolutionary tradition. America, born out of revolution against George III, was now exporting that tradition to the Middle East. Members of the Bush administration have argued the case that democracy in Iraq would create a model for more secular forms of democracy in the Arab world. This view of exporting democracy seems to be very different from previous histories of democracy, where democracy has very often reflected internal struggles between the elites who held power and disenfranchised populations. Furthermore, a brief study of US foreign policy would suggest that in the past, the USA has supported non-democratic governments in Argentina, Chile and Nicaragua.

Advocates for President Bush's vision of democracy are keen to show the compatibilities between the economics of market liberal ideas and the commitment to liberal democracy. Democracy and market economics are described as being inextricably linked. Since democracy guarantees people the ability to choose their governments, likewise the liberal market economy provides choices in employment, provision of health and education and also consumer products. Democracy cannot exist without a commitment to a market economy and likewise a market economy cannot exist outside the context of political democracy. The ideas of connecting market economic ideas with liberal democracy are increasingly presented as the new modernism, the irresistible force of history, the new inevitability to which there is no alternative, a new vision as defined by neo-conservatives in the USA:

'In the monocular neo-conservative view of modernisation, every society in the world will eventually follow America in becoming a secular democracy. In reality, the US is a less secular regime than Turkey . . . By embracing the neo-conservatives distorted view of the world, he [Mr Blair] has impoverished politics. We can all see that public services have collapsed and are in need of urgent reform. But why must that mean injecting market forces and private capital into practically every corner of health and education? . . . In every area of policy there are collective choices to be made. Thinking of modernisation as a single unidirectional process has the effect of narrowing these choices.' (John Gray, 'Blair is in thrall to the myth of a monolithic modernity', *The Guardian* 19 April 2003)

While it might be true that democracy cannot exist without a commitment to a market economy, it is not necessarily true to argue that a market cannot exist in the absence of democracy. While the Pinochet regime in Chile embraced the market economic ideas of Milton Friedman, they also put democracy on hold. Since the late 1980s, the Communist Party in China has continued to show that it is possible to have a thriving market economy within the context of flexible communist thinking. Similar situations exist in Saudi Arabia, Jordan and Kuwait, while these countries can claim to have thriving market economies, there is also an apparent absence of democratic governance.

The following sections seek to explore whether globalisation is purely an economic concern or whether there are inevitable overspills between economic globalisation and political globalisation? Is it possible to continue to push with the agenda of economic globalisation in the absence of wider global accountability and democratic controls? What therefore are the connections between issues of democracy including concerns about human rights and political accountability and the challenges of a changing global economy? The explosion at a chemical plant in Bhopal during the late 1980s; the degradation of the environment; oil spillages in Nigeria; disavowal of responsibilities towards workers in the Economic Progressive Zones (EPZs) of Burma and Thailand, represent the continuous blurring of economic issues and political expediency.

At present, claims on democracy and arguments for resistance seem to be in decay. The public space seems to be associated with the retreat into quietism, disenchantment, anti-politics and increased privatism. The public spaces are described as being colonised by political elites (Barber, 2000; Habermas, 1984), professional lobbyists, influential financial contributors to politicians and political parties and owners and proprietors of newspapers and TV channels, who between them, define the political and policy agenda. Resistance is eclipsed by passivity. Reflecting on the passivity of the Arab nations on the eve of the War on Iraq, the recently deceased Edward Said (2003) asked:

'Why is there such silence and such astounding helplessness. The largest power in history is about to launch a war against a sovereign Arab country now ruled by a dreadful regime the clear purpose of which is not only to destroy the Baa'ath regime but to re-redesign the entire region . . . No one can be shielded from the cataclysm if and when it comes. And yet, there is only long silence followed by a few vague bleats of polite demurral in response . . . Do we deserve such racist derision? This is not only unacceptable. It is impossible to believe. How can a region of almost 300 million Arabs wait passively for the blows to fall without attempting a collective roar of resistance'. (Edward Said, 'When will we resist?', *The Guardian* 25 January 2003)

THE PROBLEMS OF GOVERNMENT OVERLOAD AND UNGOVERNABILITY

Debates in the advanced economies during the 1970s and the early 1980s were focused on the view that democracy was being undermined by problems of 'ungovernability' (Rose, 1984), 'political paralysis' (Beer, 1982) of political parties outbidding each other during election (Brittan, 1977) and the danger of governments going bankrupt (Rose and Peters, 1979). These concerns pointed to arguments about the implications of big government defined in terms of government regulation, high levels of public expenditure, taxation and the likely influences of strategic interest groups especially trade unions, public sector employees that were often described as the beneficiaries of government subsidies and which, at the same time, was undermining the democratic process:

> 'The subsidy scramble is very much like the benefits scramble and the pay scramble . . . A principal source of syndicalist power is the 'know-how' of the producer. Such knowledge, moreover, may be not only technical and thus only accessible to technocrats with the right training but also quite particularistic and even personal . . . This etatism succumbs to syndicalism'. (Beer, 1982, p. 75)

The common thread of these arguments was the attempt to explain what seemed to be the paradox that government intervention in social policies, subsidies to employers and policies on incomes, was likely to make government and democracy weaker, rather than stronger. Intervention created professionals and knowledge estates that would advertise the benefits of their programmes, but would equally resist any change of policy. Government employees were more likely to revert to industrial militancy, since they were less likely to lose their jobs and employers would continue to lobby for their subsidies such as in agriculture and steel. Teachers, doctors and nurses represented the new knowledge estate that increased the dependency of governments to implement policy.

According to these arguments, the post-war settlement founded on the twin pillars of full employment and the welfare state had undermined the disciplines of the marketplace, which in turn had resulted in increased trade union militancy and the need for government to negotiate with strategic interest groups. Public expenditure decisions reflected the politics of the 'pig trough', with interest groups lobbying for subsidies for agriculture, steel making, coal mining and defence contracts. The result has been big government, at the expense of higher levels of taxation and the increased remoteness of citizens due to increased bureaucracy and the influence of the knowledge estates of professional elites.

Since the mid-1970s, the economic concern for Government increasingly became the control of inflationary pressures brought about by escalating wage demands in the context of full employment. While committed to the policy of full employment, governments were forced to negotiate and compromise with trade unions to moderate wage demands in exchange for higher levels of public expenditure on health, education and pensions. Government was described as weak and unable to give political leadership:

> 'In the 1950s and 1960s, economic growth produced a fiscal dividend, supplying greater tax revenues to government without any increases in tax rates. Government expanded welfare programmes providing major benefits to most citizens in child-hood, ill health and retirement. In the 1970s Western economies have grown more slowly than before – an average of 2.4 per cent – while the costs of public policy have continued to rise as before. Overloading the political economy immediately threatens a loss of effectiveness and efficiency. Citizen indifference is the other possible consequence of government overloading the political economy'. (Rose, 1984, p. 12)

THE EMERGENCE OF THE NEW INDIVIDUAL

Commenting on the rise of conservative ideas in the USA, Hayward (2001) related to the eclipse of what he called liberal hegemony after the election of President Johnson in 1964. While Johnson had won a victory with 61 per cent of the popular vote – the highest since Roosevelt's landslide in 1936 – Johnson's proposals for the Great Society; his commitment to equality and re-distribution of income; the Civil Rights Act of 1964; the race and students riots in 1968 and the slowdown of the US economy all led to a Conservative counter revolution and the eventual election of Ronald Reagan to the Presidency in 1980. The 1964 election was a 'hinge election' that reflected major controversies on the future of the USA, but it was also a 'wedge elec-tion' in that the Civil Rights Act splintered the Democratic Party and also the Republican Party. It ushered in the beginning of the end of what Hayward called the old liberal establishment:

> 'In retrospect it is clear that 1964 witnessed the end of liberalism's decay, though it was difficult to perceive . . .To the Goldwater campaign, liberalism reacted with condescension, to the restiveness represented by the Free Speech Movement, liber-alism responded with incomprehension. Both reactions would eventually prove fatal'. (Hayward, 2001, p. 49)

Senator Barry Goldwater had articulated the future conservative agenda, demand-ing less government, echoing the views of his then economic adviser Milton Friedman that the problem of inflation was the money supply, government expenditure and public sector deficits. Goldwater campaigned against increasing family allowances, pointing out that welfare would encourage the breakdown of the family, increase the number of 'illegitimate children and deadbeat dads'. Goldwater had also opposed the Civil Rights Bill and Equal Voting Rights for the black population, arguing that this was not the responsibility of the Federal Government. During the election of 1964, Goldwater had been branded as a rallying call for racists. While the passive and non-violent resistance of the civil rights movement had attracted the sympathy of the majority of white voters (around 70 per cent), the shift towards more affirmative action, together with the race riots, presented the beginning of the white backlash.

Making the case for affirmative action, President Johnson, speaking at Howard University in June 1965 explained:

> 'it is not enough to open the gates of opportunity. You do not take a person who for years has been hobbled in chains and liberate him, bring him to the starting line for a race and then say, 'You are free to compete with all the others' and shall justly believe that you have been completely fair'. (Hayward, 2001, p. 47)

Hayward argues that Johnson's vision of the Great Society had shifted from self-help, equal opportunity and obligation, towards ideas of universalism, a commitment to the re-distribution of income and equality; ideas that did not correspond with the values of individualism and self help that underpinned American Society. Furthermore, the commitment on race equality, while supported for embracing the ideas of equal citizenship, by contrast policies on affirmative action and quotas created a conservative resistance. Finally, the large increases in public expenditure (public spending increased by 17 per cent in 1968) while the economy was growing by 5 per cent, together with the threats of inflation, the slowdown in the economy spelled the end of Keynesian economic ideas. The late Patrick Moynihan who was an adviser to Johnson on the anti poverty programme had already argued in early 1965:

> 'The nation is turning conservative at a time when its serious internal problems may well be more amenable to conservative solutions than to liberal ones'. (Patrick Moynihan, as quoted in Brinkley, 1998, p. 279)

The ascendancy of a conservative political discourse in both Britain and the USA sought to embrace moral, economic and political criticisms of the collectivist politics of the post-war years. Keynesian economic ideas were criticised for contributing to the high levels of inflation, unemployment and the growth of the welfare state. According to monetarist advocates, the increases in unemployment could be attributed to workers pricing themselves out of labour markets. Inflation reflected the weakness of government, which reflected their willingness to increase the money supply. The reluctance of government to increase taxation or reduce public expenditure, but instead, relying on high government borrowing to meet the claims for higher levels of public expenditure, led to inflation, but also higher costs of borrowing, which in turn had adverse effects on private investment decisions. Conservatives argued that the priority of government was to break with the politics of the stalemate state and instead embrace the disciplines of the market through a series of policy reforms including de-regulation of the labour market, breaking up public sector monopolies and liberalisation of financial markets. The public space and democracy were to be re-defined according to market liberal principles:

> 'Indeed for liberals, public space has an exclusively prudential feel and is not intended to convey a rich sense of publicness or commonwealth or republica. Contrary to historical reality, where public space was the condition of the emergence of individuals, it exists in liberal theory only as a concession reluctantly proffered by individuals pursuing self-preservation and self-aggrandizement. It is at best the domain of prudence where individuals strike public bargains'. (Barber, 2000, p. 9)

The conservative criticisms of collectivist landscapes connected the commitments to Keynesian full employment with interest group politics, making concessions to trade unions, inflation pressures and the moral hazard of the welfare state, student sub-cultures and the decline of moral authority. The major consequence of collectivism has been the overloading of democracy with increased expectations, which in turn have led to problems of ungovernability and the danger of government going bankrupt. The market liberal counter-revolution targeted the growth of government and argued that privatisation would remove a number of claims from the public space. Privatisation of government corporations transferred public sector employees to the private sector. Trade union reforms and increases in unemployment led to a decline in trade union membership and also trade union militancy. Using monetary policy to deal with inflation downgraded the role of incomes policy and also trade union influence.

The major consequence of the ascendancy of market liberal conservatives has been the de-politicisation of the public spaces and the emergence of anti-politics ideology and the new privatised individual. According to Bauman (2000) the new individual has no essential qualities, but instead reflects the concept of modular man made up of different layers ready and able to change according to the challenge and the context:

> 'The lodestar of the first reformation was the individual freedom to enter and traverse the road leading to eternal bliss. The catchword of the second reformation is human rights, that is, the right of every individual to use her or his freedom of choice to decide what bliss she or he wants ought to be like and to select or design her or his own track, which may lead to it. That hidden potential is the emergence

and prevalence of what Ernest Gellner called the modular man'. (Bauman, 2000, p. 158)

Accordingly, the collectivism of the post-war settlement has been displaced by the ideas of the new individualism and of a consumer society that seeks to put the emphasis on opportunity, identity and lifestyles. While collectivism was connected with ideas of industrial communities characterised by shared experiences of work, life insecurities and leisure, in the context of consumer society, individual identity is no longer defined by attachment to community, employment or the nation state. Instead the new individual is involved in a continuing process of do-it-yourself (DIY) biography. Gellner's metaphor of modular man is associated with modular furniture that can be shaped to reflect consumer needs and demands. Likewise, modular man is no longer a set of fixed principles:

> 'Just as modular furniture has no single pre designed 'proper' shape, the modular man has no preordained profile and assignation. He is rather a being with too many features and aspects so that most of them can only be held for a time, ready to be put in or taken away as needs arise. The modular man is a creature with mobile, disposable and exchangeable qualities. To put it in a nutshell the modular man is first and foremost a man without essence'. (Bauman, 2000, p. 158)

The concept of modular man reflects a process of breaking anchor with traditions, institutions, collective memories and histories. Economic decisions are increasingly located in the cyber-world of financial markets removed from geographical spaces. Shareholders are the new absentee landlords who are separated from factories, production and employment. There is a disavowal of responsibility. The new corporation is weightless sub-contracting services:

> 'Companies prefer to see themselves as organisers of collections of contractors as opposed to employment organisations. One thing is certain: offering employment – the steady kind, with benefits, holiday pay, a measure of security and maybe even union representation – has fallen out of economic fashion'. (Klein, 2001a, p. 221)

THE DEMOCRATIC RESPONSE

Globalisation is at present being defined as being irreversible and that there is no alternative but to accept the consequences of globalisation and the economics of competitive markets. The language of the free market is made interchangeable with the concept of globalisation. Yet, markets are social constructs and represent outcomes of political decisions. The decision of governments to provide subsidies to agriculture creates a specific market for food, which is politicised. Rights on seed patents, subsidies to chemicals, for example, help to construct a specific market in food production. In the USA, 50 per cent of senators are elected by 16 per cent of the population – a 16 per cent that lives in rural America and where subsidies to agriculture reflect a determined political choice that is influenced both by the agribusiness and by political calculation.

Present forms of globalisation represent a series of political decisions and political choices. While in 1970 the ratio of foreign exchange trade to world trade in goods and services was 2:1, by 1990, this has increased to 50:1 and by 2001, to 70:1. The end result has been to create a convergence in interest rates within the advanced economies, thus limiting the role of fiscal policy, exchange rate policy and monetary policy (Eatwell and Taylor, 2000). Increased capital mobility has therefore put limits on the autonomy of national governments:

> 'The evidence presented so far indicates that globalisation processes and their insti-
> tutionalisation, particularly through the WTO, has weakened the effectiveness of
> national governments' traditional macroeconomic and microeconomic policy
> instruments. Further, increased trade and factor mobility may be expected to
> increase the elasticity of demand for labour and thereby reduce labour's bargaining
> power'. (Perraton, 2003, p. 29)

Sutcliffe and Glyn (2003) have questioned the assumption of global competition in labour markets. While manufacturing (which employs 18 per cent of the UK workforce), agriculture and mining are open to international competition, other economic sectors, including wholesale and retail trade, community, personal, social services utilities and construction, which include 60 per cent of the workforce, are insulated from international competition.

Similarly, the decision to de-regulate labour markets, the removal of trade union immunities and the decisions on the level of the minimum wage create specific labour markets:

> 'Markets, market systems and capitalist societies do not just happen. People create
> them. In these acts of creation, people make choices . . . These choices will usually
> have socially better results when are made in an open explicit, fully informed and
> democratic manner . . . When people say they are 'for markets' or 'for the market
> system' they are primarily making an ideological statement and not giving a practi-
> cal answer to the question of what roles market should play in economic develop-
> ment'. (MacEwan, 1999, p. 116)

Anti-globalisation protests in Seattle, London and Genoa have provided increased awareness of the consequences of economic globalisation. However, present forms of resistance remain nascent and ephemeral and a reminder of the bargaining by riot of the early nineteenth century. Protest is fragmented and very often there seem to be conflicts between the interests of groups in the advanced economies, who seek to connect labour standards and trade and those in the developing economies, who see the implementation of labour standards as a form of protectionism and against competitive labour markets:

'One thing is clear, the close relationship between the state and economic restructuring means that resistance to globalisation will continue to come from within national civil society and national social movements including organised labour. Given the extension of capital's flight from the nation state, it is necessary and urgent that resistance movements attempt a similar scale of operation. Paradoxically, the current discourse on globalisation and the end of the nation-state, the new ideologies of expanding capital, actually provides an opportunity for popular resistance movements to escape the myths of the nation-state and build new popular transnational social movements'. (Amoore, 2000, p. 25)

Amoore (2000) is right in arguing that resistance will continue to be shaped within the specific contexts of the nation state but it is open to question whether the experiences of the limits of the nation state will necessarily lead to the formation of transnational social movements. Rather than being transnational, protests have also the potential to become increasingly local and against migrant workers. Politicians expressing xenophobic concerns about the decline of the nation state, national sovereignty, identity and immigration become popular in the age of globalisation. Protectionism, demands for subsidies to protect steel making against cheap foreign imports, subsidies for agriculture have also become forms of resistance to globalisation:

'(Corporations) keep silent about misdirected xenophobic on the ground responses to their global operations. They do not foment such responses deliberately, but they can only rejoice when the anger caused by the growing helplessness of government and communities to vindicate individual grievances is channelled into enmity towards the local aliens – foreign and migrant workers. And so the public debate about the ways and means to alleviate the sorry state of local affairs tends to focus on the foreigners in our midst, on the best methods of spotting them, rounding them up and deporting them back 'to where they've come from', while coming nowhere near the true source of trouble'. (Bauman, 2000, p. 193)

What is Democracy for?

Can the democratic process deal with the challenges of globalisation? The growth of influence of multinational corporations, the increased mobility of capital and the increased separations of space between economic decisions and political autonomy indicate that forms of political accountability are now lagging behind the globalising economy. There is increasingly a globalised democratic deficit. Paradoxically, while economic influence has become global the individual has retreated from the political spaces. Globalisation has become interchangeable with the neo-liberal language of free markets and the privatised individual.

Politics and the democratic process have in the past provided the means of resistance. Public health, sanitation, provisions for unemployment, old age pensions, universal education and health care have all represented historical struggles, negotiations and comprises. During the past 130 years, modern democracy has been anchored in a specific geographic space, in the city, the region and the nation state. Politics has reflected conflicting interests of localised competing interests of the aristocracy, industrialists, labour, shop keepers, politicians, bureaucracies and the knowledge estates of health and education professionals, each making claims on the public spaces.

Definitions of democracy combine both the 'is' and the 'ought' which means that it is both a descriptive and a normative concept. In this sense, the focus on the practicalities and realisms of democracy, without exploring the hopes and optimism of democracy, only captures one level of meaning. According to Sartori (1987):

> 'To avoid starting out on the wrong foot we must keep in mind, then, that (a) the democratic ideal does not define the democratic reality and, vice versa, a real democracy is not and cannot be the same, as an ideal one and that (b) democracy results from and is shaped by, the interactions between its ideals and its reality, the pull of an ought and the resistance of an is'. (Sartori, 1987, p. 8)

Dahl (2000) has suggested that democracy needs to be measured against the criteria of effective participation, equality in voting, public spaces, control over the agenda and inclusion. Political decisions are often made by the few behind closed doors. There is unequal access to political resources. Democracy seems to serve some vested interest, while the needs of majorities are often ignored or marginalised. However, democracy still represents the best way in which societies can give shape to their social, economic, political and cultural landscapes, of being actively involved in dialogue, of being informed, of being able to express differences and diversity of opinions. Democracy provides the potential for change, so that rather than being the decision takers, societies can become the decision makers. Freedom of speech, of association, human rights and the right to choose, depend on the willingness of people to come together to claim those rights and then defend them. Thus, individual autonomy is not something that happens in a vacuum. Democracy by itself does not guarantee human rights, but that it is active participation, involvement and vigilance that ensure the rights of the individual. By contrast, the retreat into privatised lives and the retreat from public spaces undermine democracy:

> 'As a result, one of the imperative needs of democratic countries is to improve citizens' capacities to engage intelligently in political life . . . Will democratic countries,

whether old, new or in transition rise to these challenges? If they fail to do so, the gap between democratic ideals and democratic realities, already large, will grow even greater and an era of democratic triumph will be followed by an era of democratic deterioration and decline'. (Dahl, 2000, p. 188)

Market Liberals and Democracy

Market liberal views of democracy tend to put limits on the role of politics. They argue that individuals are ends, not means to an end. Individual lives should not be shaped by the views of others. In arguing the case for free markets, market liberals point out that the guarantee of individual rights and freedom depends on the rights to property, because property is attached to the individual and in consequence, the right to property gives recognition to the existence of the individual. The free market confirms the rights of the individual. Attempts to re-distribute resources through governments represent the centralising tendency of the state. The state is able to dispose of the individual. Representative democracy is replaced by functional democracy, allowing coalitions of interests to threaten the individual citizen. Market liberals including Nozick (1974), Friedman (1962) and Hayek (1982) have pointed out that there are inequalities of access to the political process. Politics is therefore described as being unjust because politics serves those with connections and knowledge of the corridors of governments. In recognising the nature of political inequality, the response is to seek retreat from politics and to put limits on government:

'Only limited government can be decent government because there does not exist (and cannot exist) general moral rules for the assignment of particular benefits'. (Hayek, 1982, p. 102)

Individual rights are therefore central to the doctrine of liberal democracy, since individual liberty is seen as the emancipation of the subject. The individual is defined as a rational agent making decisions that are of equal value and demand mutual recognition and respect. Individuals have to be treated as ends in themselves rather than means to an end:

'Individuals are ends and not merely means; they may not be sacrificed or used for the achieving of other ends without their consent'. (Nozick, 1974, p. 30)

The political process is to be treated with suspicion and caution because it is more fickle and unjust than the marketplace. Inequalities, which emerge within the marketplace, are more just, because individuals meet as sovereign individuals. In contrast, inequalities, which result from resource allocation through the political process, are unjust, because these inequalities relate to inequalities of access to the political process. Those likely to benefit through the political process are the political elite and those who have the knowledge and access to the political process.

In a democracy, people are likely to change their views between elections, which means that government do not have the mandate to bring about irreversible shifts in rights and obligations. In a democracy, people do not have the right to threaten or undermine the rights of others. Accordingly, market liberals point out that there is the need for constitutional form of governments. The Constitution should establish the rights of the individual in such a way that changes in government will not lead to changes in the rights of the individual. This means that the Constitution should state clearly what the rights of the individual should be.

The major flaws with the market liberal view of democracy are two-fold. First, market liberal views are based on the assumption that if people retreat from the public space, politics will not matter. There is, therefore, a sense of denial, with no attempt to address the question of who occupies the public space, including the impact of business influence on the public space or the continued unequal relationships between corporate vested interests and the interest of the individual citizen. Market liberals depend on written constitution as the means of protecting the individual. There is therefore a denial of inequality of power and influence, the existence of a plutocracy, of an elite of political and business connections that ensure the ascendance of their specific interests. Second, there is the assumption that political elites will voluntarily surrender political power. Market liberalism seeks to expand privatised lives where individuals seek to resolve problems through family networks, employment and neighbourhood. Individuals are asked to retreat from the public sphere because 'politics' is unpredictable, unstable and unjust. The public space is to be treated with suspicion than with hope and optimism.

Market liberal views of democracy represent an adherence to 'thin democracy' (Barber, 1996), based on the premise of individualism where democratic values correspond with the values of self-interest. Barber describes thin democracy as being precarious and provisional because the commitment to democracy is limited to the idea of self-interest. It is the democracy of the acquisitive individual of McPherson. The voter making self-interest the priority may abandon democracy for other forms of politics if other political systems seem to offer something better. Market liberals embrace a negative framework of liberty in the sense that they point to the negative nature of the state and the arbitrary nature of politics. Within the discourse of the New Right the possibility of politics as a process that enhances individual liberty and freedom is not taken seriously.

The Participatory Model of Democracy

The participatory model is characterised by an attempt to provide an agenda for democracy, for providing opportunities for participation, but also for pointing out that participation should not be left to narrow aspects of electoral democracy, but actually to promote a culture of democracy:

> 'The problem of building a democratic society is thus one of a dynamic interaction of rules and actors with the actors rendering the rules more democratic and the increasingly democratic rules rendering the actors more firmly committed to and skilled democratic participation and decision making. We term this process a democratic dynamic'. (Bowles and Gintis, 1986, p. 186)

According to this approach, it is not sufficient to understand the 'is' of democracy and how democracy works at present, but to establish a culture of hope and optimism for democracy. The ethics of participation in decision making should not be confined to the electoral process, but also to other aspects of daily life. This means the right to participate at the place of work, to be involved in decisions on investment, which are likely to effect daily lives, earnings and future pensions. People who invest their lives in their place should have equal value to those who have financial interests. Workers cannot just be dismissed as hired labour who are paid a wage, but be accepted as investors. Vaclav Havel, a Czech writer and dissident during the years of Soviet occupation and later to become the first President of the New Czech Republic, connects democracy with the spirit of hope:

> 'Either we have hope within us or we don't: it is a dimension of the soul and it's not essentially dependent on some particular observation of the world or estimate of the situation . . . It is an orientation of the spirit, an orientation of the heart, it transcends the world that immediately experienced and is anchored somewhere beyond the horizons'. (Havel, 1990, p. 181)

The hopes of deliberative democracy are therefore seen to be inextricably connected with issues of social justice, income inequalities and the access to public provision, including health and education. The vision of participatory democracy seeks to encourage a public culture where the process of participation is likely to result in a better-informed citizen. Fernando Cardoso, who became the first democratically installed President of Brazil after 20 years of military rule, described democracy as an ongoing process:

> 'It is absolutely essential to understand that democracy is not the finish line, but rather a starting point. Securing democratic freedoms does not guarantee an immediate solution to the problems that afflict the population, such as poverty, disease and social inequalities. Democracy does not put an end to injustice, but it does establish the conditions that allow us to aspire to achieve effective justice, not merely as an abstract ideal, but as a value present in the everyday life of citizens. Democracy can also contribute to making injustices more perceptible, which is the first step in combating them. The more injustice becomes visible, the greater becomes our motivation to fight it . . . At the same time, we cannot lose sight of the

negative effect that extreme inequalities and rigid social stratification have on the performance of free institutions. Democracy is rooted in equality and, for it to be fully realised, it is essential that each citizen be able to identify the possibilities for improving his situation and that of his family. It is essential that there be equality of opportunity'. (Cardoso, 2001, p. 9)

Individuals are part of their community and it is within communities that ethics of democracy and citizenship are created. Communities can be the spaces that guarantee diversity and pluralities of views and a discursive model of democracy. Freedom of the individual cannot be perceived in a void, but can only be understood within the wider social context – it is the community, which therefore defines freedom. The idea of a communicative democracy makes central the ethics of dialogue as an ongoing project, which guarantees contestation and which allows for the articulation of a plurality of demands and interests. Freedom and democracy do not depend on 'a priori' agreed definitions, but derive their meanings within specific social contexts.

'There cannot be more freedom than the right and the possibility of equal participation in decision-making processes in terms of the democratic concept of freedom. In terms of the democratic concept of freedom the more everyone has the right and the possibility to participate the freer people are. Liberation can thus be conceived as a lengthy process in which everyone has the right and the very increasing possibility for participating. And that is what democratic freedom is about'. (Heller, 1990, pp. 367–368)

THE BROKEN PROMISES OF DEMOCRACY

Dewey and Rorty (Bernstein, 1991) have defended democracy for what it is. Pragmatists favour a world of doubts and therefore have a suspicion of those who argue about the 'ought' and the hopes of democracy pointing out that such arguments overload the expectations of democracy and therefore also undermine democracy. Pragmatists seek to defend democracy as being the art of the possible. The pragmatist defends democracy because it provides a context for compromise and negotiation. Democracy is contextual in the sense that people are able to change their mind. Those who have fanatical visions of society and who have no tolerance for the visions of others, undermine the principles of democracy. Democracy is threatened by those who take advantage of liberal institutions to pursue doctrine and use democracy as a means to an end, rather than defending democracy as an end in itself. Pragmatists accept the precarious nature of democracy. Within this framework, pragmatists accept that the world is made of pluralities of 'letting a thousand flowers bloom' and for giving legitimacy to different vocabularies:

'The type of pluralism that represents what is best in our pragmatic tradition is an engaged fallibilistic pluralism. Such a pluralistic ethos places new responsibilities upon each of us. For it means taking our fallibility seriously – resolving that however much we are committed to our styles of thinking we are willing to listen to others without denying or suppressing the otherness of the other'. (Bernstein, 1991, p. 336)

Dissent and disagreement are essential pillars of a participatory democracy because the presence of opposition confirms the presence of the other. Dissent is accepted for what it is. Opposition provides the means for competing vocabularies. Opposition forces transparency and accountability. Participatory democracy means listening to the other. Nothing is static, but is open to be challenged. The nature of politics is to challenge the world as it is.

Bobbio (1987) relates what he has called the Six Broken promises of democracy. These include:

1. The Persistence of Pluralism and politics as practised through interest groups. This form of politics generates and maintains inequality. Pluralism is identified with those who organise themselves and gain access to political goods at the cost of those who are on the outside and remain marginalised. Strategic interest groups are involved in scrambles, for subsidies in agriculture and defence, pay scrambles in the public sector. Political parties seek to outbid each other in making pledges for higher levels of public expenditure on health and education. The politics of interest groups results in the stalemate state, political paralysis and the politics of the pig trough.

   'No doubt in some categories the new groups had a much greater leverage on the processes of public choice than the actors in the old group politics had typically had. The latter, for example, had operated in an essentially private economy and their syndicalist power affected public choice only indirectly. But in the managed economy the new producer groups could directly slow down, divert or even halt the implementation of policy. To this reallocation of power we might plausibly attribute the defeat of deference and the disruption of class'. (Beer, 1982, p. 210)

2. Political Parties are mainly concerned with becoming and remaining the incumbent government. The main concern is to produce policies desirable to electoral majorities. The focus is put on policy presentation rather than policy substance. The concern of the Government is how to sell a policy and how to gain favourable media headlines. According to Heller (1990), electoral majorities tend to thread together a form of political consensus, which is often oppressive to those who are on the outside of that consensus. Electoral majorities reflect a defence of the status quo. Government

is concerned with the 'spin' of policy rather than the substance. The primary aim is the favourable news coverage. Government increasingly becomes centralised and the role of the legislature marginalised. Politics is stage-managed. Costs of elections spiral, electors are treated as the passive audience and as consumers of policy. The aim is to create what Galbraith calls a politics of contentment based on a simple political arithmetic that policies should always create more winners than losers

3. The Survival of Oligarchy. Representative democracy generates new forms of political elites rather than a process of participation.

> 'Democratic political practice is best regarded neither as a method of popular participation in government nor as a means of putting into effect the people's will, but mainly as a competition for power by means of votes among competing teams, subject to endemic and growing weakness and the generation of excessive expectations among voters by the processes of political competition and the disruptive effects arising from the pursuit of self interest by rival coercive groups'. (Brittan, 1977, p. 266)

4. Limited Spaces for Democracy. The vision of participation is corrupted by the more pragmatic arguments that democracy is a method of choosing between competing political parties. Direct democracy requires too much politics because it rests on continuous debate, which in itself could result in paralysis, since any decisions will seem to take longer because of a lack of consent. Contemporary politics in the USA is described as grid-locked because of too much partisan politics at all levels of government. Supreme Court judges at Federal and State levels are nominated according to political allegiances and people are nominated to join the Government or key committees because of their financial contributions, or because of their commitment to the party. In the 1996 Congressional elections, a majority (51 per cent) of voting Americans chose not to vote. In the 1998 elections, those who did not vote increased to 64 per cent. In the meantime, turnouts for Presidential election have continuously declined since the Nixon/Kennedy Presidential campaign of 1960, when there was a 60 per cent turnout compared with the 2000 Presidential election, in which only 49 per cent of people voted. In US elections, money matters. Advertising and soft money have become crucial in election campaigns. In the 1996 Congressional elections, US$405 million were spent on TV advertising and by 1998, this had risen to US$531 million. Some 98 per cent of incumbents to congress and the senate were re-elected. Senator F. Kimberley, who recently announced his retirement, estimated that he needed to raise an average of US$3000 a day for his election campaigns (Drew, 2000). According to *The New York Times*:

'Some of the obstacles come from deliberate decisions. Some television advertisements are really intended to drive down turnout. Both parties have become
highly skilled at drawing the boundaries of Congressional and Legislative
districts so that few seats will be truly competitive. That preserves the careers
of incumbents'. (*New York Times* 2 January 2000, pp. A1 and A24)

5. Invisible Power and the 'Rule by Nobody'. The influence and impact of
    the welfare state and the bureaucracy of government reduce the impor-
    tance of the 'elected' assembly. Modern democracy is failing, mainly as
    the result of unforeseen transformations; these include the expansion of
    knowledge estates and the problem of political overload. The modern
    economy and the modern welfare state produce experts committed to
    rationale forms of knowledge, which are seen as being superior to other
    forms of knowledge (Habermas, 1987). Modern democracy is therefore
    seen as being managed by those who have certain forms of knowledge –
    the new knowledge estate of welfare professionals, bureaucracies, inter-
    national trade lawyers and policy advisers. Government becomes depen-
    dent on the advice of professionals, but also on professionals who are
    sympathetic to the ideology of government. Government hires consultants
    to give advice on privatisation policy, yet the consultants are not account-
    able to Parliament. There is little attempt to seek oppositional advice.
    Policy recommendations are not open to the scrutiny of Parliament.
6. Democracy and Citizenship. Modern democracy is corrupted because it
    encourages passivity, leaving the political stage to the few. Modern
    democracy is limited to electoral process, while other forms of participa-
    tion are discouraged. Socialist and Marxist critics have pointed out that
    liberal democracy was legitimising capitalism (O'Connor, 1973; Gough,
    1979; Poulantzas, 1980) since working class interests and oppositions are
    increasingly incorporated within the agendas of the capitalist state.

> 'The capitalist state plays an organic role in organising the political unity of the
> bourgeois and constituting it as the politically dominant class. This can only
> become possible because of the relative autonomy of the state from the vari-
> ous fractions, components and specific interests of the capitalist class'.
> (Poulantzas, 1980, pp.125 and 127)

Bobbio (1987) has argued that the future of democracy depends on lowering our normative expectations of democracy and to construct some 'minimal' expectations of those who continue to adhere to democratic principles.
He therefore urges that a minimal democracy should be characterised by a
set of rules; as to who is eligible to vote, the rights of political parties and
free and frequent elections; a set of rules which establish who is authorised
to rule and which procedures to be applied. Yet democracy needs to offer

real alternatives, while at the same time, it needs to give priority to liberal rights.

At the centre of liberal democracy are the existence of the individual and the possession of inalienable rights, for individuals to make claims to live their lives as unique individuals with personal human rights and the observance of civil liberties. It is connected with the previous discussion on the 'independent citizen' and the emphasis on markets and the rights to make choices; of having a constitutional government and putting limits on government. The model of participatory democracy offers the spaces to the 'public citizen' for involvement, for sharing in decision making, for taking responsibility for those decisions and for creating a democratic culture. In the context of participatory democracy, citizenship resistance is defined through involvement. Participatory democracy reinforces ideas of plurality, diversity and oppositions. The globalised economy requires the globalised democracy and the resistance of the cosmopolitan citizen who is not defined through belonging but through connections that can resist the degradation of the environment; the influence of the multinational corporations and geo-politics.

THE RETREAT FROM THE PUBLIC SPACE

The retreat from public spaces has been an ongoing historical process. Sennet (1979) pointed out that the emergence of political parties and bureaucracies had increasingly created a political stage that was occupied by the political actors, leaving the population as the quiet audience sitting in the dark watching in silence:

> 'public life has become passive – a sense of obligation and duties, conforming to the rules but investing less and less passion in those of conformity. Public life is bloodless; emotional energies are privatised. Citizens approach their dealings with the state in a spirit of resigned acquiescence; at best it is formal, dry and phoney. The obsession with persons at the expense of more impersonal relations is like a filter that discolours our rational understanding of society and obscures the importance of class'. (Sennet, 1979, p. 3)

One major consequence of globalisation is the dislocation of spaces. The movements of capital and knowledge are now located in cyber-spaces of financial markets, new technologies that allow for the movement of capital and where knowledge and information are located in the World Wide Web. In contrast, politics is still firmly located within geographical space. Economic decisions however, are no longer confined to a specific geographical space. The manufacturing of goods within the hard walls of factories is in decline within the advanced economies. High profits and higher wages are earned in the selling of ideas, the world of advertising and the ability to sell a product as a way of life. This is the age of the weightless corporation where the manufacturing of products is sub-contracted and where corporations do not seek to be employers. Those in employment are seen as being in transit. There is no commitment to the organisation, but the concern is with individuals to sell their ideas. There are no longer specific owners of companies, but networks of shareholding. Headquarters of companies are more often located in different spaces from the production that is taking place in factories. Management is delegated.

In the new globalised economy, politics has been eclipsed (Castells, 2000) and traditional forms of resistances, including trade unions, have lost their relevance in the context of the knowledge economy (Giddens, 2001). Politics was important in a world where the hardware of firms' companies, trade unions and other interest groups were firmly located in the local. Politics made transparent issues of power, while democracy facilitated the articulation of demands and resistance. In the new global economy, the shift is towards post-engagement:

'This is a situation radically different from the past 'hardware' era, when power and knowledge, just like other objects remained essentially 'local and earthbound. Capital tied in heavy machinery and thick factory walls as well as in the local, closely, guarded markets of labour and commodities was no more free to move than the factory hands . . . For better or worse, capital was bound to stay in one place and whatever happened in that place was for its investors, owners and managers just as it was for the rest of its residents a matter of success or defeat perhaps even life and death'. (Bauman, 2000, p. 121)

Bauman (2000) argues that the era of post-engagement is also accompanied by the political economy of insecurity. Capital and knowledge have become freed from local geographic spaces. Transactions in capital markets have become a major industry. The new absentee landlords seek to live off their investments using their cellular phones to earn their rentier incomes. Transactions in shares and in financial markets dwarf the transactions required in the transfer of commodities in the real economy. Work no longer pays. It is left for those who have no alternative but to sell their labour. The world of work is no longer the avenue to wealth. Shares values rise much faster than wages. Those with financial capital vacate the world of work. Meanwhile, discussions of poverty remind those in work of the political economy of insecurity and the precarious line between employment and unemployment.

The political economy of insecurity is also accompanied by an absence of traditional resistances and social movements. Issues can no longer be condensed within a specific geographic space. Corporations cannot be anchored in the local. There is a disavowal of responsibility. The landed aristocracy, despite being absentee landlords, was still firmly tied to the local. Bargaining by riot was therefore visible and tangible. The new absentee land-lords of financial capital are no longer anchored in the local. Capital is now highly mobile. The recent closure of Enron in the USA – a company worth some US$60 billion and seventh in the Fortune 500 of America's largest companies, confirmed the nature of the new dislocation between the two worlds of the geography of politics and the cyber spaces of economics. Workers have lost their jobs – there is little government can do about the exec-utives of the company who, on seeing the early signals, sold their share hold-ings. Overnight, Enron share prices fell from US$96 a share, to a few cents. Other losers were those who depended on pensions from Enron and those who had invested their retirement funds in Enron shares:

> 'Enron's financial bankruptcy, triggered in part by revelations of faulty financial reporting, was a shocking national calamity . . . Criminal charges may still be in store for top Enron executives who sold nearly 1 billion dollars worth of their company stock, possibly knowing it was improperly inflated, before it plummeted. Thousands of employees were not so lucky and lost their lifetime savings. Close to 60 per cent of all employee money was wasted in Enron stock. Unsuspecting Enron employees were the most direct victims of the company's lack of forthrightness, but overall investor confidence in the integrity of the marketplace took a serious hit with Enron's demise'. ('The Enron post-mortem', *The New York Times* 4 January 2002)

The attempt to make connections between democracy and the globalised econ-omy rests on the simple assumption that democracy provides the means for people to give shape to questions of resource allocation and distribution. The public space offers opportunities for political choices and decisions, while the retreat from the public space and the emergence of the privatised individual means that the public space is left to others. The liberalisation of capital, the flexibility of foreign direct investment and increasing economic integration are at present moving faster than the processes of democracy, accountability, transparency and citizenship. The shaping of the globalised economy is being defined by the priorities of market liberal ideas. Furthermore, there is at present a lack of a coherent response at the global level to create the possibil-ities of globalised democracy.

Images of the corruption of the public spaces result in further retreat and the demand to be left alone. The spaces of family and home, to get on with daily lives, going to work and looking after their children encourage passivity, while providing no avenues for forms of collective resistance. Work becomes an individualised experience. The globalised economy is taken as given, something that cannot be changed. Insecurity of employment, income, low wages, lack of health insurance etc. are part of the new insecurities:

'Behind the expanding insecurities of the millions dependent on selling their labour, lurks the absence of a potent and effective agency which could with will and resolve make their plight less insecure . . . today they speak of globalisation – something that happens to us for reasons about which we may surmise, even get to know but can hardly control'. (Bauman, 2000, p. 20)

Globalisation, the market economy and neo-liberalism are presented as facts, devoid of ideology, aiming to define the world as it is. Resistance to neo-liberal thinking is presented as the 'unreal' and an attack on freedom of choice, individualism and democracy. The argument that globalisation is happening to us seeks to provide a framework of thinking about the need to create more privatised spaces. In the meantime, governments ask to be trusted in making the private more secure. Insecurity is the stranger, the alien and the migrant. Those who protest and resist and those who strike become the cause of concern. They undermine employment and create perceptions of militancy that will send signals to financial markets. Markets need stability. Policy decisions are defined as being complex and difficult and best left to the experts, the new knowledge estates of legal advisers on international trade negotiations, for experts to make decisions on health, education transport and environment. Issues of power are denied. Policy lobbyists and political advisers live in the shadows, invisible from the public gaze. All policy decisions are presented as being in the public interest. There are no winners and losers. This is the 'end of ideology':

'The announcement of the 'end of ideology' is on the part of social commentators a declaration of intent more than it is a description of things as they are: no more criticism of the way things are being done . . . What, however, makes the neo liberal world-view view sharply different from other ideologies – indeed, a phenomenon of a separate class – is precisely the absence of questioning; its surrender to what is seen as the implacable and irreversible logic of social reality. The difference between neo-liberal discourse and the classic ideologies of modernity is, one might say, the difference between the mentality of plankton and that of swimmers or sailors'. (Bauman, 2000, p. 127)

CONCLUSIONS

The re-discovery of democracy as the awkward public spaces of both the hopes and realism, needs to encompass the following dimensions:

Proposal 1

That democracy provides opportunities and sites, which generate options, diversity and pluralities of views that reinforce the recognition of the other.

This proposal seeks to break with oligarchy. The criticisms that present forms of democracy serve specific strategic interest groups, while citizens who do not belong to such groups, are marginalised. The unemployed, the elderly women and the ethnic minorities have often been marginalised in a politics that has focused on economic strategic interests. Furthermore, a globalised democracy has to reflect greater diversities of needs. Workers in the advanced economies need alliances with workers from emerging and developing economies, to put pressure on their national governments on behalf of strangers. Campaigns against sweatshops, low pay, slave and child labour, are prime examples. Consumer boycotts of Nike shoes, Taco Bell Restaurants, etc. heightens awareness and create possibilities of alliances of producers and consumers.

Proposal 2

That democracy has to be perceived to be an ongoing project with a commitment to vigilance against the arbitrary nature of decision making within public institutions and to provide increased transparency and more accountable forms of policy making. Democrats should seek to join campaigns that promote the transparencies of governments and to commit government to the universal human rights. Campaigns against racism and other forms of social oppressions are essential in the commitment to ideas of cosmopolitan virtues. Connections between business advocacy and government policy making need to be made transparent, as are the funding of election campaigns and political advertising.

Proposal 3

That democracy needs to be constantly created in the context of new challenges. The weightless corporation and disavowal of responsibility mean new forms of accountability. Companies involved in countries that do not uphold human rights deny responsibility and knowledge on the basis that they are not directly hiring labour. Supporters of democracy have to defend democracy at the global level, defending human rights as universal rights. Democracy is not static. The 'ought to' of democracy is the commitment of involvement and participation. In addition to political rights, the commitments to economic and social rights are defined as equal essential pillars of democracy. The commitment to the politics of the republic also requires the creation of a citizen's income that acts as a base against the economic insecurities of old age, sickness and unemployment.

Proposal 4

That democracy facilitates independent opposition. The ownership of the media becomes a major concern if there is a tendency towards monopoly.

Access to the media is essential to ensure dialogue and for a plurality of views. Political parties have to be committed to financial transparency and limits should be put on the financing of election campaigns, soft money for political parties and financial contributions. The funding of political parties and election campaigns through the state have not resolved the problems of corruption.

Economic globalisation does not make the nation state redundant. Globalisation is not an exogenous event that challenges government, but rather it is a product of political decisions. Governments are not prisoners of globalisation, they are part of the decision takers on globalisation. Democracy is still the means by which citizens make governments accountable and ensure that policies are in the public interest. Transparency and accountability become more essential in a more integrated world economy.

Globalisation does create new political problems. Economic globalisation requires political accountability at the global level. Economic decisions tend to overspill national borders. Producing clothing in sweatshop conditions with forced child labour in China and Burma have spillover effects on workers in the advanced economies. The weightless corporation that sub-contracts the making of clothing is the same weightless corporation that uses employment agencies to hire and fire workers, according to the needs of the company. There is no loyalty and identity between employer and workers, whether it is the first or the third world. Globalisation is, at the same time, the opportunity to create cosmopolitan virtues and cosmopolitan forms of resistance.

At present, the retreat into privatised lives means that the public spaces are increasingly occupied by the interests of financial markets and multinational corporations. The political spaces have become de-politicised and these have to become re-politicised. Campaigns for greater political transparency and demands for more collective forms of resistance offer potential to renew democracy. New forms of politics and resistance can easily replace silence and acquiescence. It takes time for people to create appropriate forms of resistances. Between the emergence of the first industrial revolution and the first trade unions responses, there was approximately a lag of 70 years. It took a further 40 years to organise manual workers. Resistance to present forms of globalisation remains nascent and experimental, but there are already in the making, new coalitions, protests, environmental campaigns and the existence of the institutions of democracy and trade unions, which do not have to be re-invented.

5. Mapping the winners and the losers

INTRODUCTION

Globalisation as Fact and as Policy Choice

Definitions of globalisation conflate two separate themes. First, the theme of defining 'globalisation' in terms of a series of indisputable facts. Such facts include the new technologies and information systems, which are described as making the world into a global village. Technology makes possible the greater mobility of capital, the sharing of information, greater awareness of global interconnectedness and the potential for wider political participation, transparency and accountability. For example, it is no longer possible to argue the case of ignorance – that we do not know of the exploitation of forced labour in Burma or the unease about GM crops in India and Brazil or of increasing poverty in developing countries and the frequent floods in Bangladesh. It is therefore an indisputable 'fact' to argue that technology is a major factor making the world more globalised. Equally, there are a number of issues, which are being described as 'globalised facts' when these facts can be described as policy choices. Policy choices are not facts in the sense that they cannot be categorised as being either 'inescapable' or 'inevitable':

> 'The term 'globalisation' as too frequently used, confuses two totally different phenomena. The first is the shrinkage in space and in time that the world has experienced in consequence of the technological revolutions in transport, communication and information processing. The second usage of the term relates to matters of human policy choice – the degree to which one opens and submits oneself mindless to surrounding external forces. Individuals, firms, governments and NGOs all have choices. While globalisation (in my first meaning) is a fact and it may constrain some choices it does not totally foreclose options in the way that many imply'. (Helleiner, 2000, Raul Prebisch Lecture, Geneva, p. 6)

Governments do not have complete autonomy in the making of policy, but neither are governments prisoners of events. While it is a fact that governments have to respond to problems of inflation and rising public sector deficits, there is still the issue of autonomy in deciding at what level of inflation governments should start to worry? The question that needs to be asked is why inflation is intolerable at 3 per cent and that under the EU Stability and

Growth Pact (SGP), EU member states have agreed to adopt policies of zero inflation and balanced budgets? The convergence criteria outlined in the Maastricht Treaty in 1997 reflects the political choices of governments that had associated themselves with monetarists ideas during the 1980s. Implicitly, the policy priorities on the money supply, inflation and the role of governments represented the downgrading of Keynesian arguments about the role of fiscal policy in generating growth and employment:

> 'The relatively poor economic performance of many of the EU economies during the 1990s may to some degree be attributable to the striving of countries to meet those criteria. From 1992 to 1999 the growth of national income averaged 1.7 per cent in the Eurozone countries, compared with the UK average of 2.5 per cent per annum . . . The adoption of these criteria not only brought in a deflationary element to the Maastricht Treaty, but also reflected the general rejection of Keynesian economics and the use of fiscal policy to stimulate the economy'. (Arestis and Sawyer, 2003, p. 117)

It is therefore important to ask who gains from the policy frameworks of low inflation, low interests and low government deficits, since these represent deliberate policy priorities and policy choices and their impact on the distribution of income will be different for different income groups? Economists like to point out that inflation is bad for the poor, because it erodes the values of pensions and social security. However, governments can ensure that pensions are protected by making commitments to align pensions to earnings or the cost of living. Anti-inflation policy is implicitly a political decision. Independent central banks are asked to deliver on inflation targets set by governments. Workers are then faced with a dilemma of pushing for higher wage demands, which in turn are likely to result in higher interests rates and higher mortgage costs or allowing wages to decline. In the early 1980s, The Republican Party in the USA argued that government deficits were bad because they crowded out private investment. In 2004, the Bush proposals to reduce taxation have been presented as a necessary stimulus to the economy. The forecasts that the government budget deficits will increase to nearly 5 per cent of GDP are dismissed as not being important. Republican deficits in 2004 are 'good' and do not crowd out private investment.

Economic Globalisation

Ohmae (1990) has argued that contemporary globalisation represents the emergence of competition and the ascendancy of the sovereign consumer. Globalisation breaks national borders and allows for the free movement of capital, goods and labour:

'The country to which they (the consumers) are all migrating – helped along the way by shared exposure to the English language, to the internet, Fox TV, the BBC, CNN and MTV and by interactive tools – is the global economy of the borderless world. Using a telephone, fax machine or personal consumer linked to the internet, for example a Japanese consumer in Sapporo can place an order for clothing with Lands End in Wisconsin or LL Bean in Maine and have the merchandise delivered by UPS or Yamato and charge the purchase to American Express, Visa or Mastercard'. (Ohmae, 1990, p. 39)

According to market liberal thinkers, present forms of globalisation are to be celebrated, because they reinforce the ascendancy of the sovereign consumer. Consumers can at last purchase products outside the limits of their national borders, thus increasing competition on prices and choices. Consumption is tied to web pages and virtual shopping malls, where all purchases are possible with the click of a button. Car components are produced in Portugal and Germany, assembled in Britain, while the car company is owned by a US corporation. Just-in-time production removes the needs for keeping parts in stores and warehouses when instant delivery allows for flexible production methods that meet consumer designed requirements. According to this approach, the vision of the invisible hand and competitive markets envisaged by Adam Smith in 1776, has become a reality in the process of economic globalisation. Consumers are now in the driving seat. There are no barriers to entry because internet facilities ensure the breakdown of monopoly over products or prices. Producers are forced to compete to meet consumer choices. There is a shift of power from the vested interests of producers to consumers.

In the new global economy, individuals are the new owners of knowledge. The added value of a new car is no longer located at the stage of production, but rather in the selling of that car as a concept and a philosophy of life. Successful business organisations depend on the ability to transfer products into concepts and ideas.

Castells (2000) has pointed out that contemporary globalisation has given ascendancy to the interests of financial markets and financial institutions. Capital flows in a new liberalised climate are giving shape to the globalised economy dominated by financial communities. The IMF and the World Bank define the priorities of economic policies. Trading in financial markets allow for the mobility of investment between countries. Financial liberalisation and the removal of exchange controls allows for greater financial flows. Governments become increasingly dependent on the sentiments of financial markets. In an era of floating exchange rates, currencies become vulnerable to international trading:

'In the electronically operated global casino specific capitals boom and bust set the fate of corporations, household savings, national currencies and regional economies. The net result sums to zero while the losers pay for the winners. But who are the winners and the losers changes by the year, the month, the day, the second and permeates down to the world of firms, jobs, salaries taxes and public services. To the world of what is sometimes called 'the real economy' and I would be tempted to call the unreal economy since in the age of networked capitalism the fundamental reality where what is made and lost, invested or saved is the financial sphere. All other activities are primarily the basis to generate the necessary surplus to invest in the global flows or the result of investment originated in these financial networks'. (Castells, 2000, p. 472)

In a speech in Ontario on 12 November 2001, the Secretary General of the World Trade Organisation (WTO) pointed to the limits of present globalisation:

'1.2 billion people live on less than $1 a day; another 1.6 billion people live on less than $2 a day . . . the international community can and must help. Poor countries need to grow their way out of poverty. Trade is a key engine for growth but currently developing country products face many obstacles entering rich country markets. By opening these markets, we can help lift millions of people out of poverty. And the most effective way to achieve these market openings is by launching a new round. It is true some imbalances exist in the trading system. But the only way the system can be adjusted and the imbalances addressed is in a wider process of negotiation'. (John Moore, Chair opening address, WTO Meeting, Ontario, 12 November 2001).

The World Bank Report (World Bank, 2001) on World Poverty also claimed that present globalisation is contributing to the reduction of world poverty. James Wolfensohn went as far as to claim that world poverty had declined from 29 per cent in the world population in 1990, to 23 per cent by 1998:

'Over the past few years, [these] better policies have contributed to more rapid growth in developing countries' per capita incomes than at any point since the mid-1970s. And faster growth has meant poverty reduction: the proportion of people worldwide living in absolute poverty has dropped steadily in recent decades, from 29 per cent in 1990 to a record low of 23 per cent in 1998'. (James D. Wolfensohn, the Bank's President, remarks to the G-20 Finance Ministers and Central Governors, Ottawa, 17 November 2001).

However, not all of the world' s poor experience the world in the same way. Reddy and Pogge (2003) have criticised the Bank's assessment of world poverty, arguing that the Bank was not measuring like with like. The World Bank measure using Purchasing Power Parity (PPP) makes the assumption that consumption is similar between all countries. This does not take into account, for example, that the cost of food in poor countries takes a higher percentage of income:

'Income poverty is only one aspect of poverty and other poverty estimates, based on under-nutrition, infant mortality, access to health services and other indicators can continue to inform us even in the absence of usable figures concerning global income poverty. International development targets should appropriately continue to focus on these measures of deprivation in the world, while a new procedure for the global assessment of income poverty is developed and implemented'. (Reddy and Pogge, 2003, p. 4)

Reddy and Pogge (2002 and 2003) have questioned the validity of $1/day to define poverty and have suggested that the Bank has underestimated the true levels of poverty by between 30 and 40 per cent – measuring poverty using a basket of goods that includes services irrelevant to the poor, when the focus should be a poverty line that takes into consideration food and nutrition:

'For example, the food component of a global standard for poverty avoidance could be defined in terms of the calorie and micro-nutrient content of foods, without specifying these foods exactly. This would permit wheat to be consumed in wheat eating regions and rice in rice eating regions, so long as the calorie standard was met. This approach, isolating the *characteristics* of commodities rather than commodities themselves, has been widely used in poverty assessments at the national level. The global standard, once specified, should be given specific regional and local content in a transparent, participatory and rigorous way. We see no reason why this approach should be more controversial than the decidedly controversial $1/day approach. As we have argued, the seeming uniformity of this approach masks hidden variations in the meaning of the $1/day standard'. (Reddy and Pogge, 2002, p. 7)

There are winners and losers in both the developed countries and the developing economies. The world economy can be described by the analogy of three boats in an ocean, where in the first boat are 80 per cent of the people of the advanced economies, in the second boat, 60 per cent of the population of the developing countries and in the third, 10 per cent of the people in the least developed countries. In the water, are the losers from all three worlds. Globalisation is creating losers and winners. The total losers make up 40 per cent of the world population. While workers in the advanced economies are relatively better off than their counterparts in developing countries, their status is as precarious. Equally, the elites in developing countries are racing to riches as much as their counterparts in the advanced economies. Devaluation of currencies, liberalisation of financial markets and the sale of state assets provide financial gains for those who hold foreign bank accounts, those who can afford assets at low prices and those who can afford to take advantage of liberalised financial markets.

In the UK, the unemployment rate in 2003 fell to 5.5 per cent of the working population, the lowest rate recorded since 1975. At the same time, incomes from wages have either stagnated or declined for ~80 per cent of the working population. The inequality gap between the top 10 per cent and the bottom 10 per cent has increased from 3 to 4 times. The number of men within the age group 25–54, who are inactive, has increased from 12 per cent in 1979 to 16 per cent in 2000. There were 400 000 inactive men in 1974, compared with 2.2 million in 2000. The male labour participation rate has declined from 95 per cent in 1950 to 74 per cent in 2000 (Upchurch, 1999; Danford, 1998). The decline of male employment in manufacturing is also reflected in the decline of trade union membership, from a peak of 50 per cent in 1975, to 30 per cent in 2000 (Nickell, 2001). The Joseph Rowntree Study (2001) confirmed that the total number of people who lacked three or more basic necessities because they could not afford them, had increased from 14 per cent in 1983, to 21 per cent in 1990, to 24 per cent in 1999. In 1999, there were 9.6 million people who could not afford adequate housing, while 7.5 million people were too poor to engage in common social activities. The same story applies to the USA, were the incomes of the top 5 per cent have increased by 24 per cent since the mid-1980s, while those of the bottom 10 per cent have declined by 10 per cent. The Gini coefficient for the USA is at its highest since the mid-1950s.

More than half of the world's population is living close to poverty. While there are 60 million people connected to internet facilities, 90 per cent of these are concentrated in the advanced economies. The advanced economies have continued to maintain their tariffs on agriculture, textiles and manufacturing, making it impossible for the developing countries to compete. In the advanced economies, there is over production in agriculture, which in turn undermines and displaces the small farmers in the developing countries. Furthermore, rules on intellectual property rights (TRIPS) and on trade in goods and services (GATS) are also likely to be to the disadvantage of the developing countries. The concept of the sovereign consumer is limited to the one with the ability to pay. Drugs and medicines might be available, but people in poor countries earning less than $2/day are unable to enter the markets for these medicines. Their Governments are unable to purchase cheaper generic drugs because of WTO rules and the threat of court action brought forward by pharmaceutical companies. Lower production costs do not necessarily lead to low prices, since supply is increasingly dominated by a few large multinational corporations.

Globalisation and Political Choices

Globalisation reflects continuing political choices and decisions that directly influence the outcomes in distribution of incomes and wealth between and within countries, which in turn shape the landscapes of inclusion, exclusion and the idea of belonging. Advocates for globalisation point out that free trade, the removal of barriers and the retreat of government create an environment of

greater consumer choices, lower prices and higher living standards, which
benefit the global community. Commitment to free trade is connected to ideas
of economic growth, which in turn, it is argued, will lead to income re-distribution. The 'trickle down' argument is based on the assumption that as *per
capita* incomes increase, these will also benefit those defined as being in
poverty. It is a view that corresponds with the Kuznets theory of development
that has associated income distribution with levels of development, so that
countries with low levels of development are associated with high levels of
income inequality and as development increases so income inequalities
decrease.

By contrast, critics point to income inequalities, increases in world poverty,
the dominance of multinational corporations and the ascendancy of neo-liberalism as a set of ideas that seek to shape and arrange the world economic order.
Kofi Annan, UN Secretary General, in his Report to the Millennium Assembly
pointed out that:

> 'The central challenge we face today is to ensure that globalisation becomes a posi-
> tive force for all the world's people instead of leaving billions of them behind in
> squalor. Inclusive globalisation must be built on the great enabling force of the
> market but market forces alone will not achieve it. It requires a broader effort to
> create a shared future, based upon our common humanity in all its diversity'. (Kofi
> Annan, remarks to the UN Millenium Assembly, Washington DC, 20 April 2000)

The process of globalisation can be beneficial. The problem is the way globalisation is being shaped and defined. Allowing globalisation to be shaped by
market liberal ideas is creating a landscape of income inequalities and social
exclusion. Globalisation needs government intervention at the global, the
national and the local level to ensure social inclusion and political decision
making that provide for the making of the global citizen.

Despite year on year increases in world trade and output, the income shares
of people in poor countries have actually declined since the mid-1980s. Free
trade does not necessarily improve the incomes of the poor; there has to be the
political will of governments to improve incomes through social security,
pensions, access to health care and education. The top four billionaires have
the equivalent of the total GDP of 36 least developed economies, where there
are 600 million people. The UN Commission (UNDP, 2001) has reported that
while those dying from malnutrition have declined from 960 million to 770
million, this still represents some 17 per cent of the world's population.

According to Save the Children:

> 'In an era of unprecedented global wealth, millions of children across the world are
> facing a health crisis. Trade liberalisation has exposed some of the most vulnerable
> communities to dangerous new challenges, with devastating effects on children's

nutrition and basic health. Yet despite widespread evidence of these new dangers, the world's most powerful economies are trying to use the Doha Ministerial to push ahead with their agenda of further trade liberalisation. The WTO is also hoping to use Doha to boost liberalisation of trade in services, as part of the ongoing negotiations under the General Agreement on Trade in Services (GATS). Yet our research shows that liberalisation of trade in health services is the wrong model to follow if countries wish to develop strong public health systems for all their people. It is time to give trade liberalisation a 'health check' – to assess which elements of GATS and other WTO agreements are a threat to public health and revise them accordingly'.

Public health, the provision of education and social security payments are still the major functions of the nation state. In all of the advanced economies, public expenditure amounts to between 40 and 50 per cent of the GDP, while expenditure on social protection is approximately 27 per cent of the GDP. Social policy still continues to be the best means available for the re-distribution of income and for ensuring greater access to health care and education provision. The health of young children in developing countries improves in relation to the education of the mother, the awareness of nutrition and healthy eating and also the provision of preventive health care:

'Three major developments in recent decades have altered the economic, political and ideological context of the welfare state in important ways. They are: the collapse of the socialist alternative, the globalisation of the economy and the relative decline of the nation state'. (Mishra, 1999, p. 1)

When globalisation is defined as being an exogenous event to which governments have to respond, issues of political sovereignty are likely to be undermined under the pressures of the global straitjacket. Developing countries with high debt burdens are directed by the IMF and the World Bank to open their economies to free trade, phase out subsidies, privatise government corporations and reduce social spending, all which have adverse effects on the poor. By contrast, globalisation can be described as a series of political decisions and political choices where the outcomes can therefore be different if there is the political will. In accepting the model of globalisation as an event that demands a response of government, then it becomes an argument that allows globalisation to define the limits of politics. The argument that points out that globalisation represents political decisions also asks for greater political accountability and transparency, so that citizens can shape and define globalisation.

Globalisation is becoming associated with issues of power and influence and the ability of multinational corporations to bring about change both at national and international levels. Agricultural lobbies in the USA and Europe ensure the payments of subsidies that advantage domestic vested interests, despite the international commitments to free trade. Globalisation makes transparent growing income inequalities both within countries and also between the rich industrialised economies and poor third world countries. Multinational corporations in their continuous search for lower labour costs seek and find free trade zones and pay wages of around 80 US cents an hour. Deals are made between governments and multinational corporations in the organisation of tax regimes and the non-recognition of national labour standards.

Present forms of globalisation are qualitatively different and represent a break with the past. The potential of new technologies and how they facilitate major inflows and outflows of capital in between countries do create a borderless world. In the meantime, governments have facilitated the process of globalisation by promoting policies of liberalisation of financial markets and also their commitment to floating exchange rates. Capital flows between different stock markets and exchanges dwarf the ability of governments to give priority to national economic priorities. There is now increasingly interconnectedness of political, economic and social decisions, which when made in one locality, are likely to have ripple effects somewhere else. Drinking a cup of coffee at the local Starbucks or eating at MacDonald's or Pizza Hut have ripple effects on share prices, on pensions funds, as much as on coffee growers. The decline in share values on dot.coms eventually means jobs losses in Silicone Valley California, in West Lothian and in Coventry.

There is concern about the nature of globalisation: how globalisation has become interchangeable with a neo-liberal perspective of individualism and markets. To market liberals, the new globalised economy represents the triumph of liberal thinking. The market confirms the freedom of individual choice and competition. The globalised economy offers more choices, cheaper prices and higher living standards. The role of government should be confined to de-regulation policies of labour market, privatisation of state monopolies and providing incentives for private pensions and health insurance. Globalisation leads to the re-invention of government. High marginal taxes on higher income earners represent a disincentive to innovation, while demands for higher wages are likely to result in unemployment.

Globalisation seems to present a policy framework of passivity, fear and insecurity. Multinationals are defined as being footloose, having the choice to move around the world. Some 80 per cent of foreign direct investment is invested in the advanced economies, including the USA, Japan, Britain and Germany (UNCTAD, 2001). The nature of employment has changed. In manufacturing, the employed workforce declined from around 40 per cent in the 1950s, to 26 per cent in the 1970s, to 18 per cent in the 1990s. Industrial communities in coal, textiles and steel have disappeared, as have the collectivist values that facilitated the development of welfare states. The information economy is more of an individualised experience of individuals making choices about careers, life projects and life styles. Employment and unemployment become an individualised risk. There are now highly qualified employees on a global scale competing for jobs.

Implicitly, the suggestion is that national governments can 'no longer go at it alone'. The Government of Francois Mitterand was forced to devalue during the early 1980s, when the Government attempted to reflate the economy. Financial markets now swamp the abilities of government to intervene in support of their currencies. The French franc and UK sterling were put under increased pressure by financial markets, despite the attempts by the world financial institutions to stem the speculative tide. Liberalisation of financial markets has resulted in major foreign currencies' inflows and outflows between countries. In 1973, international trade in foreign exchange amounted to US$15 billion a day, in 1992 this had increased to US$900 billion dollars a day and to over US$1000 billion in 2000. Most of these inflows and outflows are speculative in nature. It is estimated that only 2 per cent of flows are in traded payments (Eatwell, 1998).

In 1900, the world population totalled some 1.6 billion and by 1950, this had grown to 2.5 billion, while in the following 50 years, world population expanded rapidly to over 6 billion people by the year 2000. During the past 50 years, average incomes have increased by a factor of 2.5 times, while global GDP has increased six-fold. In the meantime, world trade had increased 14-fold (World Bank, 2002). Growth in incomes over the last 50 years, together with the expansion in world trade and world output, has reduced infant mortality rates. The world today is able to feed 4 times as many people as 100 years ago. During the past 50 years, the world economy has also become more integrated because of increases in communications and technology, reductions in barriers to trade and reductions in barriers to foreign investment. These three factors have reduced transition costs and have provided for greater mobility of capital and of companies:

> '54 years ago on 30 October, representatives of 23 nations assembled in Geneva to sign what would become an historic agreement: the Geneva Agreement on Tariffs and Trade. It was clear to those individuals meeting in Geneva in the dangerous Autumn of 1947 that trade was inextricably linked to recovery, development and even their security . . . So now we are gathered here in a different era with different challenges . . . The very fact of this meeting now with nearly 150 nations present underscores how much progress has been made over the past half century'. (Robert Zolleinick, US Trade Minister at Doha Ministerial Meeting, 10 November 2001)

Globalisation and Distribution of Income

Since the process of globalisation is shaped by political decisions, issues of who benefits also involve political choices about distribution and re-distribution of resources. Bhagwati (2002) and Dollar and Kraay (2001) have argued the case that while economic growth is the mechanism that ensures reductions in poverty, the major contributor to growth has been the decisions of government to integrate their economies into the world economy by adopting free trade policies. Dollar and Kraay (2001) have highlighted the progress achieved in Vietnam and Uganda in reducing poverty and Vietnam, where after 10 years of greater global integration, has been associated with an estimated decline in poverty rate from 75 to 37 per cent:

> 'the only developing countries which have registered significant declines in poverty are those that also have integrated faster into the world economy on the dimensions of trade and direct investment. It is hard therefore to concur with the many critics of freer trade (and direct foreign investment) that see the heavy hand of such globalisation casting its evil spell on the poor of the poor countries. The empirical truth seems to be exactly the opposite'. (Dollar and Kraay, 2001, p. 17)

Citing the progress made by China and India in reducing poverty, Bhagwati (2002) has pointed to the World Bank Report (2000), which estimated that real GDP grew at an annual average rate of 10 per cent in China and 6 per cent in India, during the period 1980–2000:

> 'No country in the world had as rapid growth as China whereas fewer than ten countries exceeded the Indian growth rate. The effect on reduction in poverty in both countries was dramatic, entirely in keeping with the Bhagwati hypothesis of the early 1960s that growth is a principal driver of reduced poverty. Thus, according to the Asian Development Bank (2000) estimates, the incidence of poverty, by agreed measures, declined from 28 per cent in 1978 to 9 per cent in 1998 in China. By the Government of India's estimates, poverty incidence fell from 51 per cent in 1977–78 to 27 per cent in 1999–2000'. (Bhagwati, 2002, p. 12)

The assumption that free trade promotes economic growth, which in turn redistributes income rests on the view that free trade is a lump sum, which does not take into consideration the winners and losers of policies of liberalisation, de-regulation and less government. Free trade creates winners and losers, in that companies and workers sheltered by tariffs and subsidies are likely to be displaced by removing barriers. Furthermore, in the context of unequal access to resources the freeing of markets is likely to lead to further inequalities since those with resources can take advantage of changing economic contexts in contrast to those who lack the resources who are left behind. In the changing economic context those with skills can migrate to other countries or to new areas of employment; those with low skills have less choice. At the level of countries policies of liberalisation are likely to favour the richer countries at the cost of poor countries. At the level of labour markets the process of globalisation increases labour supply since companies and financial capital become more mobile. For workers, the discipline of the market creates insecurity of employment and a reluctance to bargain for higher wages. Wage inequalities widen between skilled and unskilled workers while the share of wages and profits in relation to GDP shifts towards higher profits.

Advocates of globalisation, including the World Bank, the IMF and the WTO argue the case that the reduction of poverty requires economic prosperity, which in turn depends on the expansion of world trade. Growth in *per capita* GDP benefits the whole community. The World Bank has continually pointed out that the removal of tariffs agreed in the Uruguay Round in 1994 would increase world GDP by US$550 billion, while the phasing out of all trade barriers would increase world GDP by US$1300 billion, an equivalent of adding three Chinas to the world economy. According to the WTO view:

'The multilateral trading system has probably done more to boost living standards and lift people out of poverty over the past 50 years than any other government intervention. The 17-fold rise in world trade since 1950 has gone hand-in-hand with a six-fold rise in world output. This has benefited both developed and developing countries: in both, living standards have risen three-fold. Life expectancy in developing countries has risen from 41 to 62 years, infant mortality has more than halved, while the adult literacy rate is up from 40 per cent to 70 per cent'. (John Moore, WTO Secretariat speech, Ontario, 19 February 2001)

The studies by Dollard and Kraay (2001), on behalf of the World Bank, showed that for every 1 per cent of growth in the economy, there is a 1 per cent improvement in the income of the poor. The authors point out that in 108 episodes in which *per capita* GDP grew at a rate of at least 2 per cent per year, in 102 of these episodes, income of the poor also rose. The World Bank and the IMF policy prescriptions of fiscal discipline, austerity reduced welfare expenditures and free trade had benefited the poor. The IMF and World Bank recommendations encourage governments to reform macroeconomic policy, reduce government deficits, reduce taxes, liberalise trade and de-regulate the labour market, creating climates of employability and flexibility. The growth in world trade is defined as being in the interests of those on low incomes. The expansion of imports and competition leads to falling prices, which benefit consumers and those on low incomes. Trade liberalisation means that developing countries can become involved in new export markets and employ more people, which benefit the poor through employment. Liberalisation of financial markets breaks the monopoly of domestic interests, while foreign direct investment brings new companies, technologies and skills that benefit developing countries:

'growth generally does benefit the poor and that anyone who cares about the poor should favour the growth-enhancing policies of good rule of law, fiscal discipline and openness to international trade'. (Dollar and Kraay, 2001, p. 27)

These findings have been heavily criticised in research by Weisbrot *et al.* (2000) who suggested that the policy prescriptions of the World Bank and the IMF have actually slowed down growth and contributed to greater poverty and income inequalities:

> 'In Latin America GDP per capita grew by 75 percent from 1960 to 1980 whereas from 1980 to 1998 it has only risen 6 per cent. For Sub Sahara Africa GDP per capita grew by 36 per cent in the first period while it has since fallen by 15 per cent'. (Weisbrot *et al.*, 2000, p. 1)

For the developing countries, globalisation has been accompanied with deteriorating incomes. Most of the developing countries were better off between 1950 and 1970, than in the 1980s and 1990s. The 48 countries that make up the Least Developed Countries (LDCs) have seen their share of world trade decline from 0.7 per cent of world GDP in 1994, to 0.4 per cent in 2000. Developing countries as a whole have seen an increase in world trade from 19 per cent in 1972, to 22 per cent in 2001, while during the same period, the volume in world trade has expanded by 14 times. Poor countries have become poorer because of declining commodity prices and declining food prices, which are their major exports. The OECD subsidies to agriculture of US$ 320 billion have resulted in over production of food within the EU, USA and Japan, which in turn has reduced prices to the extent that the developed countries are now accused of dumping food, including rice and meat, on Africa and Asia. Developing countries are unable to offer the same levels of subsidies to their agriculture. The World Bank estimates that the subsidies are costing the developing countries some US$19.8 billion a year and that if the subsidies were removed, the incomes *per capita* would improve by US$1 a day in South East Asia and US$6 in Sub-Saharan Africa. Considering that there are 1.3 billion people living on less than US$1/day, such a policy reform would bring a qualitative change to people in the Philippines, Chad, Bangladesh and Burundi.

UNCTAD (2001) has pointed out that in the 1990s, the top 20 per cent of the world population who lived mainly in the advanced economies of the OECD received 83 per cent of the world's income, while the bottom 20 per cent received 1.4 per cent. The World Gini coefficient increased from 0.68 per cent in 1980 to 0.74 per cent in 2000 (UNCTAD, 2001). Between 1980 and 1997, there were 33 countries that had growth rates of 3 per cent per year, while another 59 countries experienced negative growth rates. Between 1980 and 1990, inequality increased in 15 of the industrialised countries, while all the economies in transition became more unequal. In Latin America, eight out of 13 countries became more unequal, while in Asia inequality increased in seven out of 10 countries (UNDP, 1999).

The impact of economic growth on the distribution of income in the world economy can be described, as being 'distribution neutral' in that economic growth alone does not improve income inequality. It is the political choices and decisions of government that shape income distribution. In Brazil, 48 per cent of income goes to the top 10 per cent of earners, while 0.8 per cent is the income of the bottom 10 per cent. By contrast, in India the top 10 per cent of earners received 25 per cent of income, while 4.1 per cent went to the bottom 10 per cent. In Taiwan, China and the Republic of Korea, the key policies of land reforms provided the means for a better re-distribution of income. In Malaysia, a policy of low taxes and support for agriculture resulted in a growth rate of 5 per cent per annum in incomes to agriculture, in contrast to Ghana, which has seen a decline of 1 per cent per annum in agriculture. Expenditure on education in East Asia gives access to adult literacy classes to 80 per cent of the population, compared with 13 per cent in Niger and 36 per cent in Pakistan. In Zambia, enrolments in tertiary education are around 2 per cent of the adult population, compared with 3 per cent in Bangladesh and the Republic of Korea, which has 48 per cent. Countries with high growth rates, including China and Korea have also high-income distribution policies. Equally, other countries that have high growth rates are also associated with low distribution of income policies, such as Brazil.

Since the mid-1980s, the major losers of globalisation have been wage earners, while the gainers have been the holders of financial assets. Wage earners in both the developed and developing countries have seen their wages either stagnate or even decline in value. In the developed countries, people who lost their jobs in manufacturing never returned to work. The labour shake-outs since the mid-1980s in textiles, steel and coal resulted in the decline of industrial communities. In the meantime, world trade increased from 6 per cent of the world GDP in 1950, to 17 per cent of the world GDP in 2000. The top 200 multinational corporations were responsible for 80 foreign direct investments and the 24 per cent of the world GDP in 1982 that had increased to 26.8 per cent in 2000. Furthermore, 70 per cent of total world trade takes place within the advanced economies.

The real median wage of US workers was no higher in 2002 than it was in 1973. Real wages for the bottom quintile of the labour force actually dropped by about 9 per cent between 1973 and 1997. In the meantime, *per capita* income had risen by 70 per cent. For the median and the bottom-quintile, wages actually fell during this same period. During the first half of the post-Second World War era, the wages of the bottom three quintiles increased roughly in step with the average (which rose 80 per cent from 1946–1973). Since the mid-1980s, the majority of the US labour force has been excluded from sharing in the gains from economic growth. In Latin America, income distribution became more equal in the 1970s and has worsened since the

1980s. Cornia and Kiiski's (2001) study of 73 countries, which amount to 80 per cent of the world population, have shown that in 48 of those countries, income inequalities increased between 1980 and 2000.

National Governments and central banks are unable to match the flows of financial transactions, which result in governments having to increasingly take heed of market sentiment. The making of macroeconomic policy increasingly has to correspond with the expectations of financial markets. The emphasis on transparency and stability in the making of macroeconomic policy reflects the view that governments are committed to a policy framework that ensures a path of low inflation, low government borrowing and low interest rates – a policy framework that is compatible in the context of globalised economic policy making. In the control of inflation the independence of the central bank is essential for monetary policy. Inflation is perceived as destabilising, because of the predictability of wage pressures and rising prices. The fine-tuning of monetary policy is judged as being more effective than fiscal policy. Economic cycles can be smoothed through marginal changes in interest rates, according to the New Economic Orthodoxy. Developing countries faced with balance of payments deficits are presented with programmes by the IMF and the World Bank that seek to re-structure debt financing through reductions in public expenditure, reductions in taxation liberalisation, de-regulation and privatisation. For the developed economy, the new economic orthodoxy points to the priorities of balanced budgets; reducing the costs of government, retreating from areas of social protection including health, pensions and social security expenditures and making labour market more flexible.

Globalisation and Market Liberalism

Globalisation is at present being defined by neo-liberal ideas of free markets, liberalisation and de-regulation and the urgency to push back the frontiers of government intervention. The twin commitments to free trade and economic liberalisation have been the pillars of economic globalisation since the mid-1970s. The neo-liberal argument advocating free markets and less government has been the prevailing paradigm. Free trade has been associated with economic prosperity, with higher living standards, lower mortality rates and for advancing ideas of individual freedom and democracy. Governments and political parties have increasingly accepted the logic of neo-liberal views of globalisation.

Throughout modern history, the concepts of market liberalism have been presented as de-politicised arguments. Market economics is defined as a science, a series of laws of supply and demand equal in status to the laws of gravity, laws that cannot be altered and which human beings have to live with. The laws of markets, of supply and demand, equilibrium and diminishing returns are even more enduring than the laws of physics, chemistry and biology. While the natural science has been revised in the light of new knowledge and new findings, by contrast, the laws of markets cannot be challenged. Despite arguments to the contrary, market liberals still hold to the basic axioms of the marginal theory of labour, the idea of equilibrium and competition. Market liberal ideas have a life of their own, difficult to challenge and difficult to dislodge:

> 'Today, most economists imperiously dismiss the notion that ideology plays any part in their thinking. The profession has in fact devised the term 'positive economics' to signify economic theory without any value judgements . . . Yet ideology lurks within 'positive' economics in the form of the core belief in equilibrium. The defence of this core belief is what has made economics so resistant to change, since virtually every challenge to economic theory has called upon it to abandon the concept of equilibrium. It has refused to do so and thus each challenge has been repulsed, ignored or belittled'. (Keen, 2001, p. 163)

In over 200 years of market liberalism, only Keynes and Keynesian economists have provided the major economic intellectual challenge to market liberalism and provided the opportunity for a paradigm shift. However, even Keynes and Keynesian thinking have continued to be downgraded since the mid-1970s. Market liberalism is presented as the only viable alternative that can protect individual rights. Furthermore, market liberalism is equated with the commitment to democratic government. Democracy and free markets become inextricably linked. However, while it might be true to argue that it is not possible to have democracy without a commitment to markets; it is not equally true that markets need a democratic form of government. Free markets seem to thrive equally well in the context of democracy, as much as within military governments and totalitarian states. The military regimes in Chile, Argentina and Burma, together with the present Communist governments in China, have shown that it is possible to promote market economic reforms in the absence of democracy. Polanyi (1957) in his criticism of nineteenth century industrial, market-based society pointed out that:

> 'To allow the market mechanism to be sole director of the fate of human beings and their natural environment would result in the demolition of society'. (Polanyi, 1957, p. 73)

However, Polanyi was also equally convinced that such a demolition could no longer happen in the post-war world because:

> 'Within the nations we are witnessing a development under which the economic system ceases to lay down the law to society and the primacy of society over that system is secured'. (Polanyi, 1957, p. 251)

Polanyi was influenced by the ascendancy of Keynesian economic ideas and the acceptance of greater government intervention. In a number of countries, governments had already committed themselves to the concept of full employment and social policies. Polanyi argued with Keynes that there was the political choice of living with the market economy or of shaping the market economy in a way that benefits humanity. There is a choice to be made between accepting the argument that globalisation is an event, which governments have to respond to or arguing that globalisation is being defined and shaped through political choices. Accepting the former leads to the view that there is no alternative to the free market economy and the ideas of market liberalism, while the emphasis on the latter points to the view that governments are not prisoners of globalisation, but have political autonomy.

The economics axioms of market liberalism eclipsed Keynesian economics ideas in the mid-1970s, when it was argued that Keynesians did not have a response to the dual problems of unemployment and inflation. According to Keynesian orthodoxy, it was not possible to have the co-existence of unemployment and inflation. Leading market liberal economists, including Friedman and Von Mises argued that the stagflation of the 1970s was attributable to big government. Governments had become involved in increased public expenditures and high deficits that had led to the crowding out of the private sector because of higher interest rates and public sector employment. According to market liberals, inflation was always the problem of government borrowing, while unemployment was the consequence of the uncertainties of inflation and higher wage demands. Market liberals blamed government for inflation, while arguing the case that unemployment represented problems of labour market rigidities that required labour market reforms.

The common theme that connects globalisation and market liberalism is that both are perceived to be exogenous processes that have a life of their own, laws, which cannot be questioned or contravened. There is therefore no alternative but to live with the impersonal forces of the market. Markets reflect human nature and individual self-interest. Pursuing self-interest is compatible with the public interest, since self-interest promotes economic prosperity. The market provides price signals for the allocation and distribution of resources.

The Maastricht Treaty of 1997, the Growth and Stability Pact and the commitment to economic convergence, lower government spending, lower inflation and lower interests have been presented as strategies for EU members to meet the challenges of globalisation. EU member states have committed themselves to balanced budgets; inflation targets lower than 3 per cent and reducing government debts to below 60 per cent of the GDP. The European Central Bank is responsible for maintaining low inflation. Globalisation demands greater competition, wider liberalisation of trade, increased consumer choice, lower prices and more flexible labour markets. Accordingly, for Europe to compete, there has to be reforms of labour markets, creating greater flexibility and reforming social policy in order to reduce labour costs. While the USA has created some 32 million jobs since the mid-1980s, by contrast, Europe has created 5 million new jobs. Over the past 15 years, unemployment in France and Germany has remained at around 9 per cent. These are described as the failures of sclerosis in Europe and of being unable to compete with the USA on indicators of productivity and living standards:

> 'Sovereign states are waging a war of competitive deregulation forced on them by the global market. A mechanism of downward harmonisation of market economies is already in operation. Every type of currently existing capitalisms is thrown into the melting pot. In this contest the socially dislocated American free market possesses powerful advantages'. (Gray, 1998, p. 78)

According to Gray (1998), present forms of globalisation are undermining social policies and welfare states, since countries with social market economies including Germany, France, Norway, Sweden and Britain are characterised by higher indirect labour costs, which make them unable to compete with countries with lower labour costs. The new economic orthodoxy points to competitive markets based on lower costs and the ability of finance capital to flow to countries that have lower costs. The priority for governments in the advanced industrial economies is therefore to embrace economic policies that seek to reduce the role of government, reduce government deficits and national debt burdens and reduce interest rates. With regard to employment, the role of government is limited to ensure that it provides the opportunities that create a framework for flexible labour markets and employability through better training, education and de-regulation of working hours. Accordingly, there is no alternative but to follow the logic of the free market economy:

> 'national policy makers face a prisoner's dilemma; democratically elected governments ... face strong incentives to engage in competition to retain and attract transnationally fluid investment through reductions in social benefits, market-oriented reforms of social services and cuts in associated tax burdens'. (Swank, 2001, p. 5)

Markets are made and defined by people. Rather than assuming that it is the impersonal laws of supply and demand, the laws of markets, the invisible hands that are shaping the global economy, it is essential to point out that it is policies that define markets and therefore there is the element of political choice. If it is people who are making political choices then it is appropriate to ask why is market liberalism presented as the only set of ideas that should guide the ethics of the globalised economy? Are there no other sets of economic ideas that challenge *laissez faire*? Furthermore, it might be appropriate to ask whether the concept of free markets is value-free or whether there are interests groups that benefit from the ideas of free markets. Free markets ideas represent yet another set of ideas of yet another vested interest group and should be treated as such, rather than as a series of impersonal laws.

The WTO rules seek to give priority to free trade, removing what are defined as unnecessary barriers to trade and to protect intellectual property rights. Attempting to connect ideas of free trade with issues of social justice, including core labour standards, the rights to freedom of association in the workplace, access to public health, education and protection of the environment, have been defined as barriers to trade. This approach to policy making has adversely affected the quality of life for those on low incomes.

In the aftermath of the protests in Genoa, the Prime Minister of Belgium, Guy Verhofstadt, in his capacity of President of the EU, issued an open letter under the heading 'The paradox of anti globalisation', in which he introduced the concept of ethical globalisation. He argued that the agenda of globalisation needed to be greater free trade, more democracy, greater respect for human rights and more concern about development. Verhofstadt suggested the major limit of present globalisation was that the interests of the wealthy nations dominated policy priorities and what was lacking was a global political body. He urged that the present G8 meetings should be replaced by a G8 of world regions rather than the present eight dominant countries:

> 'More free trade, more democracy, greater respect for human rights and more development aid is that enough to make ethical globalisation a reality? Certainly not! What is missing is a powerful instrument to enforce it. We need a global political body that is as powerful as the globalised market in which we already live. The G8 of the rich countries must be replaced by a G8 of existing regional partnerships. A G8 where the South is given an important and deserved place at the table to ensure that the globalisation of the economy is headed in the right direction. In other words we need to create a forum where the leading continental partnerships can all speak on an equal footing'. (*Financial Times*, 27 September 2001)

Implicit in the argument is the view that there is now a mismatch between economic globalisation and political accountability. His argument is that the challenge of globalisation is to create a framework of political institutions that ensure political equality. It is an interpretation that is founded on the theme that globalisation is an event which is happening, that has its own logic and that this process requires a political response and therefore underestimates the extent to which globalisation represents political decisions. The problem of globalisation is therefore not a lack of appropriate political institutions, but rather the understanding of the nature of the politics that is giving shape to globalisation; a form of politics that appears to be remote, beyond political accountability that seems to serve the interests of large business organisations and results in social exclusion.

THE POLITICS OF GLOBALISATION

Globalisation is continually being defined and reshaped through political choices and political decisions. This means that globalisation is not something that is beyond control or that there is somehow a logic of globalisation. The process of economic globalisation is not inevitable. Governments are not prisoners responding to economic globalisation, as if the process was beyond their control, but rather governments shape globalisation, which suggests that economic globalisation reflects political choices. Accepting the premise that globalisation is political, the next question is to ask who is involved in making the political decisions? Are the decision makers accountable for these decisions and are the decisions transparent?

Economic globalisation is associated with greater liberalisation of trade, including the removal of barriers and tariffs against imports. However, the concept of barriers to trade is not innocent and judging and defining necessary barriers to trade involve political decisions. Protecting the rights of employees, their working conditions and limits of hours in work can be defined as artificial barriers to trade, even when these rights represent people's political wishes. Public sector health and education provision can be defined as public sector monopolies, which act as barriers to trade. Inevitably, the commitments to free trade and liberalisation are likely to increase tensions between the spaces of democracy and accountability and the commitment to free trade, liberalisation and de-regulation.

The Secretary to the WTO has recently defended the WTO's democratic credentials by pointing out that all 142 members had an equal vote and that by contrast to the United Nations, the WTO did not have a General Council. Equally, decisions taken by the WTO are decisions taken by elected governments and these governments are accountable to their Parliaments. By contrast, critics of the WTO have pointed to the inequality of access to decision making and to the ascendancy of corporate-government alliances:

'Overall the spoils of the WTO dispute system seem to go to the wealthiest participants . . . developed countries have the resources to take advantage of the WTO pattern of ruling in favour of the challenger. Many developing countries not only cannot afford to bring cases but also cannot afford the costs of a WTO defence. Indeed an alarming trend under the WTO is that developing countries faced with the enormous expertise and resources involved in mounting a WTO defence in Geneva are changing laws merely after the threat of a WTO challenge from wealthy countries'. (Wallach, Public Citizen Testimony on the WTO Dispute Settlement System to the US Senate Finance Committee, 20 June 2000)

Blackhurst (1997) estimated that there are, on average, 45 WTO meetings in Geneva each week, dealing with highly technical and legal processes. It is at these meetings that rules are made. These are the meetings that require high levels of staffing and resources, utilising trade lawyers and specific advisers on pharmaceuticals, finance and services. Developing countries do not have the financial or personnel to staff these meetings. The lack of transparency, the lobbying by business interests and the making of trade coalitions between the EU and the USA make the nature of WTO decisions a pyramid, with decisions being taken by a very few at the top, while the poor countries are bounced into agreements.

Recent protocols including TRIPS (Treaty Related to Intellectual Property Rights) and GATS (General Agreement on Trade and Services) confirm the nature of decision making within WTO and the influence of trade lawyers shaping the nature of political decisions. The recent anthrax cases in the USA have also shown the inequalities that exist between the richer countries and the much weaker developing countries. The anthrax scares in the USA have allowed the US governments to force Bayer to accept a price reduction from US$4 a tablet, to US$1 under the threat that government was going to produce a generic for CIPRO. Similarly, the government in Canada reached a similar contract with Bayer. These settlements contrast sharply with the way drug patents are threatening public health in the developing counties and the inability of the poor to purchase generic medicines to deal with major problems such as malaria, smallpox and HIV/AIDS. In the USA, three people had died of anthrax before the US government decided to act. There are some 360 people dying each day of AIDS/HIV in South Africa.

IATP (2003) have also reported how major companies are moving to India and other African Countries and removing plants and seeds, claiming patents for natural plants. According to Action Aid, four major companies now own between 670 patents that, in turn, are leading to a monopoly in the production of food. Poor farmers in the meantime, have to purchase seeds under patent. Multinationals including Monsanto have the resources and the legal capacities to challenge national governments in court, to recover costs, if there has been discrimination on trade and infringement on intellectual property. The implications of TRIPS are having major ripple effects in public health.

The WTO has received submissions from the EU emphasising the importance of TRIPS, arguing that intellectual property rights were important because they provided the incentives for continued research into new drugs, while developing countries have continued to argue about the monopoly of patented drugs. In the developing countries, people tend to purchase medicines and drugs privately, where the costs of these drugs are usually equivalent to between 50 and 90 per cent of household incomes. When children become sick, this very often spells tragedy for families, because they need to make decisions between food and buying medicines.

In a more recent case, US multinationals have argued that the French Government were creating a barrier to trade in banning the import of asbestos, because the government made a commitment to protect the health risks of workers in France. The asbestos companies appealed to the WTO that the policy was an unnecessary restriction to trade. The dispute on trade and bananas between the USA and Europe also confirms the limits of political autonomy. In the banana dispute, the EU policy of preferential treatment for the ACP group (Asia, Caribbean Pacific countries) in the imports of bananas, was defined as a barrier to free trade by the government of Venezuela. The USA pledged that they would retaliate with imposing tariffs on EU products worth US$180 billion, unless the EU committed itself to a policy of free trade in bananas. The EU agreed to import more bananas from outside the ACP. The major beneficiary of the dispute was a US multinational, located in Venezuela that had used the government of Venezuela as proxy in the dispute with the EU, with the US Government coming to the aid of the government of Venezuela.

Multinational corporations increasingly lobby their governments to make their case within an international forum, to bring about favourable policy shifts in the name of free trade. Farmers from poor countries still wait for the Uruguay Round to be implemented, while still facing 40 per cent tariffs, with Europe and the USA continuing to subsidise their agriculture.

At present, the WTO is also providing frameworks for GATS that will influence the provision of health, social services and education. Under GATS, governments will come under pressure to ensure that the public provision of health and education services does not constitute artificial barriers to trade. Under GATS, the NHS could be defined as a monopoly and therefore a barrier to free trade in health care. Pollock and Price, writing in *The Lancet* (December 2000) have suggested that GATS could lead to the privatisation of the health service even if people in the UK are supportive of the NHS:

> 'At present the NHS is funded through the tax system it is therefore a form of cross subsidy between high and low income earners a form of universal risking polling and solidarity. These foundations can be described as anti market and anti competition and therefore can be defined as unnecessary obstacles to free trade'. (Pollock and Price, 2000, p. 4)

Article VI: 4 of the GATS agreement put a focus on measures relating to qualifications requirements and technical standards, which according to the WTO seek to eliminate artificial barriers to labour mobility procedures. According to *The Lancet* commentary therefore, there seems to be a tension between trade interests and health policy objectives. *The Lancet* goes on to quote the case of banning asbestos as a health risk, while preferring other fibres – the WTO ruled against France for using the asbestos ruling as a form of protection against trade, rather than a public health concern.

In 1994, the US Government argued that the free trade agreement between the USA, Canada and Mexico was to benefit the US consumers through lower prices, more competitive markets and greater opportunities for US employment. Studies of the benefits of NAFTA (North America Free Trade Agreement), 7 years after it was signed between the USA, Canada and Mexico have shown that consumers, small farmers and growers have been the losers, while large corporations have been the major winners. The studies (*Public Citizen*, 2001) estimate that about 15 million Mexican small farmers have been displaced by large agri-business. Mexico in 2001 became dependent on US corn exports because of cheap US imports. Transnational companies including Smithfield Foods, Tyson Foods and Murphy Family Foods have re-located to Mexico, where wages are US$3.6 per day for rural workers. These companies are able to exploit the use of pesticides, which are banned in the USA, putting Mexican workers and US consumers increasingly at risk. The flood of cheap imports has displaced small wheat growers in the Mid-West, ranchers in Texas and vegetable and fruit growers in California. The paradox is, that despite the falling prices in the production of food, the concentration of ownership has ensured larger profits for suppliers and retailers and higher prices for US consumers. The top five grain suppliers in the USA now control 75 per cent of the cereal commodity markets, while the top five food retailers control 42 per cent of all retails of food. Con Agra profits have increased from US$143 billion in 1994, to US$413 billion in 2001. Archer Midland has also increased profits from US$11 billion to US$310 billion during the same period. In the meantime, the US consumer prices index has increased by 20 per cent, during the first 7 years of NAFTA.

In shaping WTO regulations, governments are becoming increasingly dependent on business organisations to provide expertise and knowledge in defining trade regulations. Michael Treschone, the co-chair of the Transatlantic Business Dialogue (TABD) that represents the interests of business in the EU and the USA and which meets regularly with EU Ministers and EU Commissioners and US Trade Representatives said:

'We (TABD) are not a lobby group but invited advisors. That contributes to the fact that the TABD has made great progress and in the course of the years has succeeded in pushing many of our priorities into practical policy'. (M. Treschone, Chair TABD, January 2001)

The role of TABD is to ensure that the EU and USA speak with one voice in putting together a view at WTO negotiations. While other transatlantic groups, including the consumer, labour and environment, also meet on a regular basis, it is the TABD, which has managed to secure 50–80 per cent of their policy proposals on liberalisation and great free trade. Most often, these policy proposals run counter to issues of environment concerns, health and safety and worker rights. In the meantime, within the EU, the European Roundtable of Industrialists has continued to lobby for greater liberalisation, the removing of EU Governments red tape, the de-regulation of labour markets and the reduction of non-labour costs to ensure greater European competitiveness in the context of globalisation.

The Corporate Europe Observatory has recently pointed to the blurred relationships between UK civil servants, the DTI and the LOTIS committee and International Finances Services London that have helped advise the DTI:

'The strength and effectiveness of the LOTIS Committee derives from the open and co-operative interface which exists in its work between its private sector members and the British Government officials who are involved in the negotiating process in Brussels and Geneva This enables the UK position on financial and related professional services interests to be represented in the most direct way possible'. (E. Wesselius, Liberalisation of Trade in Services Corporate Power at Work, *Corporate Europe Observatory*, November 2001)

The politics of globalisation is increasingly being shaped by the interest of multinational corporations. Business interests have ready access to the corridors of their national governments and are therefore able to articulate their priorities and to advise their governments in trade negotiations. In the meantime, trade negotiations become increasingly complex and governments become more dependent on the advice of business. This relationship between business organisations and governments is criticised for the lack of political transparency and accountability, but also for the narrowness of perspective:

'While it is useful and justified for governments to take business concerns into account when formulating trade policy' privileged co-operative arrangements between business and government do not belong in a truly democratic policy making process . . . High priority should be given to the development of balanced and truly democratic mechanisms for civil society input in trade policy preparation'. (*Corporate Europe Observatory*, November 2001)

CONCLUSIONS

Critics of the present forms of globalisation are confronted with the view that there is no alternative to the neo-liberal paradigm of globalisation. Economic globalisation since the 1970s has been driven by market liberal ideas. The view that economic reforms need to be made compatible with the economic laws of supply and demand, have also resulted in the ascendancy of multinational corporations in shaping and influencing the economics but also the politics of world trade. The advocacy of free trade has tended to benefit the advanced industrial economies, while developing countries are still waiting for agreements to remove tariffs on textiles and agriculture to be implemented. The governments in the industrial economies still give priority to their domestic constituencies of farming and manufacturing interests through the provision of export subsidies, while imposing tariffs on imports from developing economies. Furthermore, protocols on intellectual property rights and safeguards on foreign investment have established a climate where the priorities of free trade put into question concerns on public health, environment and protection of worker rights. TRIPS has prevented developing countries from purchasing cheaper medicines to deal with malaria, smallpox and HIV/AIDS.

Market liberals argue the case for less government. Public sector monopolies need to be broken up to provide greater choices for consumers and increase competition. Privatisation of public sector monopolies, contracting out of services, liberalisation of financial markets and the de-regulation of labour markets become the new economic priorities. The concept of the rational individual is interpreted as a policy that favours reductions in taxation, since people can make better choices on how to spend their money, than governments. Monetary policy is put at arm's length from government. The independent central bank becomes the custodian of monetary policy and the control of inflation. The instrument of economic fine-tuning is monetary policy and interest rates. Contemporary globalisation represents the ascendancy of market liberalism. It is presented as an argument between free trade and protectionism. Those who argue for human rights, for decent wages and labour standards, are depicted as promoting their vested interests.

At present, globalisation has become interchangeable with the policy choice of neo-liberal perspectives on individualism and markets. To neo-liberals, the new globalised economy represents the triumph of liberal thinking. The market confirms the freedom of individual choice and competition. The globalised economy offers more choices, cheaper prices and higher living standards. The role of government should be confined to de-regulation policies of the labour market, the privatisation of state monopolies and the provision of incentives for private pensions and health insurance. Globalisation leads to the re-invention of government. High marginal taxes on higher income earners are a disincentive to innovation, while demands for higher wages are likely to result in unemployment.

Globalisation is increasingly equated with political passivity. It seems to serve as a form of fear and insecurity – the fear of a loss of jobs and insecurity about the long term. The concern about globalisation and the nature of the challenge takes different forms. There is concern about what Hertz (Hertz, 2001) has recently described as the 'silent takeover' and the relevance of the nation state when a number of multinational companies have incomes higher than the GDP of a number of countries. The concern is whether national governments can still provide social programmes for the protection of rights and the well being of their citizens. Beck (2000c) has argued for the need to transform the nation state into a 'transnation' state, a hybrid between the nation and the international state; an attempt at the pooling of sovereignty. In a similar vein, Held *et al.* (2000) has pointed to the need to create a cosmopolitan democracy. The aim is to create a space for political accountability on environment issues and to put a stop to further degradation by making multinationals more transparent and accountable and to prevent nation states competing with each other with policies of social dumping, further de-regulation, privatisation and liberalisation, falling tax yields, threatened social programmes, unemployment and greater income inequalities.

6. Globalisation and empowerment

INTRODUCTION

Bhagwati (2002) in his WIDER memorial lecture argued the case that globalisation was good for the dignity of women. To illustrate his point, he questioned feminists' criticisms that had attempted to show that one of the main implications of globalisation was for women from the third world to go and become nannies in upper-middle-class homes in the USA, leaving their own children with nannies back in their countries of origin. Bhagwati felt this experience actually benefited women from the third world, because they in turn experienced American ways of life and therefore were able to go home and argue the case of human rights and question male dominance:

> 'The same goes for women in the 'global childcare chain' who go abroad for work. It is even suggested by some critics that the migrant women in such occupations lose a sense of self-respect because they work for other women's children while missing their own. But the opposite is also possible, in my experience in my own household and seems more likely. The key is that these women come from poor and traditional, almost feudal, societies where women's rights are far less recognized, if at all. Seeing how the women they work for are treated with greater respect and dignity and also how they themselves are generally treated by their men and women employers with the regard and courtesy that is often missing in the feudal or traditional cultures they come from, acts as an eye-opener that reinforces their search for autonomy and individuality that unsettle the straitjacket of traditional, repressive roles that they were born into and conditioned by. Also, looking at it from the viewpoint of the employing women in the rich countries, the childcare chain enables them to go to work, a feminist gain again'. (Bhagwati, 2002, 'Globalisation and appropriate governance', WIDER Annual Lecture No. 4, p. 17)

Implicit within this argument is the idea the people should be thankful for the jobs that they have because through employment there is a path out of poverty and therefore to break with dependency on the state for social assistance. Chinese and Burmese women working in EPZs (Export Processing Zones), which are usually de-regulated factories set up by local sub-contractors working for large multinationals such as Nike or Gap are better off working under these conditions than doing back breaking work on small farms in their villages.

'Thus, consider that, even when young girls in EPZs are not turned into long-term employees, many come from the rural countryside to which they return, having acquired, not skills, but an experience out of the home and even some savings that give them a certain autonomy, plus what some economists studying household behavior today call 'bargaining power' within the household. This would have been missing if they had not left home for the globalised EPZs. Surely, this works towards feminist objectives as UNIFEM, the UN organization dealing with women's issues, recognizes'. (Bhagwati, 2002, p. 16)

According to Bhagwati, economic globalisation generates individual empowerment. Studies about trade, growth and their impact on poverty and income inequalities seek to deal with questions of empowerment. Less poverty is correlated with better health, better education, high wages and higher life expectancy. Poverty is associated with illiteracy, ill health, high child mortality rates and low life expectancy. In contrast to the optimism of Bhagwati, Barber (1996) has utilised the concept of McWorld to describe the growth of sameness that describes the consumer society of designer labelled clothing, shopping malls, surfing the internet and mobile phones:

'of shimmering pastels, a busy portrait of on rushing economic, technological and ecological forces that demand integration and uniformity and that mesmerise peoples everywhere with fast music, fast computers and fast food – pressing nations into one homogenous global theme park'. (Barber, 1996, p. 4)

According to this argument, governments are under pressure to acquiesce to the global straitjacket. In that same world of glittering shopping malls, there are major problems of widespread poverty, child labour, sweatshops of low wages, longer hours and fewer holidays, where the work experience is still about repetition, whether it is making a high-tech running shoe, telephone sales or selling cheeseburgers. This is the narrative of disempowerment and the corruption of the public space that serves particular interests, rather than public interests. It is the language of community and belonging that denies the existence of poverty or hardships. There is increased erosion of intermediate agencies of local governments, trade unions and political institutions that mediated between centralised forms of power and the individual. The marginalised, including the new economic migrants and asylum seekers, often working very long hours in dangerous work places, with no trade union rights or employment protection, do not make the news. The public spaces are filled with the glittering celebrities. In the context of disempowerment, the individual becomes more remote and depoliticised, having to create a narrative that gives meaning to a life that is changing, but where the political economy of citizenship and self-government are replaced by ideas of the passive consumer:

'politics creates a way of living with social problems by defining them as inevitable or as equitable – problems that are attributed to human nature, to economics laws encouraging both the powerful and the powerless to accept their situation. This results in the continuation of broad public support for recurrent policies'. (Edelman, 1977, p. 141)

According to Barber (1996) 'McWorld' creates a political response, which he terms as Jihad. Jihad is the politics that seeks the return to tribalism, community and the exclusion of the stranger and the migrant. Right wing candidates make inroads in the decaying parts of inner cities and on social housing estates where there is high unemployment and where the local residents feel that they no longer have a voice in politics. Politics no longer makes a difference to their lives. The attraction of right wing candidates in part reflects resistance to the globalised economy and the increased feelings of remoteness, which is blamed on the politics of elites, migrants and asylum seekers. The experience of disempowerment in a world of global markets creates a need for community and for de-centralised forms of government as a means of breaking with the feeling of remoteness. Both McWorld and the world of Jihad undermine citizenship and democracy:

'Yet Jihad and McWorld have this in common: they both make war on the sovereign nation-state and thus undermine the nation-state's democratic institutions. Each eschews civil society and belittles democratic citizenship neither seeking alternative democratic institutions. Their common thread is indifference to civil liberty. Jihad forges communities rooted in exclusion and hatred. McWorld forges global markets rooted in consumption and profit'. (Barber, 1996, p. 6)

This chapter seeks to examine the dual concepts of empowerment and disempowerment. In the previous chapters, it was pointed out that definitions of citizenship are continually being shaped and defined in the context of political decisions. Making the public citizen a reality required the commitment to transparency and accountability of political institutions. However, the language of the independent and consumer citizen disempowers by putting the focus on the retreat to the safety of the homes, family and the private space. Citizenship is shaped by policy making. However, it has also been suggested that citizenship represents a form of resistance in the sense that the claims on democracy also provide the opportunities for continued dissent. While in the context of market liberal thinking, individual empowerment is guaranteed, in the context of market competition and consumer society the argument for citizenship as a form resistance puts the emphasis on the need to continually unmask hidden issues of power and hypocrisies that are the result of languages of power, which, in turn, marginalise, devalue and ignore languages of social injustice. Studying the implications of the retreat from the public space into privatised lives in the context of contemporary globalisation Barber (1996) and Sennet (2000) have pointed to the implications of increased indifference and disavowal of responsibilities at both the levels of the economy and of governments.

The attempt to connect the issues of empowerment, disempowerment and globalisation does not imply that there existed some previous 'golden age' of the empowered individual and of community in a world we have lost. Indeed, even a cursory look at agricultural communities of the seventeenth century suggests that people experienced community in terms of class differences. Land ownership, the church, trade and many occupational differences defined the fit and proper persons who made the political decisions. The ties of tradition and authority defined the economic, political and social contours that provided the rhythms of village life. A sense of belonging existed because people moved house very little and when someone died, their home or cottage would remain and stay empty. Landscapes hardly changed. Equally, there was little room for those who did not belong, the strangers, the vagrants, those who dissented or challenged the symbols of community:

> 'At the lowest level even the poor were drawn into the system; the respectable those for whom powerful friends, squire, parson or prominent townsman or parishioner would vouch had first access to local charities. Even the paupers were those acknowledged by 'the gentlemen of the parish' as their own. Only the poor stranger, the vagrant, the miscreant, the 'masterless man' without a friend to speak for him was whipped and turned away'. (Perkin, 1969, p. 50)

Equally, people experienced disintegration in the age of industrial capitalism, as towns and cities became the places that reflected diversity, plurality and difference. The industrial communities of coal, textiles, engineering, shipbuilding and steel making, produced shared economic, social and political experiences, but again there were differences between the corner-shop owners, the self-employed and the small businesses that served these communities. Industrial communities were structured and layered. There were 'in-groups' and 'out-groups', those who moralised and those who were marginalised. When coal mines or steel mills shut down, business was always more mobile and could move to the next town.

THE INDIVIDUAL CITIZEN AND RESISTANCE

Citizenship as resistance includes resistance to the institutions that govern the global economy and the lack of transparency of organisation such as the WTO, the World Bank and the IMF. Resistance as citizenship points to the influence of business interests on governments, their lack of accountability, the expansion and influence of bureaucracy and the 'rule by nobody' and, by contrast, giving priority to the processes of democratic politics, accountability and transparency. It embraces resistance to the new knowledge estates of the so-called experts, including health professionals, military, environmental and economics experts, their language of exclusion and their disavowal of responsibility (Beck, 2000c).

New forms of resistance including consumer and rent boycotts in South Africa, protests against water privatisation in Nigeria and protest meetings against globalisation, whether in Davos, Seattle, Prague or Genoa, reflect the ephemeral nature of contemporary protest in the context of globalisation. People in employment no longer look at traditional means of trade union resistance. Trade union membership has been in decline since the 1980s, unable to replace the lost membership of manufacturing, with those in the new transitional jobs of, e.g. McDonalds and Gap. In the context of work, despite the low levels of unemployment, there is reluctance by workers to become involved in workplace disputes. The privatised individual searching for quiet, for stability of wages and mortgage repayments, replaces the collective forms of resistance of trade unions, industrial disputes, protest and involvement in the public space. Issues of principle come at a price. It is better to live with the continuity of income rather than the uncertainties of strikes and disruption:

> 'Our interpretation is that such a retreat and the associated reduction of demands would place trade unions in a losing position (in part because they would then be weakened organisationally and also because they would be made vulnerable externally to their claims to representation. The retreat would sooner or later initiate a spiral of continuous restrictions of trade claims to responsibility'. (Offe, 1985, p. 169)

Very often, citizenship is associated with the individual, the nation state and with institutions and issues of inequality of access. However, static definitions tend to construct a vision of citizen as a form of clothing and asks who is dressed and who is not dressed for the citizens parade. The concern of definition assumes that there is some agreed vision of what a citizen should look like when there is no agreed yardstick that compares whether a person living in Germany or France is citizen and whether this applies to a person living in Italy or in Britain. Citizenship as resistance makes the definition of citizenship fluid, permeable and a continuing agenda that does not come to a stop. Citizenship becomes a journey of resistances, of trying to create accountability, transparency and involvement in decisions that impact on the individual's lived experiences. Citizenship as resistance, is associated with awkwardness and discomfort. It provides the climate that seeks to deconstruct languages of power and oppression. Citizenship as dialogue resists the limits of government, so that what is perceived as being inevitable comes to be understood as choice and autonomy. Citizenship in the context of globalisation means resistance to the argument that there is no alternative. Citizenship in the global context by contrast is approximated with the world of alternatives.

In thinking of citizenship as resistance, there is a need to reflect on hybrid biographies, of young Muslims in Britain who see themselves as British, but also as coming from Pakistan. I reflect on my own personal biography. I was born in Malta. I am Maltese, but I am not Maltese. I have English origins. I have lived in England for 30 years, but I have brothers and sisters in Malta and also in England. I am an exile and a migrant, but I have UK citizenship. I have a hybrid identity. That hybrid nature of identity suggests to me that my identity cannot be confined with the territory of the nation state, but rather that I am a cosmopolitan citizen and cannot be rooted in community or tradition and that my resistance is shaped by defining myself as the other who continues to resist those who seek to define who I am.

Citizenship as resistance is related to the concept of the self-constituted individual who constructs identity as part of life's journey and personal biography founded on reflection. In the context of personhood, identity is very often defined by external factors, which on reflection are contingent. The person attempts to resist those parts of identity that are increasingly experienced as suppressive, including sexual orientation and gender oppression. The process of negotiating personal biographies reinforces the view that many dispositions of identity are contingent and could have been otherwise different in a different context. Resistance in the context of collective identity is the attempt to create a context that questions assumptions and points to the world as we know it, as being contingent rather than inevitable and that it is also a world which is susceptible to change.

'The one who construes her identity to be laced with contingency, including branded contingencies, is in a better position to question and resist the drive to convert difference into otherness to be defeated, converted or marginalised'. (Connolly, 1994, p. 180)

Within the context of democratic politics, citizenship is the artery between personal and collective identity. Democracy is perceived as having the potential for promoting the collective good – a collective good that is not mobilised by the state in a way that marginalises and devalues the other. It is a democracy that allows for plurality and resistance both at the level of the person and state, a context of agonal relationships that are continuously awkward, open and transparent.

THE STRONG ECONOMY AND THE STRONG STATE

The commitment to privatise gas, electricity and other public utilities changes the landscape of industrial relations. Employees in the newly, privatised industries are no longer in the employment of government. The sub-contracting of services by local government, private finance initiatives and public-private partnerships seeks to alter working conditions of public sector employees who find themselves doing the same work, but working for private contractors. Creating school governing bodies and executive agencies to administer social security means that responsibility is decentralised to executive agencies, rather than government. The aim is to de-politicise areas of government, while at the same time, the process seeks to dissolve collective resistance and the influence of interest groups such as trade unions. The defeat of the steelworkers and the year-long miners' strike in 1984, together with major reforms of industrial relations laws, helped to disconnect the influence of organised labour. However, the strong state also aims to re-integrate people as individuals. Government policies de-centralise public policies to regions, local government, local schools and hospitals empower local communities, but at the same time, erode ideas of universal expectations. With people paying taxes to local districts, the political focus becomes the local. There is little distribution of income between the affluence of the suburbs and the low incomes of inner cities, so that public schools no longer deliver a public good, but a service according to the tax yields of local communities. Affluent communities pay higher property taxes, which then can be used to pay for better teachers, books and school repairs. In the USA, state legislatures have taken over the delivery of social policy, so there is no longer a standardised delivery of medical care or social security payments. Some states behave like the Poor Law guardians of Britain in the 1840s, delivering welfare with different levels of harshness in defining the deserving and undeserving poor.

In the meantime, those who earn high incomes in the cities, are concerned with working in the city and eating in the vast number of restaurants. They are not concerned with the politics and the public interest of the cities. In contrast to the fit and proper persons that had constructed libraries and city halls in the nineteenth century, the new elite rush to catch trains and make their way to the quietness of their suburban castles. The city is threatening. It is not a safe place to bring up children:

'a regime of power operating on the principle of indifference to those in its grip, a regime seeking to evade, in the workplace, being held accountable for its acts. The essence of the politics of globalisation is finding ways to hold this regime of indifference to account. If we fail in this political effort, we will suffer a profound personal wound'. (Sennet, 2000, p. 190)

INDIVIDUAL EMPOWERMENT

This section examines two possible discourses of empowerment whose home domains are very different, yet seem to converge in their conclusions. Initially, it may seem strange to put into the same category the theory of individualism of market economists, including those of Hayek, Friedman and Nozick, with the postmodern views of Foucault and Bauman. However, in their different ways, both perspectives argue the case for individual empowerment. Furthermore, each seeks to dismiss the idea of politics in that the primacy is the individual's life project and the possibility of each making life into a work of art, taking responsibility for his or her own lives, free from community rules and from political constraints.

Empowerment, Liberalism and the Market Economy Way

Market economists put the individual at the centre by arguing for the concept of rational individualism and the competence of individuals to make choices about their well being. People's ability to make choices create market economies, which are influenced by prices, which are flexible and reflect people's priorities. In the context of the market economy, there is no attempt to moralise about the good society because it is plural and fragmented. In the market economy, people sell their talents and the income they receive reflects the willingness of others to pay for these talents. Income inequality reflects different abilities and talents. People receive the income they deserve. Top executives demand higher incomes because they create new companies and take risks in the creation of employment and wealth for others. Footballers, tennis players, golfers and film stars demand high incomes because of their individual attributes and people are willing to pay to watch their unique talent.

Governments distort the market when they introduce pay policies because they hinder people in utilising their abilities and incentives. Pay differentials become squeezed and training and investment in human capital become less important because those without skills start to earn similar incomes to those with higher skills. Empowerment in the context of market liberal thinking is equated with the right of parents to purchase private education for their children, investing in private health plans and private pension schemes. Empowerment reflects the individual's right to make choices,

'so long as effective freedom of exchange is maintained, the central feature of the market organisation of economic activity is that it prevents one person from interfering with another in respect of most of his activities. The consumer is protected from coercion by the seller because of the presence of other sellers . . . The seller is protected from the coercion by the consumer because of other consumers . . . The employee is protected from the coercion by the employer because of other

employers for whom he can work and so on. And the market does this imperson-
ally and without centralised authority'. (Friedman, 1962, pp. 14–15)

Empowerment the Postmodern Way

Postmodern thinking challenged the uses of meta theories, which it is argued,
attempted to explain everything, but really explained nothing. Postmodern
thinking therefore challenged the paradigms of big theories and argued instead
about the need of understanding plurality, diversity and fragmentation. Hassan
(Wellmer, 1985) defines postmodernity as the process of deconstruction and
unmaking:

> 'It is an antinomian moment that assumes a vast unmaking of the Western mind . . .
> I say 'unmaking' though other terms are now de rigueur for instance deconstruction,
> decentering, disappearance, demystification, discontinuity, difference, dispersion
> etc . . . Such terms express an ontological rejection of the traditional full subject . . .
> To think well, to fell well to act well, to read well according to this episteme of
> unmaking is to refuse the tyranny of wholes'. (Hassan, quoted in Wellmer, 1985, p.
> 338)

Market theories represent a hidden discourse of power, while arguing about
individual equality. Equally, Marxist analysis fails to deal with the more
complex issues of fragmentation and elites, while putting an emphasis on class
struggles. The methodology of postmodernity is the deconstruction of
language and the attempt to unmake ideology in the hope of creating a better
understanding of social structures, of the uses of power and the assumptions
that underpin policy processes. At the centre of postmodern thinking is 'the
other', the stranger who has so often been marginalised and devalued for being
different.

> 'I will use the term modern to designate any science that legitimates itself with
> reference to a meta discourse making explicit appeal to some grand narrative . . . I
> define postmodern as incredulity toward meta narratives . . . Our working hypothe-
> sis is that the status of knowledge is altered as societies enter what is known as the
> post industrial age and culture enters what is known as the postmodern age'.
> (Lyotard, 1984, pp. xxv and 3)

The world of postmodernity is about empowerment of the other and the
recognition that the global economy is made up increasingly of strangers. In
this world of strangers, we aim to create individual identities. The ethic of
postmodernity is the respect for the other who is different, but equal. This
celebration of difference is the awareness of uniqueness of individuals with
their own life projects. Postmodernity seeks to break with universal demands
and therefore universal forms of discourses of resistance. In the context of

postmodernity therefore there is no claim on universal human rights on universal citizenship. Postmodernity points to plurality and diversity as being the reason for celebrating greater individual autonomy. It points to the displacement of claims of community and solidarity, which in themselves have contributed to social exclusion. Individual empowerment is equated with the idea of the self-constituted individual.

Explaining disempowerment

Disempowerment reflects the lack of ability to bring about change in a world where the elite define the world for the rest. While most people experience the market economy as given or something they have to live with, it is others who are making and defining the market. Increased disempowerment is experienced when the boundaries and limits of government are redefined. Increasingly in politics, there seems to be the desire to expunge contestability, a desire to rationalise public life and to construct a consensus making politics marginal and unimportant. Governments increasingly focus on selling policies to focus groups, where winning elections depends of changing the minds of voters in marginal constituencies. There is no attempt to give political leadership, but instead an attempt to justify consumer politics.

Between 1945 and 1976 people in the advanced industrial economies of Europe and the USA experienced continuing growth in the economy, with low levels of unemployment and an expanding welfare state. The relationships between governments, markets and individualism had created a more humane form of capitalism than the previous 100 years. The post-war settlement aimed to address problems of income inequality through better pensions, social security payments, minimum wages and policies of child support:

'Among the great political achievements of the twentieth century was the domesticating of laissez faire capitalism's brute power under democratic auspices . . . It (the nation-state) pursued economic stabilisation and steady growth through an active macro-economic policy. It regulated the more self destructive tendencies of markets . . . It empowered trade unions and put a floor under labour and later created environmental standards'. (Kuttner, 2000, p. 152)

By contrast, the experience of stagflation in the mid-1970s undermined Keynesian thinking at the intellectual and practical levels of policy making. The experience of both rising unemployment and inflation was explained by monetarist economists to be the fault of big government. Governments had over three decades of expanded welfare and increased spending and borrowing that had contributed to the expansion of the money supply and inflation. Unemployment was also rising because of high interest rates and the disincentive of social costs created by the welfare state.

Governments after the mid-1970s abandoned fiscal policy as the means of generating employment. Unemployment has been high for most of the last 20 years. In Britain, it twice reached peaks of over three million and stayed around 2 million for most of the 1980s and 1990s. These levels of unemployment have to be compared with the 250 000 experienced in the three decades after the Second World War. This experience was shared in Europe and the USA, as governments made the control of inflation their priority.

So what is the role of Government in the context of the globalised economy? While Governments argue in favour of policies of inclusion, citizenship and belonging, there are increases in disparities of income inequality. The increasing globalisation of economies is re-defining the limits of national governments. A car made in the UK or the USA now has at least 50 per cent of parts imported from different parts of the world. Shock absorbers come from Taiwan, steel from India, lights and engine parts from Germany, but all are assembled at Dagenham. Mercedes Benz has moved production from the high-cost labour of Germany, 30 km down the road into the Czech Republic, where wages are 40 times lower. In the globalised economy, there is increased convergence in the making of economic policy, since market sentiments and the flows of capital in financial markets have a direct influence on exchange rate and interest rates:

> 'Markets abhor frontiers as nature abhors a vacuum. Within their expansive and permeable domains, interests are private, trade is free, currencies are convertible, access to banking is open, contracts are enforceable and the laws of production and consumption are sovereign, trumping the laws of legislatures and courts. While mills and factories sit somewhere on sovereign territory, under the eye and potential regulation of nation-states, currency markets and the Internet exists everywhere, but nowhere in particular. Without an address or a national affiliation, they are altogether beyond the devices of sovereignty'. (Barber, 1996, p. 14)

The new capitalism is no longer about production, but about the selling of an idea. The weightless economy and the knowledge society are often perceived as shaping the contours of the global economy. The influences of new technologies are changing the nature of capitalism and the market economy. The success of companies and their competitive edge now rests with the human capital of employees who hold knowledge and who are able to design a product and the ability to turn the product into a philosophy of life. The competitive edge is the style and image attached to a car such as harmony with the environment and the attraction of colour. Selling a car is now the selling of safety, the selling of a sexual symbol, a lifestyle, harmony and escape to the countryside, leisure and comfort. Clothing is no longer about function, but about concepts of design and image, creating a designer-labelled society.

'It is a quantum leap because the essence of the economy has changed. What matters isn't how or where goods are manufactured, but the definition of the 'product' that is bought and sold. It is the idea that sells not the material built into construction. Human capital counts far more than anything else in giving companies a competitive edge'. (Giddens, 2001, p. 24)

The Velvet Revolutions in Eastern Europe are still in the process of unwinding. The Czech Republic, Hungary and Poland were always the more advanced industrial countries before they became part of the Soviet bloc economies after 1948. With the break-up of the Soviet Union, all three countries have gone through a process of creating democratic institutions. Wages are still very low when compared with those of the EU – the average wage of skilled workers is around 40 per cent of those in Germany. There are still major problems with tax reforms and reforming the welfare state. Old people are completely dependent on state pensions and they have experienced real hardships. Women have lost child care benefits and there are major problems of deteriorating housing stocks. The new economic elites who opened businesses after the break up of the Soviet Union are able to build spacious houses in the new suburbs, while escaping the welfare state by looking to private medicine and private education. Although there are still collectivist ties, the model of welfare, which is emerging, is more influenced by American ideas of private insurance, private health and private education for those who can afford them, rather than European views of solidarity.

In these countries, privatisation policy came too quickly, with no real public discussion or evaluation, so those who benefited were the old elites who seemed to be equally very competent capitalists. The merchant bankers from Western Europe and the USA who set up camp in Prague, Moscow, Kiev and Budapest found they could only talk with the existing elites when it came to the sell off in the energy sectors, engineering and textiles. Major tracts of manufacturing have been shut down and subsidies from coal and steel making have been phased out. The agriculture sector needs huge investment and there are major problems of pollution. All three countries have a highly educated workforce. There are also problems of racism emerging, as Slovaks in the Czech Republic lose their citizens and gypsies become increasingly marginalised.

In 1998, Russia devalued the rouble by 30 per cent and set up a moratorium in the paying of external debts. There have been real hardships for the people of Russia with people not receiving wages for up to 6 months. The elderly have not received pensions and there are food queues in Moscow. Average wages in Russia are around 100 dollars per month and those who can, have two jobs to meet the higher costs of rents and energy prices. Every Saturday and Sunday on the streets of Kiev and Moscow, there are queues of elderly selling personal treasures on street pavements in order to buy food. Some have not received any state pensions for months. The latest Russian commodity is hair. Women have their hair cut off for a price – a commodity that will eventually find its way to the more affluent European cities.

Over a period of 10 years, all the countries of Eastern Europe made transitions to the new market economy. Governments elected in these countries quickly replaced the broad coalitions and forums that heralded in the velvet revolutions. Organised political parties quickly replaced the alliances with ready-made ideologies imported from Western Europe and the USA. While the alliances sought to work across parties and aimed to create programmes of slow transition, the political parties, often better funded and better organised, won the early elections and then quickly sought economic transformation putting privatisation and liberalisation central to their political agendas. The beneficiaries of privatisation of gas and oil and other essential resources tended to be the old communists managers who had managed the plants in the Soviet era. By contrast, the elderly had no stake and no influence on the emerging economy and continued to be dependent on the government for pensions health care and social services.

The employed young are in low paid jobs, their families will continue to live in their overcrowded apartments, paying higher rents to new landlords. Labour costs in Eastern Europe are highly competitive when compared with wages costs in Western Europe. Wages in both Hungary and Poland are about 80 per cent lower than those in Germany. At present, the unemployed in Germany is about 11 per cent of the workforce. Major manufacturing companies are re-locating in the New Europe. In the Czech Republic and Poland, the newly elected Governments attempted to sell the housing stock to local trade unions and cooperatives in order to reduce the burden of subsidies and public expenditure. There is therefore a scissor effect on the living standards for the majority of people in the transitional economies. On the one hand, there are job losses, unemployment and low wages, while on the other, there are reduced welfare programmes, with many health services in crisis as doctors look to higher incomes in Europe and the USA.

The break-up of the Eastern Bloc also produced ripple effects on Western Europe, with the decline of socialist and social democratic politics. Market capitalism is increasingly presented as the only viable economic system making resistance to the paradigm of markets, less attractive. Mishra (1999) argued that the dual commitments to the welfare state and full employment during the post-war period represented concessions to social democratic parties and trade unions:

'until the 1970s an evolutionary as well as a revolutionary road to socialism seemed a real possibility in the West. The presence of a socialist world outside and a socialist labour opposition within made the inequities and insecurities of a market economy hard to justify . . . Moreover, the full employment welfare state came to be seen as the accommodation of a market society to collective values and aspirations – a middle way between laissez faire capitalism on the one hand and state socialism on the other'. (Mishra, 1999, p. 2)

By contrast, the concept of the global economy, together with the collapse of the Soviet Union have provided a new and stronger legitimacy for the ideas of free markets:

'Clearly with no rival in sight and as the only system capable of delivering economic growth and the cornucopia of consumer goods, capitalism has become almost self legitimising. In so far as the system no longer faces a legitimisation problem the incentive for attending to problems of social justice has weakened substantially'. (Mishra, 1999, p. 3)

Since 2000, the Dow Jones Index, the NASDAQ and the FTSE 100 have experienced falls of about 30 per cent. Those with small savings in pensions funds have seen their incomes decline. The globalised economy has been beneficial to companies and shareholders, as their shares of national income have increased, while the ratios of national income going to wages have declined or remained steady, with little resistance from trade unions. In contrast with other periods of full employment when trade unions saw the increases in company profitability as the signal to secure higher wage settlements, there is now industrial quietism, which would suggest that trade union members are trading-off higher wage demands for the security of employment. Unemployment throughout the EU has remained relatively high for the past two decades. Both Germany and France have continued to experience unemployment of 10 per cent for the last 15 years, while unemployment continues to be high in Spain, at 16 per cent of the workforce. Trade union density has declined sharply since the 1980s. In France trade union membership has fallen from 23 per cent in 1975, to 9 per cent of the workforce in 2000. In Germany, trade union membership declined from 37 per cent to 32 per cent during the same period. In the UK, trade union membership fell sharply during the Thatcher years, from a peak of 52 per cent in 1975, to 32 per cent in 2001(Nickell, 2001).

Since the early 1980s, in both Britain and the USA, those in employment have experienced low wage settlements, which on average have grown at around 2.3 per cent per year. Despite the unprecedented growth of the US economy, recent surveys show that wages declined by 0.4 per cent during 2000, while the chief executives of large companies received large increases, so their income has increased from 44 times the average wage in 1980, to over 200 times in 2000. Chief executives of companies now compete with football and film personalities in seeking higher incomes. Child labour is on the increase in the US agricultural sectors, with young children being used to harvest tomatoes, while farmers use the illegal immigrants as a means of reducing their unit costs. The continuing inflows of migrants make trade union membership difficult. The white Anglo American population comprises some 70 per cent of the US population, while the remainder is made up of Afro Americans, Hispanics and Asians. Employers take advantage of the continuous influx of new labour, usually paying the migrants cash in hand after a day's work, thus avoiding payments for insurance and health. Those who complain or seek to join trade unions are often reported to the immigration authorities.

CONCLUSIONS

Disempowerment and the Erosion of Public Space

Despite falling income for most people, election turnouts continue to decline. While 61 per cent of people voted in the US Presidential election in 1960, this had fallen to 49 per cent in 1996, which was the lowest turnout since the 1920s. This decline in voting is also present in most of the industrialised world. Since the 1950s, 18 of the 20 advanced countries have experienced a 10 per cent decline in the number of those who vote. In Switzerland, there was a 61 per cent turnout at elections in the 1950s, which fell to 37 per cent in the 1990s. In New Zealand, the turnout fell from 93 per cent to 75 per cent in the same era, while in France this declined from 70 per cent to 56 per cent. For the UK, the decline has been from 82 per cent in 1951 to 72 per cent in the 1980s. Britain recorded the lowest turnout at the 2001 general election, which showed that only 59 per cent of the population actually voted:

> 'The blame has to go to a corruption that encourages non voting and a citizenry that does not care enough to vote even when they are hurting. Perhaps the median and the below median households have lost faith in democratic processes knowing that whoever is elected will not address their problems'. (Thurow, 2000, p. 213)

The central argument of this chapter is that while the globalised economy seems to be creating new jobs, more optimism about economic prosperity and visions of the new individualism, there is at the same time the increasing disempowered individual who cannot find connections with others in the political spaces, in the remoteness of the economy and the erosion of collective welfare:

> 'people are integrated into society only in their partial aspects as taxpayers, car drivers, students, consumers, voters, patients, producers, fathers, mothers, sisters . . .

Modern society does not integrate them as whole persons into a functional system rather, it relies on the fact that individuals are not integrated but only partly and temporarily involved as they wander between different functional worlds'. (Beck, 2000c, p. 165)

Life is increasingly experienced as disconnected, diverse, plural and fragmented. There is no such thing as employment for life. There is no community of shared lived experiences, but only imagined communities. Throughout the industrialised world, employment in manufacturing has declined from around 26 per cent of the labour force to around 18 per cent. Since the 1980s, there have been major labour shakeouts in textiles, in steel making, automobile, manufacturing and coal, with the USA leading the march towards downsizing of companies. Even in Japan, with its long history of commitment to loyalty between companies and employees, there are moves towards ideas of flexible labour markets and of living with the insecurities of employment and unemployment. However, the weightless economy of information technology has not produced the promised productivity gains. Recent studies for the USA show that, while the economy has experienced unprecedented growth rates of 4 per cent a year since the late 1990s, productivity has only increased at around 1.1 per cent per year and has therefore not reached the productivity gains of the 1970s. In 2003, the USA had an unemployment rate of 6 per cent – a similar level to that of 1971, when Nixon declared he was now a Keynesian and sought to stimulate the US economy through increased demand and price and wage controls. By contrast, President Bush is relying on tax reductions.

At one level, it seems to be a paradox to suggest that while the economies are transcending national boundaries that people are being asked to make sense of the new globalised economy as a form of a personal biography. Furthermore, it would seem that governments' economic priorities are focused on policy frameworks of price stability, reducing governments' deficits and reducing interest rates. Labour markets are de-regulated with increased demand for greater flexibility and longer hours.

Disempowerment has a long history and the process continues to take different turns. In politics, the public meeting, the hustings and the mobilisation of party activists, were once described as being essential pillars to the making of political parties. However, the age of technology, TV and the internet make these political party structures less relevant and less important. Leaders of political parties feel increasingly less need to mobilise the party grassroots, when they can address voters directly through the media. Party conferences and conventions are no longer a place of debate of policy formulation, but have become platforms managed to catch the political sound bite that is likely to make news headlines. Election campaigns are focused on target groups and marginal seats. Politics needs an increasing amount of money. Political voices are not heard unless money is available for television advertisements. During his election campaign for a second term, President Clinton invited major contributors to have dinner with him for a cost of US$100 000 a plate (Gross, 1996). George W. Bush raised US$92 million from 200 contributors in the 2001 Presidential Election. Election pioneers were nominated to raise major dollar donations for the election. The three major contributors to his election campaign were the American Rifle Association, Microsoft and Enron, all three companies faced regulation and pending penalties in the courts.

In Germany, the UK and Ireland, there have been continuing scandals of Prime Ministers mixing donations to political parties, with personal gifts. Helmut Kohl who led Germany for 17 years and his Christian Democrat party were surrounded by scandal because of the large donations received from individuals not being declared as campaign expenses. Both the Conservative and Labour Party in Britain receive large donations from individuals. Scrutiny of public officials is weak. Declaration of interests is voluntary. Politics is perceived to be increasingly remote and corrupt.

The problem with these allegations and findings is that overall, they erode and corrode the political spaces. Individuals who run large business organisations make donations to political parties because they hope and are assured of some sort of pay back. The right people are appointed to government boards and ministries and therefore give guidance to the policy-making process and implementation. The problem is that the decay of public spaces also undermines hope and optimism in the ability to bring change through the democratic process. When the commitment to democracy declines, other forms of resistance start to take shape, which undermine the democratic process.

7. Policy rhetoric and policy realities

INTRODUCTION

Public policy can be described as being the explicit action of government. Such action involves 'policy inputs' and implies public expenditure, while the policy outputs represent what government seeks to achieve for a level of policy inputs. In this sense therefore, policy action has to be separated from policy rhetoric. It is relatively easy for the government to declare they want to alleviate child poverty, the issue is what level of resources are governments willing to direct to families to deal with child poverty. Equally, government can make a commitment to increase the numbers going into higher education, but again, unless the policy is funded, it stays at the level of rhetoric, rather than action. Politicians continuously seek to persuade voters that their primary reason for entering politics is to be their public servants, to make politics a vocation, to bring about policy change, to make a difference in promoting the interests of their citizens. Political parties provide visions and principles that will guide their actions. However, when politicians become the government, arguments about values and principles are down-played and replaced with the discourse of the national interests, however that is defined. Many studies of the Thatcher Government very often quote the first speech by Mrs Thatcher from outside 10 Downing Street, when she quoted a passage from St Francis of Assisi, to argue the case that her Government had been elected to heal the wounds of the nation; a text selected for her by her speechwriter Ronald Miller:

> 'Where there is discord, may we bring harmony', she claimed 'Where there is error may we bring truth. Where there is doubt may we bring faith. Where there is despair may we bring hope'. (M. Thatcher, as quoted in Young, 1989, p. 136)

It is important to re-examine carefully the context of that speech. First, the context of the 1979 election had been the so-called winter of discontent, when the Labour Government under James Callaghan had been undermined by a series of public sector strikes. The Conservative opposition and Mrs Thatcher had been very strident in their arguments that trade unions were too strong and for the need of trade union reform and to impose strong government that would look after the interests of individual citizens against group interests. It is therefore important to recognise that while the policy action promised by the Conservative Party in opposition had been to establish and to re-define the relationships between government and trade unions, Mrs Thatcher in her speech mentioned the twin words 'discord' and the need for 'harmony'. Strikes represented 'discord' – the government in turn sought 'harmony' – no mention here about the need to curb trade union militancy. To many people listening to that speech, there was either the hope that Mrs Thatcher's promise to be strident in opposition had been rhetorical and that there was a chance for dialogue and therefore harmony with the trade unions. Second, the Conservative Party had also made much about the need to break with public sector monopolies and to bring about more privatisation of public utilities. Again, Mrs Thatcher in her Assisi vision, pointed for the need of people to have faith in her vision. Privatisation needed to be about faith in the future. Finally, there was the problem of unemployment and poverty and here again, Mrs Thatcher aimed to be reassuring about recognising the despair of the poor in Britain's inner cities and how her government was going to bring hope, through economic regeneration. The speech was therefore about healing wounds and the caring of the nation.

In his State of the Nation Address, President George W. Bush (2002) defended his tax reductions policy as follows:

'My budget is to fight the recession and build economic security for the American people. Government doesn't create jobs, but it can encourage an environment in which jobs are created. Every budget reflects fundamental choices, and my administration has made choices to fit the times. We'll work to create jobs and renew the strength of our economy'. (George W. Bush, State of the Nation Address, 28 January 2002)

According to President Bush, the actions of the economic strategy were in the interest of all American People. While acknowledging that the two budgets of 2002 and 2003 reflected political choices, the government described their actions as being to create employment and prosperity for all the American people. The packages of US$1.3 trillion of tax reductions in 2002 and US$ 670 billion in 2003 continue to be central to the Bush Administration. The tax reductions have been justified as being essential for creating business incentives to invest and employ more people. The Democrats have opposed the strategy because of continuing budget deficits – it is now estimated the US budget deficit is likely to increase to US$400 billion, which is equivalent to 4 per cent of the GDP and also that the tax reductions are aimed at the top 1 per cent of earners. The top 1 per cent will receive windfall taxes of US$250 000, while the bottom 10 per cent of earners will received about US$300. Furthermore, the deficit is likely to impact the health and social security budgets. The tax reductions will be financed from the surpluses in the social security budget, which means that low-income groups will bear the brunt. So, while President Bush points to his policy as being in the interests of the nation, the opposition puts an emphasis on the winners and the losers:

'The Bush administration is actually fighting two wars, one against Iraq and another against the very idea of humane and responsive government at home. On Tuesday, as President Bush was asking Congress for the first instalment of the hundreds of billions of dollars needed to finance the war in Iraq and its aftermath, the students and teachers at a high school within walking distance of the White House were struggling through their daily routine in a building that has no cafeteria, no gymnasium, no student lockers, not even a fully reliable source of electricity. A few weeks ago bricks were falling from the facade of the building, which is now more than 100 years old'. (Herbert, *The New York Times*, 27 March 2003)

Action is about resources. Making room for a tax reduction package of US$550 billion inevitably means reducing expenditure elsewhere. Many States faced with large deficits are focusing on reducing expenditure on Medicaid, which mainly includes the financing for nursing home places for the elderly and the subsidy for prescriptions. Many States have also focused their budget reductions on school building and public buildings:

'It's still chilly in north-western Oregon, and there's a real bite to the wind in the evenings. But for the 19,000 students in the sprawling Hillsboro public school district, summer vacation is coming real soon. Starved for money, Hillsboro lopped 17 days off the school year. Oregon is experiencing a budget meltdown. Home to Intel and other high-tech highfliers, it suffered disproportionately from the bursting of the technology bubble. Its jobless rate is the highest in the U.S. And it is being squeezed, like many other states, by a dismal national economy. The result has been a haemorrhaging of state revenues so severe that such fundamental services as schools, basic health care and law enforcement have been undermined. A ballot proposal to raise the state income tax temporarily and thus ward off at least some of the cuts to schools and to services desperately needed by the sick and the disabled was rejected by voters in January. Something ugly is happening in Oregon, ... school funding in Oregon is a state responsibility, and neither the Legislature nor the voters have been willing to raise the additional money needed to keep the system going'. (Herbert, *The New York Times*, 1 May 2003)

Governments argue that their actions serve the interests of the community. Policy is not driven by ideology, but by the expediency of what needs to be done. There is therefore a denial that policy can be particularistic and that they might serve a specific group of interests. There are no winners and losers, only winners. Mrs Thatcher denied that her government was driven by ideology. The Community Charge (poll tax) was defended for its sense of fairness where obviously that was not the case. Prime Minister Blair and ex President Clinton argued the case that the Third Way was not an ideology, but an approach to make policy work. Blair has, for example, argued that Labour will be tough on crime (a Conservative perspective), but also that Labour would be tough on the causes of crime (a Labour principle). For a Labour audience being tough on the causes of crime, Blair was signalling a commitment to deal with problems of deprivation, unemployment, housing and poverty – all good Labour Party priorities. At the same time, Blair wanted to shift the image of the Labour as being soft on crime by arguing a Conservative case of being tough on crime:

> 'The debate about New Labour ideology, or its absence, has consumed many trees over the past decade, as an increasingly repelled leftist intelligentsia wrote essays to show Blair wanting in what they prize most: an account of himself and his policy framed in some version that is recognisably socialist, or at least social democratic. These trees have perished to no avail. Blair, for the most part, has no patience with or use for leftist intellectuals. And once he achieved power, he did not need an ideology to guide his beliefs. He believes in himself'. (Blitz, 2003, p. 17)

In the context of globalisation, policy making is perceived to be an inevitable response. There is no alternative. Globalisation poses the challenge of competitive markets. Governments have to ensure they respond to the challenges of competition. Competition means flexibility and de-regulation, reducing non-labour costs such as the cost of pensions and social security, removing the burdens on business. All policies are designed to make a country attractive to the dance of foreign direct investment. Countries are seen to be in some beauty contest parading their competitiveness. Some point to the soft regulation on business, the flexibility of their workforce, trade unions law, the nimble fingers of their female labour force. That is the policy action. But what about the consequences? Who benefits from a policy of privatisation and liberalisation? Are these policies in the national interests?

ACTIONS AND CONSEQUENCES

The Policy Process

The World Trade Organisation (WTO) was created in 1995 to ensure that members adhere to regulations on free trade. It now boasts a membership of 152 countries. Describing the nature of the WTO, the former Secretary General, John Moore, continually emphasised the institution's democratic credentials, arguing out that each member country has one vote and unlike the United Nations, there is no Security Council deciding policy behind closed doors. The policies adopted by the WTO were made by elected heads of Government and all agreements were transparent. Moore described the WTO as:

'It's like trying to run a parliament with no parties, no whip, no speaker, no speaking limits and no majority voting system'. (Moore, 2003, p. 37)

However, Moore's optimism has been criticised, because it implicitly excludes the possibilities of power and domination. In Moore's model, all countries appear as equals, all members have an equal vote, but Moore fails to make distinctions between appearances and reality. Countries are bullied and cajoled in the corridors of the WTO. Aid donors have more leverage than those who depend on aid. The WTO makes decisions so that the results' institutionalise' and therefore legitimise the advantage of the North, specifically the United States'. Furthermore the behind doors meetings in Geneva (and it is estimated there are some 2000 meetings a year) ensure that trade lawyers and the business community structure the agenda that defines world trade.

'The WTO is a member-driven organisation in which delegates from member countries must be actively involved in its day to day activities if their interests are not be ignored. It has been estimated that WTO processes involve at least 45 meetings per week in Geneva most of which are technically complex and highly legalised. The requirements for effective participation place an enormous burden on resource constrained smaller and poor countries. When they are represented at all their staffing is inadequate for handling the ever increasing complexity of issues and the rising numbers of meetings . . . Hence they are purely rule takers as opposed to rule makers'. (Helleiner, 2000, p. 17)

Developing countries are unable to provide the technical knowledge and infrastructure to ensure that their views are continuously represented in Geneva, while the pharmaceutical, the banking and financial lobbies and advisers shaped and defined the WTO rulings on intellectual property rights (TRIPS) and financial services agreements (GATS):

'Large private corporations purchase influence within all the so-called democratic societies. As all Geneva trade diplomats know, their influence over secretive international negotiations is also considerable; witness the role of the pharmaceuticals industry in intellectual property debates and the banking and financial sector in those over capital accounts regimes and trade in financial services. The international activities of business lobbies are subject to no limits, registration requirements or regulation. The bulk of their activity is not transparent to the public . . . Their activities though usually formally legal, constitute a grave threat to the prospect of democratic and accountable global economic governance'. (Helleiner, 2000, p. 12)

While at the formal and procedural levels the WTO has the potential for being a forum in the democratic governance of trade – there are major discrepancies between the 'potential' and the 'reality' of the WTO policy process, which has become the space for trade negotiators and trade lawyers representing the interests of large corporations. Very often, the distorting relationship is developed at the national level with Government ministers making their office available to trade experts and the trade policy community, so that the position taken by government at WTO meetings is the policy developed between the ministers and their experts. The 'interests' of the community are defined narrowly by the experts. Since the mid-1990s, it has become more apparent that governments have become the advocates and promoters of leading corporate interests. Governments acknowledge that they do listen to trade lobbyists, but also that in the new complex world of international trade negotiations, they need to listen to the expertise of professionals and to promote the business interests of their country, which in turn is assumed to be the interests of the nation:

> 'There is now a huge asymmetry between multilateral rules – and particularly enforcement – to protect broadly defined commercial trading interests and multilateral rule-making and enforcement in vital areas such as environmental protection, human rights, public health and cultural diversity'. (Sinclair, 2003, p. 260)

While it is legitimate for Governments to point to increased policy complexity and the need to co-opt suitable policy advisers, the issue is that opposing views are not given an equal hearing. Policy making therefore becomes selective, since competing policy options are not given equal weighting. There is a lack of policy transparency, which, in turn, contributes to worries of corruption in decision making. In the reconstruction of Iraq, USAID has given contracts to the Betchel Group, which includes, on its advisory board, George Schultz, who was Secretary of State during the years of President Reagan. The Chairman of the Betchel group sits on the President's Export Committee. The Betchel Group has been awarded a US$680 million contract to repair waterways, the electric grid and sewage works in Iraq. The Kellogg Brown and Root (KBR) company has won contracts to extinguish fires and provide maintenance for the oil fields in Iraq. There was no bidding process. KBR is a subsidiary of the Halliburton Group, which includes, on its board of directors, Dick Cheney, who is at present also the Vice President of the USA. The Chief Executive of Cargill, which is one of the largest food producers in the USA has been appointed to the President's Export Committee, while Mr Dan Amstutz, who was an executive at Cargill, has now been appointed to the Ministry of Agriculture in Iraq, to restructure agriculture in Iraq. Critics of the appointment including Oxfam, have pointed out that Cargill will use the opportunity to 'dump' cheap grain on Iraq and Kevin Watkins, policy director of Oxfam, described the appointment as follows:

> 'Putting Dan Amstutz in charge of agricultural reconstruction in Iraq is like putting Saddam Hussein in the chair of a human rights commission. This guy is uniquely well-placed to advance the commercial interests of American grain companies and

bust open the Iraqi market – but singularly ill-equipped to lead a reconstruction effort in a developing country'. (*The Guardian*, 28 April 2003)

All the major contractors in the reconstruction in Iraq have made major financial contributions to the Republican Party (Centre for Responsive Politics, 2003). In the meantime, Krugman (2002) has pointed to the emergence of a plutocracy of new elites, made up of Chief Executive Officers (CEOs of large multinationals, their connections with political elites and civil servants that are in different ways undermining democracy:

'Between 1970 and 2001, in an orgy of mutual back-scratching by C.E.O.s and their boards, median pay among the top 100 executives soared from 35 times that of the average worker to more than 500 times as much. Last summer it seemed, briefly, as if the torrent of scandals – and the revelations about how closely some of our politicians were tied to scandal-ridden companies – would bring about a public backlash against corporate malfeasance. But then the topic largely vanished from the news, driven out by reports about Iraq's nuclear weapons program and all that … Bill Clinton didn't invent sex, and the Bush administration didn't invent greed. But when insiders at major corporations see top officials getting away with it – moving unscathed between stints as crony capitalists and high office – they have to feel that old rules no longer apply, and that they can get away with even more self-dealing than before. In the end the corruption of our corporate system will bring retribution; even if political action never comes, investors will eventually lose faith and put their money elsewhere. But right now the bad guys, though they lose an occasional battle, are winning the war'. (Krugman, 2002, 'The acid test', *The New York Times*, 2 May 2003)

Appointments to major Pentagon Committees depend on loyalty and financial contributions to the incumbent government. Members of these committees are also representing major companies bidding for major government contracts. It is a policy of revolving doors of senior military personnel from the Armed Forces retiring from the military, key advisors to the government taking posts as advisors to key corporations seeking defence contracts. Nine of the 30 advisers on the Defence Policy Committee that advises the Pentagon have links to companies involved on government contracts. These companies received US$76 billion in contracts between 2001 and 2002.

'Retired Gen. Jack Sheehan joined Bechtel in 1998 after 35 years in the U.S. Marine Corp. Bechtel, one of the world's largest engineering-construction firms, is among the companies bidding for contracts to rebuild Iraq. The company had defense contracts worth close to $650 million in 2001 and more than $1 billion in 2002. Sheehan is currently a senior vice president and partner and responsible for the execution and strategy for the region that includes Europe, Africa, the Middle East and Southwest Asia. The four-star general served as NATO's Supreme Allied Commander, Atlantic and Commander in Chief U.S. Atlantic Command before his retirement in 1997. After his leaving active duty, he served as Special Advisor for Central Asia for two secretaries of Defense'. (Centre for Public Integrity, 2004).

There is now increased awareness and worry as to the lack of transparency in the discussions that take place behind closed doors within government ministries; questions are asked about who is invited to these discussions and how these experts and lobbyists influence the policy process. At present, the secrecy of these meetings provide little opportunity for independent judgement as to the nature of government decisions and to ask whether the advisers who seek to influence the policy process are doing so to serve the narrow interests of people they represent. It is this lack of transparency, which is contributing to the undermining of the democratic process. According to Weiss (1998), for the Centre for Responsive Politics:

> 'It raises the possibility that the companies specially invited to bid on this huge government contract were those with deep pockets and strong connections ... companies that may have been just as qualified but didn't have as much money or didn't have the connections weren't invited'. (Weiss, 1998; Centre for Responsive Politics)

The policies of globalisation are presented in the innocent language of markets, competition, openness, free trade flexibility de-regulation and liberalisation. There are no conflicts of interests, no conflicts of ideology and no winners and losers. The nature of policy making is described as being pragmatic and expedient, since policy makers find themselves responding to events that very often are beyond their control. From this perspective therefore, policy failings represent the unintended consequences of policy making – the unforeseen issues that could not be forecasted. Policy is described as being founded on universal principles. There is a denial that policies might benefit narrow specific interests. Policy is presented as a universal value. De-regulation of labour markets creates employment for all. De-regulation is presented as a policy of universal principles. Privatisation is good because it aims to break with government monopoly, therefore creating more competition and more choice. There are universal winners. Lobbying and influence of specific interests are denied. Governments do of course listen to business interests, but this is justified since business offers government advice on policy making. Leaders of the business community do give advice, but governments make the policy.

Advocates of markets liberalism promote the ideas of free markets. World poverty is defined to be unconnected with globalisation. The problem of poverty is attributed to the failures of governments, their reluctance to open markets to free trade or remove subsidies that benefit narrow interests. Unemployment is voluntary because people price themselves out of labour markets. Liberalisation of financial markets, de-regulation, privatisation and industrial relations legislation have created labour market landscapes that encourage the greater mobility of capital, which in turn have increased the insecurity and uncertainty of employment. Since the mid-1980s, wages as a ratio of national incomes have declined, while profits have increased. For the majority of people, incomes from employment have remained stagnant or declined. In a decade of continuing economic growth, wage earners have not benefited from that new prosperity. World poverty can be attributed to political choices and decisions. WTO enforcement of intellectual property rights acts against the interest of developing countries, while benefiting pharmaceutical companies and other multinational corporations that seek to patent seeds, which they then sell to small farmers who are displaced from the land because of high costs:

'Farmers who traditionally grew pulses and millets and paddy have been lured by seed companies to buy hybrid cotton seeds referred to by the seed merchants as 'white gold' which were supposed to make them millionaires. Instead they became paupers. Their native seeds have been displaced with hybrids, which cannot be saved, and need to be purchased every year at high costs. Hybrids are also very vulnerable to pest attacks . . . The wells are now dry, as are the wells in Gujarat and Rajasthan where more than 50 million people face a water famine. The drought is not a natural disaster. It is man made. It is the result of mining of scarce ground water in arid regions to grow thirsty cash crops for export instead of water prudent food crops for local needs'. (Shiva, 2000, p. 1)

Of the 10 000 species of seed that can been used for human food, just 12 seeds provide over 70 per cent of food, while four – rice, maize, wheat and potatoes – make up over 50 per cent of the food supply. At present, it is estimated that the US Government provides US$22.5 billion in subsidies to US agriculture every year, out of which over one-third is directed to the 10 biggest recipients directly involved in researching hybrids and patenting seeds. The whole subsidy to agriculture within the OECD is estimated at US$330 billion. The net result is over-production of rice, maize and wheat protected by subsidies, which is being dumped on the developing countries at low prices. Developing countries in the meantime cannot provide the same levels of subsidies to their small farmers. Furthermore, developing countries come under pressure from the World Bank and the IMF to remove subsidies, de-regulate markets and liberalise trade. Having to meet IMF and World Bank conditions means that developing countries have to meet the conditionality of liberalising trade and reducing public expenditure. The Minister of Trade for Pakistan, Abdul Razak Dawood responding to the November 2001 WTO settlement at Doha came to the following conclusion:

'The impact of the unfair system of agricultural trade has been devastating for developing countries which do not have the resources to subsidize their farmers. We cannot let the livelihoods of the most vulnerable in our countries be blocked by the commercial interests of other countries. Already, the impact of unfair agricultural trade has been devastating for our small farmers, forcing many out of their traditional source of livelihood. We have formed the 'Friends of the Development Box' as a Third Force in agriculture negotiations, and will fight for the 'Development Box' to be a core component of the Agreement on Agriculture. We need the flexibility to take measures to protect our rural poor'.(Helleiner, 2000)

In November 2001, the 'International Treaty on Plant Genetic Resources for Food and Agriculture' was adopted by the United Nations Food and Agriculture Organisation (FAO), with a vote of 116–0, with the USA and Japan abstaining. The treaty established a multilateral system, providing access to seeds and germ plasma for much of the world's food supply, as well as fair and equitable sharing of the benefits. It also included a provision on farmers' rights to save, use, exchange and sell farm-saved seed.

'This treaty represents a major step forward for farmers around the world by improving their access to seeds . . . It is also a blow to the biotech industry, which may no longer patent the raw material of food crops in countries that sign on to the treaty'. (Helleiner, 2000)

Ultimately, conflicts over attempts to patent seeds or genes received through the multilateral system may end up in the dispute settlement system of either the WTO or the genetic resources treaty, or both. Under the new treaty, disputes that cannot be settled through negotiation, mediation or arbitration may be referred to the International Court of Justice.

CONSEQUENCES

Explaining the Unintended

Explanations are important because they provide competing discourses as to what is possible, what is feasible and what are the limits of resistance. Interpretations of actions and consequences are located with competing discourses. Consequences can always be defined as being unintended, not foreseen, unintentional, something that happens in the wider cause of progress. Actions are linked to an event, the connection is made transparent, demands for action and resistance become feasible. The understanding of causes and consequences leads to different forms of responses and resistances.

At present, neo-liberal ideas of markets are the guiding principles of globalisation. Unemployment and poverty are described as the unintended consequences of economic growth and prosperity. These are the consequences of the impersonal forces of the market, the invisible hand of Adam Smith, the spontaneity of Hayek and the creative destruction of Schumpeter. In the global market, no-one is to blame. If farmers become displaced in Mexico, it is the laws of the market. They are flexible workers, they have to move into new areas of labour demand and learn to live with the market. Unemployment and low incomes present the lags and adjustment of markets. Alternative experiments to markets have failed, whether Khrushchev in Russia or Chairman Mao TseTung in China, both experiments at planning failed. This is therefore the triumph of capitalism. There is a disavowal of responsibility. Outcomes reflect the laws of supply and demand, the results of a myriad of impersonal transactions. Markets have a life of their own, they reflect human nature, history and development:

'equally exciting is mankind's struggle to satisfy his second imperative, the individual's craving, separately and collectively for material betterment which for brevity we may all wealth or welfare. It is in fact, part of the same story, man's success in the evolutionary stakes being linked to his success as an economic agent'. (Jay, 2000, p. 2)

According to market liberal views, globalisation is one part of the ongoing human story, of the individual as economic agent continuously striving to improve his or her material well being. Technology and inventions including electricity, railways, telegraphy and the computer reflect the human spirit of striving and searching for a better material life. Globalisation makes instant communications possible and connections immediate. Exploiting resources and technology drive prices lower and make possible access to food, health, television motorcars, Coca Cola, The Gap shirts and Nike Shoes. The UK Labour Government has defined present globalisation as:

'globalisation means the growing interdependence and interconnectedness of the modern world. The increased ease of movement of goods and services capital, people and information across national borders is rapidly creating a single global economy. The process is driven by technological advance and reductions in the cost of international transactions which spread technology and ideas, raise the share of trade in world production and increase the mobility of capital'. (HMSO, 2000, pp. 15 and 16)

Globalisation is defined as being technology driven, which in turn results in lower transaction costs, which in turn, results in increases in world trade and greater mobility of capital. These dynamics benefit the world's population in providing more food and better access to health care and literacy. Technology is defined as being value neutral, with no issues of power and influence. Ideas are researched and developed, multinational companies develop products, which results in lower costs. There are mutual benefits. Inequalities of access reflect different talents and abilities, the just entitlements of a free society. The market is taken as given. It is the nature of humanity to pursue individual self-interest. The rise in intellectual property rights reflects the new individualism in the knowledge economy. Poverty and unemployment are the structural adjustments of lead and lags in the marketplace. Unemployment can be blamed on rigidities and lack of flexibility. The problems are not the market, but government intervention and the impact of trade unions on labour markets. Unemployment becomes the consequence of not adjusting to the market and not the cause.

The emphasis on the connections between principles and actions allow for the outcomes of policy to be described as the undesired or the unintended consequence of policy action. The assumption is that principles are universal, rather than being directed at particular interests. The policy of labour market de-regulation is defined as a desirable universal policy with no winners and losers. It assumes that organisations and workers meet as equal individuals. However, the policy of de-regulation re-defines the balance of power to employers. When the focus of policy analysis is the mapping out of the winners and losers of policy, then policy is studied in terms of whose particular interests are being met and who is being ignored. A study of Mrs Thatcher's 'Right to Buy' policy may point to the connections between principles of free markets, the break up of monopoly and freedom of choice and argue that the present problem of homelessness is a consequence, since the aim of the policy was to create a home-owning democracy and greater consumer choice. By contrast the study of the policy would suggest that there was political calculation and political judgement in that the winners tended to be those tenants with high quality housing stock. The losers were tenants who lived in less attractive high-rise buildings and the homeless, who were also politically invisible. Mapping out policy outcomes makes the connection between action and consequence more transparent:

> 'Power must be analysed as something which circulates, or rather as something which only functions in the form of a chain. It is never localised here or there, never in anybody's hands, never appropriated as a commodity or piece of wealth. Power is employed and exercised through a net-like organisation . . . They (individuals) are not only its inert or consenting target; they are also always also the elements of its articulation. In other words individuals are the vehicles of power, not its points of application'. (Foucault, 1986, p. 234)

Making distances between principles and consequence have important policy implications. The preference for tax reductions has the consequence of less public provision. Decisions to reduce taxation by Republican, President Ronald Reagan, in the USA and Prime Minister, Margaret Thatcher, in the UK during the 1980s, reduced the Government's tax base and therefore their ability to expand social programmes. These policy frameworks created the landscapes for future governments by redefining the boundaries between public and private provision. The justification of the policy was that people had the right to keep what they earned and to spend their incomes according to their priorities and not on priorities decided for them by big government. The guiding principle was the market and the concept of rational individualism.

At one level, market liberal policies seem to be at best benign and have been described as being beneficial to those on low incomes, since lower taxes directly improves the take-home pay. However, the outcomes of a policy of tax reductions is that those on higher incomes gain more from the policy, while reductions in social spending programmes adversely effect lower income groups. A policy of tax reductions means less revenue to government and therefore a lowering of the quality of public services. Tax reductions imply that people have to use the additional incomes to take out private insurance, since there is an overall retreat of government provision. The costs and benefits of tax reductions are not spelled out, instead they became conflated in an argument that it is possible to have both tax reductions and high quality public services – there are no costs but only benefits. Reductions in government expenditure are focused on waste, on additional bureaucracy and on fraud and abuse of social security.

Globalised Causes and Consequences

What is the nature of contemporary globalisation? Does the present era represent some qualitative break with the past? These questions influence present debates about the nature of globalisation. Proponents of globalisation point to the qualitative break with the past. Castells (2000) has pointed to the concepts of the borderless and the networked economy, Klein (2001a) to the idea of the new weightless corporation, Hertz (2001) to the silent takeover and the decay of democracy, while Bauman (2000) has pointed to the disparities between financial capital that occupies the cyber spaces and politics still located in geographic spaces. Beck (2000c) has pointed to the conflation of globalisation and globalism and the impact of neo-liberal thinking on present economic reforms. By contrast, critics of globalisation argue that globalisation is part of history – there is nothing new, trade and economic integration have a long historic process. The impact of new technologies is no different from the inventions of railways or electricity. According to Mokyr (1992) and Foreman-Peck (1995), the invention of the telegraph in 1906 contributed to the shrinkage of the globe and made possible the acceleration of international trade:

'The telegraph had an enormous impact on nineteenth century society – possibly as great as that of the railroads. Its military and political value was vast, as was its effect in co-ordinating financial and commodity markets'. (Mokyr, 1992, p. 144)

Foreman-Peck (1995) stated that:

> 'By introducing greater certainty into international transactions the telegraphy cut stock levels and allowed the money markets to finance the inventories previously held by great merchants. The level of raw cotton stocks held in British ports and mills was much lower after the spread of the telegraph than in the 1840s despite the far greater volume of business'. (Foreman-Peck, 1995, pp. 67 and 79)

The mobility of financial capital was made possible with the invention of the telegraph. International trade expanded between 1880 and 1910:

> 'it was as though the very expansiveness of the economy the general euphoria and prosperity had persuaded nations and people to let their guard down, to trade control for freedom parochialism for universalism, tradition for change, the safety of exclusiveness for the dangerous yet potential profit of the open world'. (Landes, 1969, p. 200)

While agreeing a definition of globalisation might be difficult, explaining the process of globalisation is less difficult. Shopping in town centres, dressing the same and trying to look the same, eating at Pizza Hut and McDonald's, or buying Gap Shirts and Nike Shoes, whether it is in Florida, Cologne, Prague or Leeds, is the uniform and universal globalised experience. Watching world events unfold as they happen in London or Bogotá reinforces the experience that the world is increasingly becoming a global village and economies increasingly becoming borderless. Women and children working in sweat-shops in Burma and China, while textile workers in Blackburn are made redundant, creates the increased awareness of the mobility of capital and the continuous search for lower costs. Knowing that nearly 50 per cent of the world population is living on starvation wages, creates insecurity to those in work. The global economy is transparent. Digital TV, Fox News, CBS, MTV and Nickelodeon provide common information, portrays celebrities who need global audiences. Contemporary globalisation is a consumer global economy:

> 'There is now a world culture . . . It is marked by an organization of diversity rather than a replication of uniformity. No total homogenisation of systems of meaning and expression has occurred nor does it appear likely that there will be one anytime soon. But the world has become one network of social relationships, and between its different regions there is a flow of meanings as well as of people and goods'. (Hannerz, 1990, p. 237)

The study of globalisation is more than the study of consumer society. There is also the globalisation of social, economic and political relationships. The mobility of capital and multinational corporations directly impact employer–labour relations, wages, profits stock market prices and company dividends. In a world of expanding labour markets and more people dependant on the world of employment and jobs, there are, as would be expected, increased pressures for wages to fall. There are not enough jobs to go around, yet more and more people need jobs as their only means to survive. Furthermore, there are problems of over production. The investment in capital equipment, new technologies and robotics has increased production.

Asking the question: 'who are the winners and losers of a globalisation that is shaped by neo-liberal thinking?' then it becomes a conscious decision to make links between the particular interest of multinational corporations, their financial donations to political parties and their influence on the political process. Advocating a policy of labour market de-regulation or energy de-regulation is not a policy influenced by principles, but rather a policy stream to meet particular interests.

The political decisions of government to de-regulate and create more flexible labour markets contribute to define specific labour markets. Labour markets, like other markets, are not a given, but are socially constructed and the legislative process helps to define labour markets. Revoking trade union immunities, prohibiting secondary action and picket lines, while at the same time enforcing secret ballots on trade union membership and the right to strike, provide a specific perspective on industrial relations. Reform of social security, reducing the duration of entitlement and the rates of benefit payments again give shape to the emerging labour market landscapes. The net results have been for wages to fall as ratios of national incomes, while profit ratios have increased. At the global level, income inequalities have increased. There is now an excess of labour in relation to demand at the global level. As small farmers and landholders are displaced by large agribusiness, more people lose their independence and move to cities in search of work.

'While more of us enjoy better standards of living than ever before, many others remain desperately poor. Nearly half the world's population still has to make do on less than $2 per day. Approximately 1.2 billion–500 million in South Asia and 300 million in Africa – struggle on less than $1. People living in Africa south of the Sahara are almost as poor today as they were 20 years ago. With this kind of deprivation, comes pain, powerlessness, despair and lack of fundamental freedom – all of which in turn perpetuate poverty. Of a total world labour of some 3 billion, 140 million workers are out of work altogether and a quarter to a third are underemployed'. (UNDP, 2001, p. 19)

Governments are not in the habit of explaining the connections of the causes and consequences in policy making. Policy choices are seldom made transparent; instead the emphasis is put on opaqueness and policy complexity. Citizens are always at arm's length from policy formulation. Discussions between professional political advisers, lobbyists and business policy advocates and key politicians are by their nature secretive and kept at a distance from public gaze. There is no scrutiny of documents. No public record is kept of such meetings. Parliaments are unable to analyse the impact of business interests on the policy process. There are cabinets within cabinets. Ministers and Parliaments are often bounced into accepting already formulated policy decisions. An elite comprised of advisers, of lawyers and narrow business groups, increasingly construct policy. The increased complexity of policy making means that elected politicians need advisers to construct policy. In the meantime, Parliament finds it difficult to disentangle, scrutinise and make transparent, the processes of policy. The process of economic globalisation – concern with trade negotiations, complex issues of intellectual property rights, environmental protocols, subsidies and directives on competition and free trade have increasingly become removed from the scrutiny and democratic accountability.

At present, anti-globalisation protests, resistance and social movements continue to be coalitions of coalitions (Klein, 2001), operating as swarms of bees with no centre, no leadership and lacking durable organisation. Protesters come together using the internet and web pages. The strategy is equated with the hub and spokes approach – the hub being the internet and home pages that organise protests, while the protesters decide their own agendas and priorities:

> 'Rather than a single movement what is emerging is thousands of movements intricately linked to one another, much as hot links connect their websites on the Internet ...Although many have observed that the recent mass protests would have been impossible without the Internet what has been overlooked is how the communications technology that facilitates these campaigns is shaping the movements in its own image. Thanks to the net mobilisations are able to unfold with sparse bureaucracy and minimal hierarchy forced consensus and laboured manifestos are fading into the background replaced instead by a culture of constant loosely structured and sometimes compulsive information swapping'. (Klein, 2001a, p. 4)

Klein (2001a) refers to the Zapatista movement in Mexico as an example of the social protest. When invited to Mexico City to negotiate with ministers, the Zapatista council did not seek to become the government, instead, they asked for greater autonomy for their region. Their objective was to create less government, rather than more government. The concern was to create participatory and direct local democracy:

> 'But when the Zapatistas travelled to Mexico City in March 2001 they weren't interested in overthrowing the state or naming their leader as president ... If anything in their demands, they asked for more direct political representation and the right to protect their language and culture, the Zapatistas are demanding less state power over their lives not more. For the Zapatistas creating autonomous zones isn't a recipe for dropping out of the capitalist economy but a base from which to confront it'. (Klein, 2001a, p. 12)

The ability of the anti-globalisation protesters to include different and diverse concerns ranging from campaigns against oil drilling, sweatshops, forced child labour, McDonalds, low pay and nuclear disarmament reflects the nature of the challenges of economic globalisation. They also reflect a break with seeking to provide competing priorities. Each concern is seen of being of equal value and of equal importance. There is no longer one essential explanation of the nature of the dynamics capitalism and globalisation.

The anti-globalisation protests reflect post modern thinking since they also represent the end of meta theory and the rejection of the big explanation. Liberal, Marxist, Socialist ideologies can no longer explain the nature of globalisation. Ideologies are seen to be what they are – a series of competing perspectives each offering different views of the world. There was no one essential explanation. The concern is the continuous deconstruction of the hidden languages of power:

> 'It is precisely for strategic reasons that I found it necessary to recast the concept of the text by generalising it almost without limit. That is why there is nothing 'beyond the text'. That is why the text is always a field of forces . . . That's why deconstructive readings and writing are concerned not only with library books, with discourses. They are not simply analyses of discourse . . . they are also effective or active interventions in particular political and institutional interventions'. (Derrida, as quoted in Bernstein, 1991, p. 197)

CONCLUSIONS

Advocates of postmodernity pointed to an ethic of transparency. The study of archaeology and genealogy connects the language of policy with issues of power. The language of the family influenced a specific form of thinking about men as breadwinners and women staying at home looking after children. The acknowledgement of domestic violence and child abuse allowed for the privacy of the family to be made public. These challenges have provided the opportunity to develop a commitment to honesty:

> 'What the postmodern mind is aware of is that there are problems in human and social life with no good solutions, twisted trajectories that cannot be straightened up . . . The postmodern mind does not expect any more to find the all embracing, total and ultimate formula of life without ambiguity, risk danger and terror and is deeply suspicious of any voice that promises otherwise'. (Bauman, 1993, p. 245)

Modernity was equated with the Enlightenment Project and the Age of Reason. The mood of modernity was influenced by the promises of science, rationality and the influence of experts. The industrial evolution, the ascendancy of manufacturing and industrial capitalism were the products of science.

Modernity created its own rhymes and rhythms, traditions and institutions of work, factories, employment cities, industrial communities and family lives. The end of full employment and the decline of manufacturing resulted in the demise of collective experiences and histories. Collective resistance was replaced by fragmentation of experiences and greater individualisation. The risk society (Beck, 1994) offered the spaces for greater reflexivity and criticism. The demise of modernity was accompanied by the decline of expert knowledge. The connections became causes and consequences were made more transparent. The degradation of the environment and global warming created the connections between economic growth, emissions and global warming. The use of pesticides was harmful to the health of workers and damaged the water supply. Disagreements between environmental experts, conflict of knowledge created increased insecurities. Greater knowledge does not create the hoped stability and the age of reason. Knowledge, by its nature, provides opposing options. Knowledge and information continuously change. In the context of uncertainty, the nature of risks becomes individualised. Individuals now have to make choices. Women dealing with the menopause can choose between conventional and complementary forms of care – decisions include the risks the individual is left to choose. Cancer patients search web pages for alternative forms of care, become aware of new drugs and also the risks. They become more knowledgeable than the clinician. Expertocracy is eroded:

> 'In other words, risk society is by tendency also a self-critical society. Insurance experts contradict safety engineers. While the latter diagnose zero risk, the former decide uninsurable. Experts are undercut or deposed by opposing experts. Politicians encounter the resistance of citizen's groups and industrial management encounters morally and politically motivated organised consumer boycott. Indeed the risk issue splits families, occupational groups from skilled chemical workers all the way to the management often enough even individuals themselves. What the head wants and the tongue says might not be what the hand (eventually) wants'. (Beck, 1994, p. 11)

The break with modernity provides the possibility for the self constituted individual. The individual does not need the language of the state, nationalism and patriotism to construct identity. Identity is the outcome of life's journey. There is no need for ideology to create understanding, nor experts or intellectuals to mediate:

> 'But what is a 'self constituting individual'? We say that the first step towards self constitution . . . is the recognition that the individual has not been given her or his identity ready made, but that identity is something to be built by the individuals themselves and taken responsibility for that, in other words rather than 'having an identity' the individuals are faced with the long and arduous never to be finished job of identification'. (Bauman, 2000, p. 138)

The events of 11 September 2001 have closed down some of the potential spaces of the self-constituted individual. The meta narrative is back. The discourses of the state and patriotism have again become the pillars of identity. There is a return to big theory, a return to the expert knowledge of the military experts giving details on smart bombs and collateral damage. The mistreatment of Afghan prisoners' is received in silence with the minimum of protest. In the immediate aftermath of 11 September, the USA was united behind the red, white and blue. Flags on cars, T shirts and skirts, motorcycles re-painted in the flag of the USA – a booming new business of patriotism emerged alongside the pathways to Ground Zero. Consumption and shopping confirmed the new nationalism – consumerism was promoted as patriotic and equated with the well being of America. Adverts for people to re-visit New York, the Broadway shows, the hotels became symbols of national identity. Flagging automobile industries, steel-making airlines queued for government subsidies. Allegiance to the nation, to its history, to collective memories, have again become essential pillars in the making of the imagined community.

> 'The absurdity of individual mortality does not haunt any more, thanks to the immortality of the nation. The inherited immortality of nationhood endows mortal life with meaning, perpetuation of that immortality gives mortal acts an added value of transcendence . . . As abstract – imagined – totalities nations fit the bill well: there hovered high above the world of immediate face to face and personal experience and so there could be little doubt as to their supra-individual nature'. (Bauman, 2000, p. 36)

September 11 also confirmed that the nation state was alive and kicking. Those who had heralded the demise of the state in the emerging context of the borderless economy found that the nation state was still the most important geographic space. The terrorist attacks have provided Governments with the opportunities to redefine expectations. The new priority is the defence of the citizen against external threat. The nation state has returned to the classical home of the defence of its people. Expenditure on internal security and also the expenditure on new military equipment are justified. The peace dividend ushered in by the collapse of the Soviet Union had allowed defence expenditures to fall in and in turn had acted as an enabling factor to provide resources for social expenditure. The reversal of this policy demands new and additional expenditures on defence and therefore is likely to create tensions in priorities between security and social expenditure.

8.   Globalisation by whom and for whom?

INTRODUCTION

The focus of this chapter is the relationship between globalisation and the distribution of income. Who is getting what shares from the rewards of the global economy? Does economic globalisation contribute to a better re-distribution of income or is there is still a role for government and social policy interventions? Advocates of globalisation have argued the case that increased openness of economies; the commitment to free trade and economic growth represented the means for eliminating world poverty. It seems therefore appropriate to ask how the fruits of the world economy are being distributed and who is getting what from the expansion of trade and economic prosperity? Such advocates point to the alleviation of poverty in China and India. However, does the study of *per capita* income growth provide a sufficient indicator of prosperity and income distribution? Many advocates have argued the case that economic growth would lift all boats and that economic growth is to be celebrated because there will always be trickle down factors that ensure some of the fruits of prosperity will eventually reach the poor. The poor are more likely to benefit from a context of economic prosperity rather than economic stagnation and decline. But is this assumption 'right'? Has there been a trickle down of prosperity? Have the poor benefited from globalisation?

Commenting on the shape of the world economy, the UNCTAD Report (2001) came to the conclusion that the developing economies were in worse shape in 2000 than in 1970. In the poor countries, average growth rates between 1980 and 2000 were 2 per cent a year compared with 3.4 per cent between 1960 and 1980. In the meantime, trade deficits with the developed world have widened, these are now 3 per cent higher than in 1970. During the 1970s, the Philippines were an exporter of food, producing a surplus of US$6.7 billion. In 2002, they reported a trade deficit on food of US$670 million. Increased subsidies on agriculture have resulted in the over-production of food in OECD countries, which has contributed to increased food dumping on developing countries since they cannot provide similar levels of subsidies for their own agriculture. Food production, supply and distribution has become increasingly centralised, controlled by a very small number of US multinational corporations. In the year 2000, the top five US cereal companies, including Cargill, ADM and Zen Noh controlled 75 per cent of the world cereal commodity market, the top five US retailers controlled 42 per cent of all retail food and the top four cattle producers owned 82 per cent of the US meat market (IATP, 2003):

> 'Wheat is selling for 40 per cent less than its costs to produce. For cotton the level of dumping for 2001 rose to a remarkable 57 per cent and for rice it has stabilised at 20 per cent. Developing countries need healthy agricultural sectors to eliminate poverty. Dumping is a gross distortion . . . it undermines the livelihoods of 70 per cent of the world's poorest people'. (IATP, 2003, p. 3)

Developing countries have liberalised and opened their markets to meet conditions set by the IMF and the World Bank. In Thailand, prices for rice have fallen from Bht 8000 per kg to Bht 4000 per kg. In the year 2002, developing countries imported US$225 billion in food, which represented a 62 per cent increase since 1988. In 2000, the USA was exporting wheat at a price of US$34 for a metric ton. It exported a total of 28 million metric tons at a cost of US$1 billion in subsidies. In the meantime, subsidised wheat from the USA has displaced some 15 million small farmers in Mexico. The added consideration is that the subsidy is a cost to US taxpayers and also small farmers, who are at the mercy of the large multinational companies that can dictate the price at which to buy products from small farmers; a price which is usually well below the cost of production. IATP (2003) estimates that 56 per cent of the US subsidies of US$23 billion to agriculture are directed to the top 10 per cent of companies that include the large multinationals involved in agricultural exports, such as Cargill, Tyson, Corn Agra and ADM.

Real GDP per head for the Least Developed Countries (LDCs) excluding Bangladesh grew 0.4 per cent a year between 1990 and 1998 compared with other developing countries of 3.6 per cent and 3.2 per cent for the world economy as a whole. In 1950, world exports totalled US$61 billion or 6 per cent of world GDP, which by 1970, had increased to US$317 billion or 12 per cent of world GDP to US$3770 billion in 2000, equivalent to 16 per cent of world GDP. While world exports as a total have expanded, the ratios for the LDCs actually declined in 2000, to 0.3 per cent of world trade compared with 0.7 per cent in 1994. The same story can be told for most of the developing countries where the ratio of trade has fallen in 44 out of the last 48 years.

The G7 group of countries including the USA, Japan, UK and Germany contributed to 50 per cent of world trade and also received 80 per cent of foreign direct investment. Globalisation is at present being shaped by the advanced economies, by multinational corporations (corporate globalisation), political interests, health and education professionals, trade lawyers, accountants (globalisation from above) and the international financial communities (financial globalisation) (Stiglitz, 2002a; Sen, 2002). The top 50 multinational corporations have incomes which can be located in the GDP equivalent of the top 100 national economies, while the top 200 corporations are responsible for 27 per cent of world trade (Hertz, 2001). Liberalisation of financial markets has also resulted in major increases in financial inflows and outflows. In 1973, financial flows totalled some US$15 billion a day, which increased to 900 billion in 1992, to 1000 billion a day in 2000. (UNCTAD, 2000) estimated that only 2 per cent of currency flows were actually needed to meet trade payment, which meant that the other 98 per cent of financial flows were purely speculative transactions. The implication of such large financial daily flows means that there is the potential for major fluctuations in exchange rates, which are mainly driven by short-term market sentiment and which therefore are more likely to result in central banks being more cautious about inflation and therefore adopting policies that are more likely to be deflationary and therefore harmful to growth and employment.

The major consequence of present globalisation has been greater income inequalities both within nations and between nations. While the top 20 per cent of the world population who live in the advanced industrial economies consume 82.7 per cent of the world's GDP, the bottom 20 per cent of the world population living in the LDCs received 1.4 per cent of world GDP. In the year 2000, the incomes of the top 20 per cent of income earners received 60 times more than the bottom 20 per cent. It is estimated that reducing debt relief under the Heavily Indebted Poor Countries (HIPC) Initiative by 1.9 per cent of GDP will allow LDCs to increase expenditure on health and education by between 50 and 90 per cent. At present, LDCs social expenditure is around 2 per cent of GDP in contrast to 24 per cent of GDP in the OECD and 11 per cent in Latin America (Clement, 1997). According to IMF estimates, reducing debt under HIPC would allow 22 LDC countries to increase social expenditure by 45 per cent. Poor countries are using their exports to pay for historic debts owned to the advanced economies when the possibility of debt relief would allow them to channel the incomes earned from exports to be spent on health and education. The issue of odious debt created by dictatorships in Thailand and Nigeria has been ignored, but it now seems that the USA is willing to raise the issue of debt forgiveness for reconstruction in Iraq.

Since the early 1980s, the distances between the top 10 per cent of the world population and the bottom 20 per cent have continued to widen. The global Gini coefficient was higher during the period 1980 and 2000 when compared with the years between 1960 to 1980 (Cornia and Kiiski, 2001; Weisbrot, 2000). The world Gini coefficient has increased from 0.68 in 1980 to 0.74 in 2000 (UNCTAD, 1997, 2000) Between 1970 and 1990 income inequalities have continued to widen throughout Latin America. Inequality increased in eight out 13 countries in Latin America and in seven out of 10 countries in Asia. Between 1990 and 1998, the Gini coefficient for Brazil widened further from 0.57 to 0.62. The distance between the top 20 per cent of households and the bottom 20 per cent is now 32.1 times higher compared with 5.5 times higher in South East Asia and 6.3 in the OECD countries (Clement, 1997). The Gini coefficient for Mexico in 2000 was 0.57, compared with 0.49 for Latin America, with 0.34 for OECD countries. In Mexico, in the year 2000, the top 20 per cent of earners had incomes, which were 16.4 times higher than the bottom 20 per cent. (Corbacho and Schwarz, 2002). In Eastern Europe, in all of the 15 transitional economies, inequalities increased between 1980 and 1990, as welfare provision in terms of state pensions, subsidies for heating and food collapsed due to large public sector deficits and the pressures for market led reforms (ECLAC, 1997). The number of people experiencing malnutrition totalled 956 million people in 1971, which represented 37 per cent of the world population. By 1999, the numbers had fallen to 771 million and 17 per cent, respectively. The target to reduce the number to 400 million by 2015 has been now been put back to 2060 (UNDP, 2001). In addition to the 770 million suffering from malnutrition, there are another 1.2 billion people living on less than US$1/day and another 1.6 billion people living on less than US$2/day, which means that over 50 per cent of the world population is living below the World Bank poverty line.

'Deconstruction of the change in income distribution shows that the increased inequality was generally due, in part, to increased inequality in wage and salary earnings or in part to the rise in the profit share and a fall in the wage share, increasing the proportion of income arising from the ownership of assets which is invariably distributed more unequal that work income'. (UNCTAD, 2001, p. 16)

Public expenditure on health and education benefit the poor. Studies of 70 developing countries over the period 1979 to 1995 (Gupta *et al.*, 2001) confirmed that increases in health expenditure reduces infant mortality rates and that it benefits the poorest 20 per cent more than the top 20 per cent of households. An increase of 1 per cent in health expenditure reduces infant mortality among the bottom 20 per cent by twice that of the top 20 per cent. Debt relief of 0.4 per cent of GDP reduces infant mortality rates by 5 per 1000 in the LDCs. Infant mortality in poor countries is at present 157 deaths per 1000 compared with 37 in the OECD. However, it is also true that social expenditure does not always necessarily result in the redistribution of income towards those in low-income groups. In South America, the evidence points to social policy being hijacked by vested interest groups (Tanzi, 1998). Education expenditure, which is skewed towards higher education and the universities sector, benefits upper and middles class income groups. In Brazil, for example, the government spends US$304 per child in primary and secondary education compared with

US$7804 per student at University. However, there is clear evidence that governments committed to better income distribution should focus on improving access and enrolment rates into primary and secondary education, by providing direct subsidies to poor families:

> 'Higher primary and secondary school enrolment rates tend to be associated with lower inequality. On the basis of cross country analysis estimates indicate that a one per cent increase in the share of the labour force having at least secondary education increases the share of income received by the bottom 40 per cent by 6 per cent and that received by the bottom 60 per cent by 15 per cent'. (UNCTAD, 2001, p. 12)

Likewise, expenditure on health is directed towards the building of new hospitals in the cities neglecting primary and preventive medicines that would contribute to better health in rural areas. Decisions to freeze petrol and electricity prices in Brazil during the 1990s benefited the top 10 per cent of earners who also used 94 per cent of gasoline output and 65 per of electricity. Brazil spends 19 per cent of GDP on social programmes; the highest level for South America, yet it is also the most unequal country in South America (Clement, 1997). In Mexico, while social expenditure amounted to an average of 9 per cent of GDP, expenditures on subsidies for housing mortgages, agriculture, food subsidies, electricity and higher education tended to benefit higher incomes earners (Corbacho and Schwarz, 2002).

In Europe, the period between 1948 and 1974 was associated with the dual commitments of full employment and increased social expenditures. This approach contributed to the reductions in income inequalities by around 10 points in the Gini coefficient, from around 0.37 to 0.24 (Cornia and Kiiski, 2001). The experiences of full employment, together with sustained additional increases in social spending on pensions, health, education and social security contributed to the improvement in the incomes of the bottom 40 per cent of households. By contrast, after 1974, the abandonment of Keynesian economic policies and the ascendancy of monetarist orthodoxy, including policies of deregulation, privatisation and liberalisation the Gini coefficient has risen to around 0.28 and 0.32.

In the aftermath of the Second World War, the twin commitments to the economics of Keynes and Beveridge's welfare state led to continuing low levels of unemployment. The rate of unemployment stabilised at around 2 per cent of the labour force, which was very low when compared with the experiences of the inter-war years, when unemployment peaked at around 15 per cent in most of the European economies and in the USA. By contrast, after the mid-1970s and into the late 1980s, unemployment returned to the high levels experienced in the 1930s. In the USA, for example, unemployment increased from 5 per cent in 1973 to 8 per cent in 1975. Similarly, it rose again sharply to 9.5 per cent in 1982. In 1999, US unemployment fell to 4.5 per cent, but was rising again towards 6 per cent by early 2003. In the UK, unemployment rose sharply to 3 million in 1982 and fell back to 1.8 million in 1987. However, by 1992 it had climbed again to 3.3 million. In 2002, the UK unemployment was less than 1 million. In the meantime, both Germany and France experienced long periods of unemployment, above 10 per cent. Throughout the 1980s and 1990s, Europe had higher levels of unemployment than those of the USA.

The experience in Europe has been that government intervention and social policy have, in the past, been the mechanisms that provided the means for the re-distribution of incomes. However, histories of government and social policy confirm that the re-distribution of resources always reflected struggles and resistances of competing interests. Social provision in Latin America has tended to benefit higher and middle-income groups. Expenditure on education has been concentrated on the tertiary and higher education sectors, as have subsidies on electricity, mortgages and petroleum.

In the Least Developed Countries (LDCs), 15 per cent of children die before the age of 5, which is double the average of the developing countries. Life expectancy in the LDCs is 51 years, compared with 65 years in the developing countries and 78 years in the OECD countries. Health expenditure *per capita* in the LDCs between 1980 and 1990 was equivalent to US$11 per person, compared with US$100 in the developing countries and US$1700 in the OECD (UNCTAD, 2000). Studies of 15 developing countries confirm that the income shares of the bottom 20 per cent of the population was around 5.2 per cent, while the income shares of the top 10 per cent was 36 per cent compared with the developed countries, which show that income shares of the bottom 10 per cent to be around 8.7 per cent and the top 10 per cent of 22.4 per cent. There is no correlation between GDP per head and the distribution of income. Brazil had a higher GDP per head than Bangladesh and yet has a Gini coefficient of 60 compared with 28 in Bangladesh (Todaro, 2000; Cornia and Kiiski, 2001).

To ask whether those in poverty benefit from globalisation is to ask the wrong question, because it avoids the issue of income distribution and the idea of fair share and just rewards. The concern with income distribution changes the focus from issues of poverty to issues of who is benefiting from the rewards of the world economy. Sen (2002) uses the analogy of the family to argue the case that the issues of globalisation are whether the poor are getting their fair share of the benefits of globalisation:

'Even if the poor were to get a little richer, this would not necessarily imply that the poor were getting a fair share of the potentially vast benefits of global economic interrelations. It is not adequate to ask whether international inequality is getting marginally larger or smaller . . . By analogy, to argue that particularly unequal and sexist family arrangement is unfair, one does not have to show that women would have done comparatively better had there been no families at all, but only that the sharing of the benefits is seriously unequal in that particular arrangement'. (Sen, 2002, p. 4)

The issue of fair shares is a question of access to resources. The question of income distribution therefore is intrinsically connected to struggles and resistances about who gets what. The struggles are played out between those who have the large parts of income and want the world to stay as it is and the non-stakeholders, who seek change and a better life. The question of fair shares can be resolved through political decisions that reflect the political willingness to resolve issues of fair shares. Therefore, the issue of fair shares opens up the question as to the nature of present globalisation, to ask who are the beneficiaries and does the way present globalisation is being shaped and defined, act as a barrier to fair shares? The concern is therefore more about whether, under different arrangements, there will be a different distribution of resources?

The question of fair shares is inherently linked to the themes of citizenship and democracy. Recent studies by the IMF (Baqir, 2002) confirm that there is a strong correlation between commitments to democracy and expenditure on social spending including health and education. The study of 167 countries for the period 1985–1999 shows that countries with the highest levels of political participation, commitments to frequent elections and political rights, allocate an additional 1.5 per cent of their GDP on social spending and 6.7 per cent of total expenditure more than non-democracies. Countries with similar levels of economic development have different levels of social spending. The Dominican Republic spends 2.9 per cent of GDP on health and education in contrast to Namibia, which spends 12.9 per cent. *Per capita* GDP and social spending are not correlated (Baqir, 2002).

The question of how the benefits of economic prosperity are distributed is therefore contestable, reflecting conflicting interests. Levels of *per capita* GDP do not necessarily translate into the sharing of that prosperity. The free market philosophy of privatisation, reduced taxation for higher incomes groups and reduced government expenditure helped the richest 1 per cent in the USA to capture 62 per cent of the growth in pre-tax incomes between 1977 and 1998, while the bottom 40 per cent experienced little or no improvement. Democracy defines the nature of the public space, the openness, access, transparency, accountability and scrutiny. Equally, the public space can become colonised by narrow interests. Political decisions can shape and define markets and therefore issues of distribution and redistribution of resources. Political decisions give shape to labour markets, including decisions of de-regulation, trade union rights and macroeconomic decisions by governments to delegate responsibility for monetary policy to independent central banks, which each influence labour market relationships. The public space provides for deliberative democracy, increases the potential of transparency and accountability of government. Issues of fair shares are shifted from the spaces of the private, to become public issues.

The discourse of citizenship makes connections between membership and the sharing of the benefits of economic prosperity as a community. Citizens make political the issues of fair shares and exclusion. Citizenship as resistance re-defines the making of citizenship in a changing context. However, citizenship and democracy are intrinsically linked, since claims of citizenship need to be deliberated in the public space. Citizenship as resistance points to the self-constituted individual not dependent on community or the nation state, to define his or her identity, but that identity is gained through the process of dialogue and creating agendas of resistance around defining fair shares. Globalisation is a continuing changing landscape. Citizenship and belonging in the context of globalisation creates an awareness of new forms of global social exclusion and claims of fair shares that reflect that changing landscape.

Economists might argue that unemployment is of economic concern because it creates a problem of lost output, loss of revenue to government and also involves higher levels of expenditure on social security benefits. Unemployment is political when the issue becomes a concern that might decide the outcome of an election. High rates of unemployment create a threat effect on the living standards of those in work. Images of dole queues reinforce views of government incompetence in managing the economy. Unemployment is also of social concern because it results in hardship and deprivation for families who experience long unemployment periods. The unemployed become the socially excluded and the marginalised. Unemployment is the normal life experience of those involved in semi-skilled and unskilled labour markets. Those from ethnic minorities are more likely to experience unemployment than their white counterparts.

The question of what social policy seeks to achieve has to be evaluated at two levels. First, there is the layer of the definition of what social policy is and to provide a means of identifying issues of concerns, which can be readily defined as social policy. The problem is that what is defined as being of social concern is continuously changing. The impact of the environment on individual lives is already becoming of major social concern and will continue to be a major challenge during the twenty-first century. Already the expansion of supermarkets made possible with the wider use of the automobile have made high street shops less viable, which have impacted on the lives of the elderly and those without transport. Supermarkets are constructed on green field sites away from city centres, which requires the use of a car and the supermarkets need larger spaces to build car parks. Poor families and the elderly are unable to take advantage of supermarket shopping. The new conventional wisdom that the consumer reigns supreme does not apply for those on low incomes and without transport, while small shops go out of business. Furthermore, increased use of cars produce additional emissions that have adverse health effects, while ecosystems are undermined. There is increased eczema and asthma among young children.

Concerns about shopping, low prices, transport and the environment become blurred since they remain no longer confined to the environmentalist, the economist or the public health ministry. But they are social concerns because they increasingly become connected with issues of access and the distribution of income. While some have the financial resource to escape and to retreat to the relatively better quality of life in the suburbs, others become recipients of air pollution, traffic noise and degradation of the local environment. For some, the environment represents a dilemma, they tend to work with materials that undermine the environment, yet if their factory closes they lose their job. Workers in nuclear plants know the dangers, yet feel they have little choice but to say that nuclear power is safe. The automobile represents freedom of choice, while the concern with the environment is a restriction on that freedom of choice. The demand for better quality and safer public transport, carbon taxes and subsidies on roads or railways, are becoming as much of a concern as health care or education. Health care can no longer be separated from the environment or from transport or emissions.

The second layer is concerned with the who question. While the first layer asked about social policy for whom, the second layer asks: 'who are the providers?'. The involvement of the early church in providing alms to the poor to alleviate poverty, hunger and disease, the notion of the *noblesse oblige*, which provided the ethic for the rich aristocracy to take some responsibility for the poor and Elizabethan Poor Laws of the early 1600s can be described as the early foundations of the present definition of social policy. The involvement of charities, voluntary groups, philanthropy and the state have been the agents of social policy making.

In the making of the present welfare state, there were a number of resistances – the resistances of business and landowners, who saw state provision as an intervention with the laws of the markets and supply and demand, especially as the state sought to regulate the number of hours people were working, the conditions of the work place sanitation and public health in the provision of housing. There was also resistance from trade unions and mutual benefit societies and charities that had developed networks within communities in creating forms of provision for those in need through the ethics of mutual savings and mutual aid. State intervention was greeted with suspicion as being a form of social control and surveillance. Working class families resisted the idea of sending children to school into their teens, because they were an important part of household income. Mechanics Institutes funded through trade unions were providing a form of education, which was independent and which was a resistance to the state. Public education was seen as a form of social order. The provision of benefits results in increased information and knowledge, increased surveillance and the public gaze. At the end of the twentieth century, public provision continues to be experienced as a form of monopoly with little choice, little accountability and a lack of transparency. The expertocracy of teachers, doctors and civil servants resist transparency and very often the users of these services question whether services are provided for the benefits of users and clients or whether services are defined by those who work within them.

UNDERSTANDING CHANGING LANDSCAPES

Social landscapes are different today from those of 100 years ago. The year 1900 was still the heyday of Empires and colonialism. Politics in Europe were dominated by the symbolisms of Empire. In 1900, the average income tax in Europe was around 3 per cent of GDP and total social policy expenditure was less than 1 per cent of GDP. Britain still could claim the highest *per capita* GDP, yet the wealthiest of nations was reluctant to deal with problems of sanitation overcrowded housing, ill health and poverty. In 1900, people in Britain were not sharing in the benefits of being the wealthiest economy. Disraeli's commitment to One Nation was about the symbols of politics, rather than the substance of fair distribution. Furthermore, a number of court judgements between 1880 and 1890 reversed a number of trade union immunities, which further hindered the potential of collective resistance and the attempt to make claims for a different approach to the sharing of economic prosperity.

The sharing of the benefits of economic prosperity has again become a major problem. For the past two decades, increases in income inequalities have become a global experience. There have been reversals in social spending in most of the OECD countries, with governments seeking to break the links between security payments with increases in earnings, allowing for the real values of pensions to decline and retrenchment on health and education expenditure. Developing countries faced with higher costs of debt servicing have reduced social spending as part of a series of policy commitments to meet IMF conditions for debt-rescheduling. Developing countries' debt servicing over the past 20 years has fallen from 50 per cent of GDP to 16 per cent of GDP (Stiglitz, 2002a).

In the Britain of 2003, social expenditure is around 24 per cent of GDP. Britain has the highest rates of income inequalities and child poverty in the advanced economies, except for the USA and New Zealand (Joseph Rowntree Foundation, 1998) and deteriorating public investment in roads, railways, schools and hospitals. Public expenditure on infrastructure has declined from around 8.9 per cent in the 1975, to 1.7 per cent in 2001 (Mullard, 2001b; Clark, 2001):

> 'Cuts in public investment are less immediately noticeable than cuts in current spending. Which risks leaving them a soft target during a period of retrenchment . . . a decision to delay building a new school or health centre might be expected to provoke less anger than a decision to cut the pay of public sector workers'. (Clarke, 2001, p. 1)

The decision not to build a school or a hospital and to postpone investment in railways is good politics at least in the short term. Capital expenditure is less politically visible than current expenditure. Both Labour and Conservative Governments (Mullard, 1993; 2001b) have adopted this approach to public expenditure. The short-term approach unravels when the policy becomes the policy of the long term. The 30 years of continuing reductions in investment in public housing, health and education have resulted in deterioration in public services. There is now no new building of houses by the public sector. Equally, decisions not to build or repair schools have left a number of schools with leaking roofs and with inadequate accommodation. Local councils now estimate that there is a backlog of school repairs and buildings costing some £16 billion. To make up for the neglect in public provision, Governments need to rely on the private finance initiatives to provide the necessary capital expenditure. The evidence of private affluence and public squalor characterises the boundaries between private concerns and public provision in the USA. While the Federal Government and the state governments make their priority to reduce income taxes and therefore erode their tax revenue base, public services continue to deteriorate:

> 'Oregon is one of many states caught in a fiscal quagmire. There are many reasons for the budgetary distress, which has spread from coast to coast. They include a lousy national economy, a widespread unwillingness locally and nationally to levy the taxes necessary to support government services or the refusal of the Bush administration to help state and local governments that are experiencing their worst budget shortfalls since World War II . . . School financing has been cut so drastically that some districts have had to curtail the school year. And healthcare cuts that have already hurt thousands of poor and working-poor residents are expected to go much deeper'. (Herbert, *The New York Times*, 5 May 2003)

Social policy is a mechanism that influences the distribution of resources. Transfer payments including pensions and social security payments have a direct effect on the bottom 10 per cent of earners. Income in kind that includes expenditure on health and education also acts as transfers provided the tax system is also redistributed. Social provision reflects claims and expectation on resources that are located in contexts that have changed and will continue because hopes and aspirations change. In Britain, the dreams of the elderly when they received their first pensions in the early 1900s were different to those of today. People in Britain in the year 2002 hope to spend at least 15 years in retirement. Today the new 60 something are relatively young, healthier and more mobile and with expectations qualitatively to those of 100 years ago. At 60, people still have hopes to re-marry and the possibility of starting new families. Today, people are living an additional 10 years, are more active and are looking for a quality of life that confirms independence and dignity. Those on state pensions still experience hardships and poverty, but a different hardship. The elderly of today have enough food and heating, but also have ambitions to take holidays, to enjoy retirement and to have good health. Old age meant destitution for the majority 100 years ago; that destitution has virtually disappeared today. The challenge for the next 100 years is how to make an average period of retirement of 20 years more meaningful, so that the afternoons of life continue to be as exciting as the mornings of youth.

The Human Development Index (HDI) developed by the United Nations in 1997 includes the dimensions of longevity, literacy and health. While the life expectancy in the advanced economies in 2002 is around 74 years for men, in the least developed countries, life expectancy is around 46 years. Furthermore commitments to wider literacy, improvements in the quality of water and sanitation are the concerns of the LDCs.

In the context of the globalised economy, the concern with fair shares and the social dimension reflect changing expectations. The argument of the global citizen makes connections between the elderly as citizens in Britain and life expectations of people in developing countries. Constructing a universal discourse of expectations points to the argument that life expectancy at the age of 46 in the year 2002 is attributed to issues of fair shares. In the Britain of 1900, life expectancy was on average the same as that of India today.

The nature of the economy has changed during the last 100 years. The make up of the political elite has also changed. Issues of class, collective identity and resistance located in the context of an economy dependent on industry and industrial communities, with shared views and traditions have been displaced:

'In late modernity old standards of freedom and responsibility impose a new set of hard choices. One can either treat one' s life as a project, negotiating a path through a finely grained network of institutionally imposed disciplines and requirements or one can struggle against those disciplines by refusing to treat one's life as a project'. (Connolly, 1991, p. 21)

The nation state is in transition as the globalised economy blurs the importance of national boundaries. Announcements in the UK by Ford and Vauxhall to halt car production in Britain and Germany and to move to the Czech Republic where labour costs are 40 per cent lower than in EU or the USA reflect the mobility of capital. The state can no longer make claims on the ability to fine tune national economies. Countries are now involved in 'beauty contests' pointing to the flexibility of their labour market, the lightness of regulation and low corporation taxes. The nation state seeks to address issues of controlling government expenditure and reducing the government debt, allowing interest rates to fall and making provision for education and training that addresses issues of labour market flexibility and employability. Developing countries are also seeking a place in the sun of economic prosperity, seeking to improve their shares of world trade and open markets. Technology and skills become more mobile and the knowledge society replaces the world of commodities, such as oil, coal, iron and other metals that had previously guaranteed the relative advantage of some nations.

In the context of the globalised economy, accountability and transparency can only be secured if democratic nation states become part of a wider cosmopolitan democracy that guarantees cosmopolitan citizenship:

> 'In the context of contemporary forms of globalisation, for democratic law to be effective it must be internationalised. Thus, the implementation of what I call a cosmopolitan democratic law and the establishment of a community of all democratic communities – a cosmopolitan community – must become an obligation for democrats; an obligation to build a transnational, common structure of political action which alone, ultimately, can support the politics of self determination'. (Held, 1999, p. 106)

At the dawn of the new millennium, the new buzzwords were influenced by the new technologies of the internet, websites and e-commerce. The numbers connected to the net have increased from around 80 000 in the late 1980s to over 290 million in 2001. E-commerce was becoming a multi billion dollar industry. The Blair Government in Britain provided financial incentives for MIT and Microsoft to set up research in Cambridge to ensure that Britain stayed at the forefront of 'e' commerce. The 'net', the 'web' and other internet engines were described as being similar to the inventions of the railway, the light bulb, the steam engine and the telegraph, each of which had revolutionised productivity and economic prosperity during the previous 100 years. During 1990s, the US economy experienced unprecedented growth rates of around 4 per cent per annum in contrast with the historical capacity of 2.5 per cent. In the late 1990s, the UK economy became the leading economy in Europe, with the lowest rates of unemployment and high growth rates. However, the Goldilocks economy of continued growth had slowed and the world economy and had returned to the historic economic fundamentals of trying to explain the business cycle. The promising dot.com companies have seen their stock market values falling. This has over spilled into manufacturing, as consumer confidence has also started to plummet and people are buying fewer utilities, e.g. washing machines and cars.

The world of e-commerce promised the end of shopping malls and supermarkets – these centres were to become a thing of the past. Dot.com companies pointed to lower prices, as less investment was required in property on the high streets. People shopped through looking at catalogues, on internet catalogues and shopped for food on the super highway. However, the world of the internet may not be a revolution, but just another version of mail order shopping, with all the problems of delivery dates, shipping and limited ranges of choices. People will still like to feel what they buy, to look and to touch. The glitter of the mall and the shopping centre are surely here to stay.

More people are being employed in telephone shopping, but these do not offer long-term careers or job prospects. Labour turnover continues to be high as young women become bored sitting at computer terminals all day. Producing search engines and internet directories will replace mail order companies, but this will not necessarily mean that large corporations will give up their investments in shopping arcades. Some did seem to be making a quick fortune selling search engines and web pages, but surely the ordinary person will still have to work for a lifetime. We do not all become millionaires. Despite the promises of the new cyber world – the majority will still spend their lifetime in work having to deal with the insecurities of the market economy of seeking insurance against the risks of unemployment, ill health and old age. Governments will still be talking about the need for an educated workforce if countries and regions are to remain competitive and attract inward investment. The large corporations will still influence employment and growth, while the consumer is surfing the web for the best buy (provided he/she could afford the computer and the telephone bill for searching on-line).

THE CULT OF PERSONALITY AND THE NEW ARISTOCRACY

The new millennium is saturated by the cult of personality. The celebration of the personality is resulting in the ascendancy of a new aristocracy that replaces the old aristocracy of property, by the new heroes of sport, of personalities created by the media, the new owners of the cyber world and the superstars of the business world. The new TV shows of how to make a million in less than 1 hour, national lotteries that promise millions, million pound contracts for individuals, etc. make the earning of money look quick and easy. The cult of personality creates a new legitimacy of inequality. David Beckham, with reported earnings of £180 000 per week, whose job is football, is the new icon that denies the barriers of class and yet it helps to create a new class. Not every footballer reaches stardom, the majority of players will give up playing at the age of 30 and retire as unknowns only to tell stories to their grandchildren that they played in the English Premier League.

Education is no longer the necessary path to better employment. For the young, there are few incentives to study and little incentive to work. Unlike previous generations, the young of the new century will not feel betrayed because of unemployment. Nurses, teachers, doctors and surgeons do not make money; they are seen as the poor neighbours. They are not the role models in the world of the celebrity. It is not those who save lives, those who educate children who are the role models. It is the celebrities, the TV shows or actors in TV and cinema who are continuously in the public eye. It is they who define the new priorities. Those in work do not fit the images of the world of personality.

For over 1000 years the landed aristocracy became rich and highly influential because of property they had plundered in battles long forgotten or had been handed to them by a grateful monarch. In 1840, The Duke of Devonshire was told he needed to revise his annual spending. It was estimated he was spending around £15 000 a year consuming large amounts of champagne and wine. During the same period, those in work in the cotton industry were earning around £40 a year. The new aristocracy of personalities and celebrities has no similar claim to political legitimacy of the landed gentry, who claimed the historical legacy of sustaining English identity and who were paternal towards their workforce. The new aristocracy comes from the ranks of those who lead ordinary lives. This creates the new illusion that there is a new meritocracy that will allow entry to the majority and there is no exclusion. The dream is to join the ranks of the new gods.

The landed aristocracy resisted government regulation and intervention. The attempt to limit hours in factories or child labour was perceived to be an unnecessary intervention and regulation by the state. Likewise, multinational corporations form into pressure groups including the International Chamber of Commerce (ICC) or Business Action for Sustainable Development (BASD) to make the case for soft and self-regulation, again arguing the case that regulation of hours and conditions at work will increase labour costs and therefore hurt employment. In the interest of social order and the need to develop 'One Nation' in Britain and Bismarckian social order in Germany, provided the necessary arguments for the aristocracy to accept some limited intervention. In most of the OECD countries, social policy has moved from its nascent stage to maturity. Public provision is now institutionalised. The resistance of the landed aristocracy changed in the aftermath of the franchise. Their coalitions and alliances with industrialists and parts of the middle class have over the last 100 years had their views articulated through conservative political parties, flying the flag of deference, tradition, the nation and authority. The New

Aristocracy seems to be less politically homogenised than the one it eclipses. Their home is not necessarily the Conservative Party. Tony Blair's and Bill Clinton's 'Third Way' was successful in recruiting parts of the New Aristocracy. The Third Way and the emphasis on meritocracy, ability and potential seem to resonate with the new money of the theatre, the arts and cinema.

At present, most governments in Europe are spending on behalf of each person, around 40 per cent of national income on some form of social provision extending from pensions to child care. Equally, individuals are surrendering 40 per cent of their income through various forms of taxation to finance these areas of public expenditure. The boundaries between private and public provision seem to be fixed and most arguments are related to marginal questions of improvement and reform, rather than making some radical break with the present system. The present approach also assumes a world that is going to change very little during the next 100 years. A quick glance over the past 100 years tells us that such an assumption rests on very shaky ground. One hundred years ago, people found jobs in the new industrial communities of coal, steel, textiles and steel making – within a period of 70 years, these communities have collapsed. In the mid-1980s, during major labour shake outs in manufacturing, men lost their jobs and never returned to work again. Despite numerous attempts, re-structuring failed to replace manufacturing with new growth sectors. It is only since the mid-1990s that there has been major employment growth in new sectors of technology. In Britain, The Netherlands and Ireland, there has been employment growth, but unemployment remains persistently high in France, Germany and Spain. Manufacturing in most industrial countries is no longer a major form of employment. Manufacturing employment has fallen from around 45 per cent of the labour force 70 years ago, to 18 per cent in 2000. There have been equally major shake outs in the service sector, such as banking and commerce. Traditional assumptions about jobs for life and the nuclear family no longer apply.

CONCLUSIONS

One hundred years ago, in the advanced economies, social provision was still being born, a fledgling social policy with minimal provision of state pensions, some health care and tentative experiments in education. University education was still for the privileged few and the unemployed had still to submit themselves to the workhouse test. The city was still attracting people away from the countryside. The car was still a minority sport. A few families took their children to the seaside for the day. Social provision was born in the starkness of the failings of the market economy. The changing political contexts, demands for democracy, claims for fair shares in the midst of affluence of the few and the experiences of insecurities, such as illness, unemployment and old age created the necessary context for governments to intervene. While mutual benefit societies, charities, voluntary associations, trade unions and other informal networks were already involved in making provision, large numbers were still excluded from these informal welfare networks. The principles of deserving and undeserving defined by charities, marginalised those who were not in full-time employment or who were not members of trade unions and mutual benefit societies.

The state is an excellent agency of provision, because of its ability to reduce the cost of risk to the individual by providing for collective insecurities in the place of private insurance. If individuals had to insure against all risks from unemployment, to old age, to sickness, to financing children's education, it is estimated that only around 5 per cent of the population would be able to finance such a plethora of individualised insurance policies. By contrast, it would seem that through national insurance and taxation, the state is able to insure most of the population against most risks and provide some minimum income for old age, sickness and unemployment. Marshall (Bulmer and Rees, 1996), when writing about citizenship in 1949, connected the notion of social citizenship with social policy and argued the case that civil, political and social rights were the three pillars of citizenship. Marshall was defining citizenship as a form of belonging; of being part of the community, sharing the daily life experience. Those who did not belong were therefore excluded from membership. Access to education, health care and social benefits were therefore essential ingredients to the making of citizenship, because it was no longer income that determined access.

Citizenship and democracy link social policy to the political context. Democracy becomes the focus and the public space, the site for resolving conflicts of interests. In the twenty-first century, the globalised economy is described as undermining the nation state. The flows of capital, the movement of corporation between borders and frontiers makes it difficult for the nation state to make pretensions towards the management of the national economy. In Europe, the move towards greater economic and political integration acknowledges the limits of the nation state and acknowledges the advantages of a polled sovereignty.

The shift towards global governance and the super national state does not necessarily mean that social policy will follow suit. Indeed, it would seem highly inappropriate to shift social policy further away to an even more remote organisation than the nation state. Issues of accountability and transparency will become even more blurred. In the USA, federal governance in Washington is remote and people feel little optimism for the political process because the political process is no a longer a catalyst of change. The US political process ensures that present vested interests persist. There is a continued disavowal of responsibilities between different layers of government. Despite having an elected legislative assembly, there is little political accountability, transparency and scrutiny of the executive. Politicians do not take responsibility for the running of a state hospital, instead the responsibility rests with the Department of Health. Issues do not therefore become politicised.

While certain areas are shifting beyond the boundaries of the nation state to the more international public space, the nation state will continue to be a highly politicised public space. Claims for fair shares are best articulated within the spaces of the local states, decentralised to local governments, voluntary associations, charities and mutual benefit organisations. While the WTO, the ILO and the United Nations take responsibility for setting labour standards and for protecting universal human rights, social policy will be increasingly delivered by national governments. The major lesson for developing and least developing countries is that the social dimension of globalisation remains a local issue. Resistances and arguments about fair shares and who gets what will be resolved in local contexts anchored in local histories.

9. Conclusions

INTRODUCTION

Commenting on the implications of the perceived triumph of globalised capitalism after the break of the Soviet Union in the early 1990s, Dunn (2001) wrote:

'A world at last fit for capitalism will be a world in which those who have talents, good fortune and energy equip them to trade profitably profit handsomely, irrespective of where they happen to have been born. It will be a world in which property rights are highly secure, but other human claims have force only insofar as they fit comfortably with the security of property rights. In this sense, it will be a world of increasingly pure power, where the strong take what they can get and the weak endure what they have to'. (Dunn, 2001, p. 332)

According to the Dunn thesis, the ascendance of capitalism as the only viable economic system meant that the power and influence of the global financial markets, large corporations, strategic interest groups in the advanced economies and the new millionaires, were the ascendant voices that were giving shape and defining the nature of globalisation. In the meantime, workers were increasingly forced to compete with each other in a context of falling wages and also declining social provision processes that were undermining communities:

'It is crucial to make a clear distinction between for example a global flow of technology, ideas and information to rebuild sustainable local communities – i.e. a supportive internationalism – and the process of globalisation. In essence, the latter is the systematic reduction of protective barriers to the flow of goods and money by international trade rules shaped by and for big business. It pits country against country, community against community and workers against workers'. (Hines, 2003, p. 274)

FROM GLOBALISATION TO POLARISATION

The study of the privatisation of public utilities including gas, water and electricity in Argentina, Indonesia or the Philippines reinforces the nature of present forms of globalisation. First, there was the issue of under investment and neglect by national governments. This was followed by the World Bank and the IMF, in making clear prescriptive public policy guidelines that governments had, to reduce their deficits and adhere to policies of privatisation and liberalisation, if these countries were going to secure financial assistance through these financial institutions. Private contractors including Vivendi and Suez, two French multinationals that bid for the contract on the water industry in Argentina, were also backed by their respective national governments. President Chirac of France visited Argentina on a number of occasions, while President Menem went to France.

'For many of President Carlos Menem's allies, being invited to the sale of water assets was like getting their own keys to the candy store. Supporters found high-paid jobs as company executives and directors, while others got rich investing in the new firm. Menem's environment minister, Maria Julia Alsogaray, who awarded Aguas Argentinas numerous rate increases and contract concessions, is being prosecuted for illicit enrichment. After the privatisations of power and water utilities, she bought herself a Buenos Aires mansion and two apartments in New York. Furthermore, the ICIJ investigation has found that Argentine authorities are investigating others for the embezzlement of $2 million in World Bank funds. Argentina's current economic crisis is having a devastating effect on its people. A country that only 10 years earlier had Latin America's highest standard of living was now on a level with Jamaica; half of Argentina's 37 million people lived below the poverty level'. ('The Aquas Tango – cashing in on Buenos Aires privatisation', The Centre for Public Integrity, 2004, p. 4).

The third stage was the problem of corruption and the collusion of key political actors involved in privatisation contracts. Santani who owned 20 per cent of Aquas Argentinas, which he had bought for US$50 million in 1991, was able to sell his shares to the holding for US$150 million in 1996. The Secretary of State for Energy in Argentina has been accused of gross corruption. On becoming a Minister, she declared an ownership of wealth of around US$350 000. Four years later she owned two major properties in New York and a mansion in Buenos Aires. Lastly, there are the overspills for the consumers who are frequently faced with higher prices. In Buenos Aires, consumers were asked to pay US$800 to be contacted to the water and sewerage system. This was reduced to US$200 after a number of street protests. The contractor who made a number of promises before securing the contract then failed to deliver on the contract and forced the government to extend subsidies on the threat that the company would be unable to deliver (Centre for Public Integrity, 2004). In the meantime, The World Bank has pointed to water privatisation in Argentina as being a major contributor to the lowering of infant morality.

The World Bank Report (World Bank, 2001) has shown that a total of 193 loans were made in the period 1998–2000, where 58 per cent of these were directed towards water privatisation. In each case, the World Bank has not advocated a policy of privatisation, but has instead tended to emphasise the language for the need for reform as being the means for new investment. Adjustment loans have continued to expand. While during the 1980s the World Bank advanced such loans to 27 countries, totalling US$27 billion; by 1998, the Bank had made similar loans to 98 countries, totalling US$71.7 billion dollars. Leaked EU documents have also indicated that EU commissioners have written to 42 countries on their future requests to become involved in GATS proposals on water privatisation. Countries targeted for the privatisation of fresh water supply have included the Philippines, Tanzania, Mozambique and Bangladesh. In each request, the EU letter stated that it was seeking to 'encourage' the targeted country to embrace progressive liberalisation as being of benefits for all members. The closing date for GATS request was March 2003. Only 15 countries have put forward official requests. Water privatisation in developing countries is increasingly becoming a major business, with the World Bank providing the necessary funding for the process of privatisation and the EU and other countries making connections between potential customers and water companies in their member states.

> 'A close analysis of the documents and e-mails reveals that officials of the European Commission met and communicated regularly with representatives from various large water companies and that the requests put forth by the EU reflect the interests of the water companies. The World Trade Organization has often defended GATS by stating that none of the countries have to accept any of the requests. This therefore means that all 72 countries could reject the requests to open up water markets. Critics fear, however, that the privatisation of water from these GATS requests are related to the way in which many developing countries are often forced to bring in the private sector by international financial institutions. The GATS is functioning under a certain context and that is the context of IMF, World Bank policies where countries are forced to privatise their public services . . . the EU has received only 25 requests from other nations, showing that developing countries do not have a lot to ask for in service liberalisation'. (Politi, 2003, p. 8)

Politics is about choices. It would be misleading however, to suggest that there are endless choices and judgements. Indeed, in the context of present globalisation, it can be pointed out that a number of options are already closed down. The World Bank and the IMF are not democratic institutions in the sense that the advanced economies will always be the major policy makers. The CEOs of the major multinationals who meet under the umbrella of the Transatlantic Business Dialogue (TABD) will continue to ensure that the EU and the USA continue to define the trade agenda at the WTO in the interests of multinational corporations. Elgin (2002) of Transparency International has criticised the lack of transparency when it comes to government procurement:

'The international procurement environment is far from transparent. Although many countries have quite good procurement rules, they are routinely circumvented and thus largely useless. Escape clauses are common, thus ending the principle of 'open competition'. Furthermore, bids are usually evaluated by a handful of officials in secret, inviting manipulation. The WTO should be responsible or devising a functioning framework to remove distortions from public procurement'. (Elgin, 2002, p. 6)

The War on Iraq has polarised ideas about the shaping of the political community. However, there are fears that schisms about the war can overspill into areas of economic globalisation. Like the UN, the WTO also seems to be undermined by US neo-conservative criticisms of too much intervention. The USA has recently lost 12 appellant cases on free trade at the WTO, the most recent brought by the EU on USA include tax breaks on exports subsidies on steel and agriculture. There is increased anger within parts of the Bush administration with neo-conservatives demanding that the President ignores the WTO. Under the Trade Act of 2002, President Bush has been given the 'fast track' option to conclude bi-lateral trade agreements, without having to consult Congress. The objectives agreed at the WTO Doha Development Round in October 2002, as expected, were not met in Cancun in September 2003. American opposition on issues related to generic drugs, steel and American and European intransigence on farm subsidies, ensured that the talks collapsed. With Presidential elections now due in the USA in November 2004, plus EU enlargement of another 12 countries in 2004, it seems highly likely that world trade agreements will drop out of focus during the next 18 months:

'Some observers fear prolonged stalemate in the WTO will feed on itself and the growing disenchantment may lead members increasingly to ignore it in favour of bilateral and regional trade deals. Such initiatives have proliferated worldwide since the WTO Seattle meeting . . . Enthusiasts say bilateral deals offer a faster path than the WTO to liberalisation. However, they divert scarce negotiating capacity and risk fragmentation of the global economy into a patchwork of rival trade blocs. If they come to overshadow the WTO, their growth could undermine the effectiveness of the multilateral rules and disciplines that have kept world markets open for more than 50 years'. (*The Financial Times*, 31 March 2003)

The most recent Free Trade Agreement between the USA and Singapore (Polaski, 2003) highlights some of the major flaws of bi-lateral agreements. Within the framework of the US Trade Act 2002, partners in agreement have to observe commitments to labour rights, including the right to belong to a trade union, environment protection and intellectual property. The Trade Act also allows for what is called Integrated Sourcing Initiative (ISI), which means that products not directly produced in a country can also be treated as that country's products. In the case of the Singapore agreements, products being produced in the Exporting Processing Zones (EPZs) on the islands of Bintan and Batam, which include computers, semiconductors and electronics, are to be treated as coming from Singapore when these islands are part of Indonesia, which is not is not part of the agreement:

> 'However the ISI creates a very large loophole to the terms included in other parts of the FTA. Singapore does not assume any obligation to ensure that workers' rights are protected in the Indonesian islands or other territories that may be included in the agreement . . . Indonesia is not a party to the agreement and therefore it takes on no obligations at all. As a result, goods produced in Bintan and Batam may be made in violation of basic rights and laws without in any way jeopardising benefits under the agreement. This violates the fundamental reciprocity that Congress envisioned in extending trade-negotiating authority to the president, whereby access to the U.S. market would require disciplines on other matters important to the United States'. (Polaski, 2003, p. 7)

The US Department of State Report on Human Rights Indonesia, published in March 2002 (www.state.gov), has pointed to a number of human rights abuses in EPZs. The report pointed out that the enforcement of minimum wage and other labour regulations were inadequate; that allegations of corruption on the part of inspectors were common, that government enforcement of child labour laws were either weak or non-existent and that there was evidence of long-standing patterns of collusion between the local police force, military personnel and employers, which usually took the form of intimidation of workers by security personnel in civilian dress or by youth gangs. Under the Trade Act 2002, the President of the USA has been given autonomy to conclude trade agreements within a framework of rules agreed by the Congress. However, ISI has provided the loophole that allows for the possibility of concluding trade agreements that violate agreements on basic human rights as agreed by the Congress. The MNCs involved in sub-contracting and outsourcing can import goods into the USA via third countries outside the bilateral trade agreements.

CITIZENSHIP AND DEMOCRACY

At present, globalisation is dominated by the language of neo-market liberalism, of greater individualism, limited government and privatism that is resulting in increased polarisation, wider dispersions of income inequalities and over half of the world populations, who increasingly feel they are not part of the global community. The process of globalisation is influenced by the ideology of globalism that is underpinned by market liberal sentiments:

> 'The liberal element of liberal democracy has little difficulty in accommodating globalization. Liberalism is based on the natural rights and the desire for property

and comfortable self-preservation that are equally possessed by all human beings. As such, it is universal in its reach just as the principles of human rights and the laws of the market are universal. Liberalism limits the state in the name of the prepolitical or suprapolitical goals of the individual. In principle, there is no reason why a liberal order could not be administered by a wise and benevolent despot. In this sense, liberalism is a wholly cosmopolitan doctrine that is in full harmony with the trend toward globalization'. (Plattner, 2002, p. 59)

Globalisation requires an agenda that supports deliberative (thick) democracy and the need to construct public spaces that ensures wider dialogue. Deliberative democracy and the commitment to citizenship point to the urgency to replace a plutocracy by democracy which means the commitment to minimise the knowledge and information of political, financial, economic and professional elites whose influence distort democracy. There is a need to make a break with distorted forms of communication to widen access to knowledge and information. Large personal donations to political parties and individuals, the financing of TV and media, advertising campaigns contribute to the distortion of the democratic process.

The commitments to democracy and citizenship means allowing voices to be heard and listened to, voices that can influence and bring about social change. It is an argument that favours greater decentralisation of politics, which in turn will allow for the possibility of greater pluralities of ideas and for diversity to flourish. It also means making a commitment to the continuous deconstruction of distorted forms of communication. The distortion is associated with the way language is constructed and where democracy and citizenship create the resistance and the awareness of deconstruction, to excavate language and therefore to provide an understanding about the ownership and power associated with the language of government and, policy making.

The primary objective is therefore to deconstruct the language of globalisation and to create a language that makes transparent, the hidden meaning of concepts associated with globalisation, including concepts such as 'flexibility', 'employability', 'de-regulation', privatisation' – words, which at one level seem to be highly innocent and benign, yet when translated into policy practice reveal hidden issues of power and inequalities. Flexibility in the workplace might be the removing of demarcation of who does what on the assembly line in a car plant, but removing demarcation might also mean lower wages and lower overtime payments for some groups of workers who are defined as responsible for the maintenance of that assembly line. The deconstruction of globalisation provides an analysis of hidden and often denied relationships of power and the claim to make transparent the influences of business interests, international financial communities and governments in defining and shaping present forms of globalisation. Resistances against flexibility de-regulation and privatisation take many forms. De-regulation might mean long hours of opening for shop workers, while privatisation could lead to job losses and new working conditions. Resistance to globalisation require coalitions of interests that are inherently diverse and that seek, for example, to make coalitions between small farmers displaced by large agri business, environmentalists, women's groups and trade unions. It means making alliances between different NGOs involved in working alongside the global poor, disadvantaged children, climate change, campaigns for clean water and sanitation, as part of the global agenda.

RE-DEFINING GLOBALISATION

Definitions of globalisation need to go beyond economic measures of traded GDP, inflows of foreign direct investment and openness of economies. A narrow definition that depends on economic data does not capture the present influence of corporations involved in agriculture and the connections between government subsidies, chemical companies, research, the patenting of seeds, GM crops and the increased concentration of the ownership of food. Globalisation happens at both the level of ideas and the level of people's lived experiences. Information technologies have made global interconnections that overspill economic, social, political, ecological and cultural landscapes. Concerns about air pollution cannot be separated from the economics of the car industry, the culture of advertising, the social implications of private and public transport and the politics of transport policy.

This text has pointed to the nature of the relationships between business interests, finance and politics. Business groups, including the Transatlantic Business Dialogue (TABD) and the Business Action for Sustainable Development (BASD), have been specifically established to influence national governments and international political forums, advocating policies of business self-regulation, rather than government interference, putting the case for free trade and illustrating the need of a soft regulatory approach to employment rights. Business organisations have become increasingly institutionalised in the policy-making processes with ministries responsible for trade and industrial policies advising governments, on complex issues of trade negotiations. Governments have increasingly become the political advocates of business at international forums.

Concerns with contemporary globalisation reflect different responses, strategies and resistances. This text has tried to make connections between democracy and citizenship and to evaluate the relationships and coalitions of business interests, the international financial community and political elites that are defining the nature of globalisation.

The problem of globalisation is not globalisation in itself, but rather the way globalisation is at present being defined. From the late eighteenth century and into the 1950s, countries in Europe became global on their own terms, often protecting what they defined as infant industries, pursuing export-led growth, while also developing social policies. While Britain was associated with *laissez-faire* economics, Germany and Japan industrialised under the direction of the state. However, under present forms of globalisation, countries are forced to join the globalised economy on rules being defined by international financial institutions. The emergence of the economies in East Asia, including Thailand, Indonesia, Taiwan and Korea during the 1970s, was an Asian Miracle, in the sense that continuing growth was also accompanied by an eradication of poverty. By contrast, the imposition of IMF conditions on East Asia since the early 1990s, has been a disaster. The globalisation from above, which had forced these countries to peg their currencies to the dollar, to liberalise their trade and de-regulate industry, have resulted in property booms, in financial outflows and financial crises. The 'Washington Consensus' economic strategy, as defined by the IMF/World Bank policy prescriptions for developing countries, has also resulted in a globalisation creating increased poverty and hardship:

'The international financial institutions have pushed a particular ideology – market fundamentalism – that is both bad economics and bad politics. The IMF has these economic policies without a broader vision of society or role of economics in society ... The IMF often speaks about the importance of the discipline provided by financial markets. In so doing, it exhibits a certain paternalism, a new form of the old colonial mentality. The arrogance is offensive but the objection is more than just to style. The position is highly undemocratic'. (Stiglitz, 2002b, p. 3)

The conflation of the concept of globalisation and competitive markets reflects an ideology of globalism, rather than providing a definition of globalisation. Equating globalisation with markets represents a specific definition. The language associated with contemporary globalisation seeks to be innocent. There is a denial of exploitation, a denial of class and a denial of the existence of capitalism. The language is of flexibility, employability, the market, the individual and competition. The results are the new icons of the cult of personality and celebrities that confirm the ascendancy of the language of globalism. The cult of the celebrity reinforces the argument that individuals receive rewards according to their talents and their individual attributes. Inequalities reflect individual entitlements. Markets are taken as given. They are defined by the laws of economic science, which are more comprehensive than the laws of physics, chemistry and biology. The laws of markets are all encompassing. The market cannot be bucked. There is no alternative. The global economy is taken as given. The role of government is to respond, to intervene in a way that is compatible with the market. Markets reflect human nature, the drive of self-interest, where the individual knows what is best. The pursuing of self-interest creates the path to prosperity. Government intervention hinders markets. Those who care for the poor and say they are for the poor should advocate more open economies, liberalisation of trade, de-regulation and liberalisation:

> 'Liberal democracy clearly favours the economic arrangements that foster globalisation – namely, the market economy and an open international trading system. Moreover, liberal democracy's emphasis on the freedom of the individual and the right to information helps to promote the free flow of communications that has powered globalisation'. (Plattner, 2002, p. 59)

MAKING THE CONNECTION

Democracy/Citizenship and Social Policy

In the previous chapters, a number of discourses on citizenship and democracy were outlined. The following sections will seek to outline three narratives that seek to make the connections between the global economy and the role of social policy in the global context (Mullard, 2001b). First, there are the discourses of *modernity/enlightenment* and the attempt to connect globalisation with reason; the influence of research on people's living conditions and the willingness of government to intervene. The growth state of economic prosperity, employment and high tax revenues allow for private and public consumption. Second, there is the '*homo duplex*' discourse that points to the idea that humanity is capable of both 'barbaric' and 'civilised' habits. Market fundamentalists point to the dangers of state monopoly and the abuse of power while advocating policies of lower taxation, less government regulation and reducing public spending. This model has recently been described as the American Business Model (ABM) (Kay, 2003), which is characterised by the economics of individualism, self-interest, the minimalist state, low taxation and low public expenditure. Finally are the *postmodernists*, who put an emphasis on the context of consumer society, the commitment of living with difference and fragmentation and the attempt to connect market liberalism with the collectivists' values of the evolutionists. The Blair's Government's 'Third Way' best exemplifies the post-modern thinking on social policy. The Private Finance Initiative (PFI), the experiments in the contracting out of education provision and proposals on foundation hospitals, reflect the Third Way in dealing with consumer choice and consumer society. The Secretary of State, Alan Milburn, made the case for foundation hospitals, in a speech to the Social market foundation, using the language of postmodernity to justify the health reforms:

'Sixty years ago when the NHS was formed it was the era of the ration book. People expected little say and experienced precious little choice. Today we live in a quite different world; a consumer age; the computer age; the informed and inquiring society. People demand services tailored to their individual needs. People want choice and expect quality. We all do it and we all know it. These changes cannot be wished away. They are here to stay. And these changes challenge every one of our great public services. To meet that challenge we've got to move on from the one size fits all, take it or leave it top down health service of the 1940s towards an NHS which embraces devolution, diversity and choice – precisely so that its services can be more responsive to the way the world is today'. (Milburn, 2003, Speech to the Social Market Foundation 30 April)

1. The modern/Enlightenment approach

According to the Enlightenment perspective, human progress is perceived as reflecting the ascendance of science and rationality. The Enlightenment is associated with the role of expert knowledge and where policy is seen as being influenced by research into conditions of living, including poverty, health, housing and education and where the study of these areas have ensured a continuing critical and rational debate as to the condition of society. Condorcet, writing in 1791 in the aftermath of the Revolution in France, outlined his vision of reason, knowledge and freedom:

'The time will therefore come when the sun will shine only on free men who know no other master but their reason; when tyrants and slaves, priests and their stupid or hypocritical instruments will exist only in the works of history and on the stage; and when we shall think of them only to pity their victims and their dupes; to maintain ourselves in a state of vigilance by thinking on their excesses; and to learn how to recognise and so to destroy by force of reason, the first seeds of tyranny and superstition that ever dare to appear amongst us'. (Condorcet in Bernstein, 1991, p. 35)

There is an implicit link between the Enlightenment perspective and democracy. The framework rests on the assumption that there is access to governments, that governments are open to persuasion and the availability of knowledge to bring about policy change once policy makers have the information. Research provides the necessary information. Democracy and open spaces allow for deliberation and dialogue. Accordingly, the future success of globalisation depends on dialogue and debate within the context of new public spaces to ensure that globalisation is very much the product of deliberation:

'In Arendt's politics, institutions and individuals are always incomplete, forever calling out for augmentation and amendment. Like Nietzche's self as a work of art, like translation on Derrida's account, Arendt's politics is never a fait a accompli'. (Honig, 1993, p. 115)

The life world (Habermas, 1987) represents the dialogue, the awareness of communication, the importance of politics and making choices. By contrast, the systems world is influenced by factors perceived to be outside the control of individuals and include the impact of financial markets, the process of globalisation and competition. According to Habermas, the life world is 'colonised' by the systems world. In the globalisation economic the world of money, business interests and finance colonise the world of politics, dialogue and argument. Dialogue and communication become distorted.

The optimism of the Enlightenment is inextricably linked with the commitment to argument, deliberation, openness and dialogue. The aim is to provide thick democracy and public citizenship. Distortions to the process of dialogue emerges in the context when there is a lack of transparency and accountability and reflects the concern about the influence of business and finance in gaining ascendancy in policy making that in turn, leads to a specific form of globalisation that serves the narrow interests of large corporations and financial interests. Openness, transparency and participation prevent the take over of government. The public space provides the opportunity to make argument, to persuade and to make compromises.

2. The 'homo duplex' approach

The category of homo duplex started with the writings of Veblen and his analysis of the late nineteenth century and updated by Mestrovic (1993), in his analysis of the late twentieth century. The homo duplex argument points out that we need to balance the optimism of the Enlightenment with the pessimism that is evident in human histories. The lesson of history is that we are capable of both peaceable and barbaric habits. Genocide, the holocaust, ethnic cleansing and the treatment of the others are barbaric habits. The central theme is that the understanding of human dynamics has to be anchored and contextualised in habits. Habits are defined by Mestrovic as:

'Habits refer to settled dispositions . . . To act in certain ways which are unconscious and involuntary . . . things that are done as a matter of course . . . to act on the basis of the heart. Habits are anti modern and anti-intellectual'. (Mestrovic, 1993, p 14)

The concept of habits puts the focus on ideas of tradition, history and collective memories and on ways of thinking and behaving. It therefore asks whether it is possible that cosmopolitan virtues and the global citizen can be created, when the habit of thinking is anchored in ideas of community, nationalism and the exclusion of the stranger and the tensions between making a commitment to global connectedness and the retreat to protectionism and isolation:

'In the year ahead, I believe that this will become an increasingly contentious issue, one that may well lead to unusual political divisions and alignments. For example, even those who have been strong proponents of policies to promote the global spread of democracy are likely to split into two camps, dividing those who wish to see a world of democratically governed nation-states from those who wish to see a democratic world community – those who are concerned with preserving the sovereignty of democratic nations from those who favour the univeralisation not only of markets but also of politics and law'. (Plattner, 2002, p. 63)

Habits combine the possibilities of barbarism and civilisation. The United Nations' Millennium Report to commit nations to end malnutrition, to provide safe water, medicines and a healthy environment for future generations, reinforces the ability to think about 'the other'. Commitments to the Declaration of Human Rights, the International Criminal Court – the Kyoto protocol on the environment, all represent the possibilities of civilised habits. Globalisation can be used for the benefit of the world's population, but it requires the political will of governments. In the meantime, the use of pesticides, damage to water supplies, pollution, world poverty, the conditions of migrant workers and the treatment of asylum seekers confirms the barbaric side of present globalisation.

3. Postmodernity

Rengger (1995) highlighted that postmodernity needs to be analysed at two levels; what he calls 'postmodernity as mood' and ' postmodernity as sociocultural form'. Postmodernity as mood seeks to capture a way of thinking. In this later sense, the aim is to show a break with the ways of thinking associated with modernity, where modernity is defined in terms of industrial communities, ideas about divisions of labour scientific management. The postmodern mood can be equally pessimistic and optimistic. The idea of consumer society points to the acquisitive individual and the *me* society of designer labels and a new individualism:

'In the West we already have a society that is probably as happy as any there has ever been. But there is a danger that Me-First may pollute our way of life, now that divine punishment no longer provides the sanction for morality. If that happened, we should all be less happy. So we do need a clear philosophy. The obvious aim is the greatest happiness of all – each person counting for one. If we all really pursued that, we should all be less selfish and we should all be happier'. (Layard, 2003, p. 20)

However, Bauman (1993) has pointed to the new ethics of postmodernity. The potential of the deconstruction of oppression, of bringing hypocrisies into the light, including institutional racism and sexism, the power of bureaucracy and the monopoly power of the knowledge estates professionals:

'The postmodern perspective to which this study refers means above all the tearing off of the mask of illusions, the recognition of certain pretences as false and certain objectives as neither obtainable nor for that matter desirable . . . I suggest that the novelty of the post modern approach to ethics consists first and foremost not in the abandoning of characteristically modern concerns, but the rejection of the typically modern ways of going about its moral problems (that is responding to moral challenges with coercive normative regulation in political; practice) and the philosophical search for absolutes, universals and foundations in theory'. (Bauman, 1993, pp. 3 and 4)

Postmodernity as a sociocultural form leads to institutions, organisations and processes, while postmodernity as a mood, seeks to capture the feeling, the climate and the context. Postmodernity as a sociocultural form is located in the changes to the material aspects of life. Postmodern writers have highlighted the break with the assembly line form of manufacturing and the move towards the knowledge economy, defined by human capital, where the emphasis is not so much on production, but to the selling of concepts, of ideas and the potential shift of power away from the organisation to the knowledgeable individual. The break up of the hierarchical organisation and the move towards the flat organisation depends on knowledge workers. These are the new self-motivated workers who want to be involved in the decision making process, where knowledge continues to be the personal property of the individual and where the organisation depends on individuals sharing their intellectual property.

Contemporary globalisation reinforces diversity and plurality. Governments are no longer pivotal in economic policy making. Globalisation poses a number of challenges, which require coalitions and pluralities of responses. Class, social democracy and trade union resistance reflect one response, but equally there are coalitions that seek to deal with the global exploitation of women, of black people, a new racism, coalitions of environmental and social issues.

POLITICAL RESPONSES

Third Way Politics and Compassionate Conservatism

Giddens (2001) has suggested that the 'Politics of Third Way' and 'Compassionate Conservatism' are the two major political responses to the challenges of globalisation. He defines the Third Way as:

'Third Way thinking is driven by policy innovation and the need to react to social change. The main outlines of the Third Way remain as relevant as they ever were:

the structuring of the state and government to make them more democratic and accountable; a shake-up in welfare systems to bring them more into line with the main risks people face today; a stress upon high levels of job creation, coupled labour market reform, a commitment to fiscal discipline; investment in public services; investment in human capital as crucial to success in the knowledge economy; and the balancing of rights and responsibilities of citizens'. (Giddens, 2001, *The Guardian* 25 April 2003).

Compassionate Conservatism seeks to combine Conservative and Liberal ideologies and the ideas of one nation, an organicist view of society and the dutiful citizen, while at the same time, advocating free markets and greater individualism. Giddens (2001) has described Compassionate Conservatism as a populist revolt against globalisation:

'Compassionate Conservatism may have helped George Bush scrape into power, but is hardly a developed political philosophy. In Europe, the right has been propelled back to government largely on the back of a wave of right-wing populism. This populist revolt everywhere has the same theses. It concerns citizens' anxieties about immigration, multiculturalism and crime; it is anti-establishment, reflecting disquiet about orthodox democratic mechanisms. It taps into worries about loss of national identity in the EU and more generally about the impact of globalisation'. (Giddens, 2001)

The Blair Government, during the election campaign of June 2001, proposed putting additional resources into health and education, more people in employment, the minimum wage, increased child benefits and reducing poverty. Between 1979 and 1997, poverty doubled in Britain. Using a definition of poverty at a level of 60 per cent of median income, the experiences of the Thatcher years were: major increases in child poverty as the government failed to update child benefit, a decline in real wages and an increase in poverty, even for those who were in work. The Prime Minister Tony Blair in a key speech in January 1998 wanted to make sure that the Labour Government would make the eradication of poverty the priority during a second term:

'The last Government let poverty re-gain its hold on Britain, to an extent unseen since before the last war. To put that right we now face a task of reconstruction as intense as the one that faced the post-war Labour Government and that's why we need an anti-poverty strategy of the same ambition and breadth'.

At the 2001 win election, Labour pledged to eradicate child poverty. The Labour Government has increased child benefits, introduced a minimum wage and also established a Family Tax credit. Labour's ambition is to eradicate child poverty over a decade. When Labour came to office in 1997, the UK had the highest levels of child poverty in Europe. The commitment to reduce child poverty will put the UK at a similar level to Sweden and Norway. Blair claimed that he had returned Britain to collectivist values and that the Thatcher Revolution was over:

> 'There are 16 000 more nurses and midwives in the NHS than in 1997–98. But we need 20 000 more. The NHS plan provides them by 2004, plus 7500 more consultants, at least 2000 more GPs and over 6500 other health professionals. There are 7500 more teachers than in 1997–98. Infant class sizes of more than 30 have been virtually abolished. Some of this has already happened. Some is in the future. But the point is: we only have the money to invest because the economy is strong. And that investment can now be sustained if we choose to do it and if we don't blow the economic stability and the surplus in a short-term boom or bust'. (Prime Minister Tony Blair's Speech on 19 January 2002)

Third Way politics is described as being against ideology. The emphasis is looking for those policies that work, leaving all options open. Debates of state and market, left and right are described as being redundant. In the globalised world the priority is to construct policies that respond to the challenges of change. Globalisation is described as an external event and the role of government is to provide a policy framework that responds to that event. The challenge for progressive government is to create the knowledge economy where the role of government is to invest in human capital. Policy response needs to reflect diversity, which means blurring the divides between government and markets. The Private Finance Initiative (PFI) is to be welcomed because private finance makes possible the building of more hospitals and more schools, which in turn benefit the community.

However, as argued in previous chapters, globalisation is and continues to be the outcome of political choices and constraints. It is therefore misleading to define globalisation as being an exogenous event, since it is shaped by policy choices, but also the recognition of limits on the political autonomy of governments. Globalisation is therefore more like the ebbing and flowing of a tide defined by politics and globalised economic events, which are defined as being outside the control of political accountability. While governments might not have complete political autonomy and choice neither are they prisoners of the global context.

Policy making is a compromise between political autonomy and events. Political autonomy can be defined as being political choice, political arithmetic and political judgements. By contrast, globalisation as event, represents the constraints both of economic events. Political elites in developing countries very often argue the case that their policy agenda is being forced on them by the IMF and the World Bank, in the knowledge that there trade-offs between reducing social spending on health-care programmes and primary education, while maintaining expenditure on the military, civil servants and subsidies to strategic business interests. The concept of political choice questions the views that policy outcomes are the inevitable outcomes of constraints. Within the context of external constraints, including the IMF and World Bank adjustment programmes, there are a number of policy choices. Defining policy choice depends on how the external environment is being defined and interpreted.

In his inaugural speech as the 43rd President of the USA, George W. Bush promised to create a policy framework that emphasised the commitment for his vision of compassionate conservatism:

'America, at its best, is compassionate. In the quiet of American conscience, we know that deep, persistent poverty is unworthy of our nation's promise. And whatever our views of its cause, we can agree that children at risk are not at fault. Abandonment and abuse are not acts of God, they are failures of love. Government has great responsibilities for public safety and public health, for civil rights and common schools. Yet compassion is the work of a nation, not just a government. Many in our country do not know the pain of poverty, but we can listen to those who do. And I can pledge our nation to a goal: When we see that wounded traveller on the road to Jericho, we will not pass to the other side'. (President George W. Bush, The Inauguration Speech, as reported in *The Washington Post*, Sunday, 21 January 2001)

However, there are differences between the rhetoric of policy statements and policy substance. In his determination to reduce taxation and give electors their money back, the George Bush budget strategies of 2001 and 2003 have ensured that the top 1 per cent of earners received the highest tax reduction:

'In 2003, there will be 184,000 millionaires comprising 0.1 percent of households. Millionaires would receive average tax cuts of about $93,500 this year, far in excess of those received by other groups. The middle fifth of households would receive tax cuts averaging $217 in 2003. Millionaires would experience the largest after-tax income increases of any group. The share of the individual income tax cuts received by millionaires (27 per cent) also significantly exceeds the share of income taxes they pay (19 per cent)'. ('Millionaires and the ways and means tax plan centre on budget and policy priorities', Shapiro, 2003).

The Bush administration has not signed the Kyoto protocols on the control of emissions, has not pursued the policy of debt relief for developing countries and has not agreed to contribute to 0.7 per cent of GDP for international aid and development. Instead, the Government has reinforced the concept of the Washington consensus at both the World Bank and the IMF. The British Conservative Party makes pledges to reduce taxation, but also argues that they can provide better quality public services through a mixed economy of welfare, more privatisation of services, better managed public-private partnerships and more de-centralised decision making:

'For too long in this country we have been locked into a sterile debate. We have been told that there were only two choices. Either we have higher taxes or better public services or we have lower taxes and worse public services. Yet what we had had for the past four years is higher taxes and worse services. We will have a situation in which sclerosis in the unreformed public services will ultimately lead to sclerosis in the economy as a whole' (Iain Duncan Smith, Conservative Leader Speech, CBI Conference, 6 November 2001).

Both the politics of Third Way and Compassionate Conservatism accept that governments will continue to be involved in the public provision of health, education and social security. At the same time, both ideologies also accept the need for competitive labour markets and implicitly higher levels of income inequalities. The politics of the Third Way seeks to embrace the logic of markets, the idea of individualism and income inequalities. The aim is no longer to replace the market, but rather to show that the politics of the Third Way can create stability for free markets. Equally, compassionate conservatives recognise the need to do more about social exclusion, poverty, prescription drugs for the elderly and better coverage of health insurance for those on low income, while at the same seeking to de-regulate labour markets, social provision and environment policy.

The Third Way and Compassionate Conservatism are both organicist, in the sense that they both seek to provide arguments for community and identity in the context of globalisation. Prime Minister Blair has on many occasions argued that the Third Way is not concerned with equality. Inequality reflects different rewards for different talents and endowments. Inequality can therefore be legitimised. The politics of the Third Way is about improving the life of the poor through targeting and focused social policies, including initiatives such as New Start, the Social Exclusion Unit, Education and Health Action Zones and Employment Action Zones. The concern of the Third Way is therefore not inequality, but social justice and opportunity. Social security is to be targeted at those in need, a safety net, rather than universal commitment to social citizenship. The concern is the inclusion of those defined as being the excluded.

CONCLUSIONS

Contemporary globalisation is associated with a new individualism. However, globalisation points to a 'massive blindness' and an increasing gap between actions and consequences. There is a lack of connections between economic growth and the environment and between growth and income inequalities. Future generations have no guarantees about what sort of earth they shall inherit. They have no vote and no voice. Present generations seem to claim the rights to use all existing resources. There are equally disconnections between rich and poor countries:

'What is worse, the atomist outlook which instrumentalism fosters makes people unaware of these conditions, so that they happily support policies which undermine them – as to the recent rash of neo-conservative measures in Britain and the United States which cut welfare programmes and repressively redistribute income thus eroding the bases of community identification. Atomism has befogged our awareness of the connection between the act and consequences in society that the same people who by their mobile and growth oriented way of life have greatly increased the tasks of the public sector are the loudest to protest paying their share of the costs of fulfilling them'. (Taylor, 1994, p. 505)

There is therefore a gap between actions and consequences. Electors vote for political parties that promise tax reductions, but these actions do not spell out the consequences of such a policy. Reducing taxes erodes the government's tax base, which means that governments have less income to finance public services. In his campaign for a new package of tax reductions George W. Bush has argued that his package will create an additional 1.4 million jobs.

Since 2001, some 3 million jobs have been lost in the USA. Critics of President Bush have pointed to the fiscal crisis of many states faced with large budget deficits where the policy is resulting in laying off redundant public sector workers, closing public amenities such as parks, libraries and zoos, children learning in dilapidated schools. While capital expenditure on schools increased during the years 1992–2000 from 7.6 per cent of school expenditure, to 9.9 per cent; 50 per cent of school building continue to be in poor shape. Since 1995, states have continued to reduce personal taxes to a total of some US$36 billion. The problem is that with economic slowdown, revenues have now continued to decline more rapidly so that states have had to resort to reducing expenditure on education and Medicaid, which mainly benefits about 43 million people in the USA who do not have health insurance. Medicaid amounts to about 20 per cent of state expenditures:

'as a nation we're about to reduce spending on basic needs like education, health care and infrastructure by at least $100 billion, maybe more. And these spending cuts – the result of the fiscal crisis of the states – amount to a job destruction program bigger than any likely positive effects of the Bush tax cut . . . states are withdrawing health care for the poor and mentally ill. They are also dismissing state troopers, closing parks and schools, dropping bus routes, eliminating college scholarships and slashing a host of other services. Not to mention unscrewing every third light bulb in Missouri government offices . . . So if the administration really cared about jobs, it would provide an emergency package of aid to state governments – not to pay for new spending, but simply to maintain basic services. How about $78 billion – the same sum just allocated for the Iraq war?'. (Krugman, 'Jobs, jobs, jobs', *The New York Times* 22 April 2003)

However, tax reductions are not costed in terms of what services will stop and therefore, what people will have to buy with their tax reduction. Tax reductions are politically popular. The implication that the tax reduction has to be used for buying private health insurance or private pensions, e.g. is however never spelt out. Furthermore, those who vote for the tax reductions are also voting for lower public provision for those groups of people who do not benefit from the tax reduction, but actually experience hardships when eligibility to health care or education are reduced, to pay for the tax reductions. The third gap relates to those who think they will benefit from the tax reduction, but actually also end up being losers. The modern economy seems to require increased government intervention, including the caring of the elderly, dealing with environmental problems, public transport and making provision in higher education. Paying for these services through government must always be cheaper and more effective than individual insurance.

There seems to be a paradox between the emphasis on individualism and the increased influence of multinational corporations, bureaucracy and expert knowledge. The attempt to increase individual choice by placing more emphasis on competitive markets has resulted in day-to-day risks becoming individualised experiences, where insecurity and risk become a personal issue rather than a public concern. Unemployment is attributed to individual risk in terms of individual investment in education and training in the right skills. Risks are experienced as a series of individualised decisions.

> 'Individualisation in this sense means that each person's biography is removed from given determinations and placed in his own hands, open and dependent on decisions. The proportion of life opportunities are fundamentally closed to decision-making is decreasing and the proportion of the biography, which is open and must be constructed personally, is increasing. ... In the individualised society the individual must therefore learn, on pain of permanent disadvantage to conceive of himself or herself at the centre of action'. (Beck, 1994, p. 135)

The Role of Government

Public policy has been a major mechanism, which governments have utilised to re-distribute resources between individuals. Public provision of services and the financing of public services have been central to reducing income inequality and poverty. Economic growth does not necessarily result in the alleviation of poverty. The period from 1960 to 1980 has been referred to as the Golden Age. Continuous employment, increased expenditures on social policies and growing disposable income were essential in combating poverty. It was the era of the growth state, of growing private and public consumption. By contrast, the years 1980 to 2000 were associated with the Leaden Age of globalisation (Krugman, 2002). Economic growth has been slower; there have been sharp increases in unemployment and a decline in the incomes of those in work. During the Golden Age, the incomes of people in Latin America and the Caribbean increased by 75 per cent, while between 1980 and 2000, incomes increased by 15 per cent. On the African Continent, incomes increased by 34 per cent during the Golden Age and then fell by 15 per cent between 1980 and 2000. The problem of mass unemployment seems to have returned to some countries in Europe. The dilemma of low economic growth, together with the high costs of social security, has resulted in re-trenchment in areas of public provision. Rifkin (1995) has argued that the new knowledge economy will not result in any trickle down effects, but instead will create a small number of jobs for the elites who will be highly paid, leaving large numbers who are either low paid or unemployed:

> 'Whether a Utopian or Dystopian future awaits us depends, to a great measure, on how the productivity gains of the Information Age are distributed. A fair and equitable distribution of the productivity gains would require a shortening of the work-week around the world and a concerted effort by central governments to provide alternative employment in the third sector – the social economy . . . if, however the dramatic gains of the high-tech revolution are not shared, but rather used primarily to enhance corporate profits, to the exclusive benefit of stockholders, top corporate managers and the emerging elite of high tech knowledge workers, chances are that the growing gap between haves and the have-nots will lead to social and political upheaval on a global scale'. (Rifkin, 1995, p. 13)

Continuity

The policy strategy of continuity is founded on the argument that science, rationality and the project of the Enlightenment continue to be essential in the unfolding history of human progress. The argument for continuity is implicitly an optimistic interpretation of human progress. It is an argument, which says that present challenges are not that different from other challenges. Problems are usually dealt with incrementally, with changes at the margin and those changes tend to be experienced as evolution, rather than a series of radical breaks or watersheds.

The continuity argument therefore rejects the view that something radical is happening. The challenges of resources, citizenship ecology, political legitimacy and justice are challenges of continuity and process, since they represent voyages of discovery, rather than forces which confirm that life will be qualitatively different to that of the previous 50 years. The globalised economy is not that new. It is part of a historical legacy. The new globalisation of technology and communications make connections that much easier. The majority of the world population will continue to struggle to make a living, but indicators on life expectancy, literacy food and illness confirm the capacity for humanity to continue to progress. In the context of globalisation, governments will continue to be central in being the public space where issues of globalisation overspill.

Discontinuity

Toulmin (1992) and MacIntyre (1981) have argued that the Enlightenment 'took a wrong turn' in the seventeenth century, by concentrating too much on a narrow view of humanity. The ethics of instrumentalism, rationality, ideas of utility and individualism have all contributed to a uni-dimensional view of human nature. By contrast, as suggested earlier, postmodern ethics point to openness, to fragmentation and dislocation, the break with the oppressions of false consensus and homogeneity. The word of the experts is no longer taken for granted. Increasingly, science, expertise and professional knowledge are perceived as falling into disrepute. The crisis in health care, the loss of confidence in the medical profession, in teachers and ecology, confirm the limits of science and the undermining of trust in expertise.

The challenges of present globalisation are defined as being qualitatively different to those of the last 200 years. Economic growth has not increased happiness – growth might have resulted in more leisure opportunities, but it has also contributed to stress, pollution and environmental degradation. The disparities of incomes continue to widen and the lived experience between rich and poor is not that different than that of 100 years ago. Postmodernity challenges conventional views of progress and civilisation.

Between these visions of continuity and discontinuity, a number of overlapping themes seem to be emerging. Both arguments have a specific view of the individual. To the Enlightenment, the individual is central because the Enlightenment is intrinsically connected with the language of universal rights, freedom and the preservation of dignity. By contrast, postmodern arguments point to fragmentation to diversity and plurality implicitly resists the views of universalism. Postmodernity points to new ethics that seek to make transparent issues of hidden hypocrisy and hidden power relations.

Continuity arguments point to the need for creating a rational response to the globalised economy, by creating a global form of governance that will make the spaces for the accountability of the global economy. By contrast, postmodernity points to discontinuity, arguing that global governance will create new oligarchy that will legitimatise the politics and the economics of globalisation. Rather than global governance, postmodernity emphasises the pluralities of coalitions at the local, national and international levels. The globalised economy does not require a 'one response fits all' approach, but rather separate responses at the various levels of people's lived experiences.

References

Agosin, M. and R. Mayer (2000), 'Foreign Investment in Developing Countries', discussion paper No. 145, UNCTAD, Geneva, Switzerland.

Andersen, J. and P. Jensen (2001), *Changing Labour Markets Welfare Policies and Citizenship*, Bristol: Policy.

Amoore, L. (2000), 'Overturning "globalisation" resisting teleology, reclaiming politics', in B.K. Gills (ed.), *Globalisation and the Politics of Resistance*, Basingstoke: Palgrave, MacMillan, pp. 12–28.

Anderson, B. (1991), *Imagined Communities*, London: Verso.

Arestis, P. and M. Sawyer (2003), 'European integration and the "Euro project" ', in J. Michie (ed.), *Handbook of Globalisation*, Cheltenham, UK and Northampton, MA, USA: Edward Elgar.

Arblaster, A. (1987), *Democracy*, Milton Keynes: Open University Press.

Arendt, H. (1951), *The Origins of Totalitarianism*, New York: Harcourt.

Arunda, M. (2000), *External Debt: Brazil and the International Financial Crisis*, London: Pluto Press.

Atkinson, A. (1996), *Equity Issues in a Globalizing World: The Experience of OECD Countries*, Washington DC: IMF.

Atkinson, A. (1998), 'Is rising inequality unavoidable? a critique of the Transatlantic Consensus', WIDER Annual Lecture No. 3, WIDER, Helsinki.

Atkinson, A. (2002) 'Is rising inequality unavoidable', in P. Townsend and D. Gordon (eds), *World Poverty: New Policies to Defeat an Old Enemy*, Bristol: The Polity Press, pp. 12–31.

Bader, V.M. (ed.) (1997), *Citizenship and Exclusion*, Basingstoke: Macmillan.

Baqir, R. (2002), 'Social sector spending in a panel of countries', IMF working paper 02/35, Washington DC.

Barber, B.R. (1996), *Jihad vs McWorld: How Globalism and Tribalism are Reshaping the World*, New York: Ballantine Books.

Barber, B.R. (2000), *A Passion for Democracy: American Essays*, Princeton, NJ: Princeton University Press.

Barro, R. (1996), 'Democracy and growth', *Journal of Economic Growth*, **1** (91), 1–27.

Bauman, Z. (1992), *Imitations of Postmodernity*, London: Routledge.

Bauman, Z. (1993), *Postmodern Ethics*, Oxford: Blackwell.

Bauman, Z. (1995), *Life in Fragments: Essay in Postmodern Morality*, Oxford: Blackwell.

Bauman, Z. (2000), *In Search of Politics*, Oxford: Polity Press.

Bealey, F. (1988), *Democracy in the Contemporary State*, Oxford: Clarendon Press.

Beck, U. (1994), *Risk Society: Towards a New Modernity*, London: Sage.

Beck, U. (2000a), 'Living your own life in a runaway world', in W. Hutton and A. Giddens (ed.), *On The Edge: Living with Global Capitalism*, London: Jonathan Cape, pp. 164–74.

Beck, U. (2000b), *The Brave New World of Work*, Cambridge: Polity Press.

Beck, U. (2000c), *What is Globalisation?*, Cambridge: Polity Press.

Beck, U., A. Giddens and S. Lash (1994), *Reflexive Modernization: Politics, Tradition and Aesthetics in the Modern Social Order*, Oxford: Polity Press.

Beer, S.H. (1982), *Britain Against Itself: The Political Contradictions of Collectivism*, London: Faber and Faber.

Beetham, D. (1993), 'Liberal democracy and the limits of democratisation', in D. Held (ed.), *Prospects for Democracy*, Oxford: Polity Press, pp. 53–73.

Beetham, D. (ed.) (1994), *Defining and Measuring Democracy*, London: Sage.

Beetham, D. (1999), *Democracy and Human Rights*, Cambridge: Polity Press.

Benhabib, S. (1992), *Situating The Self: Gender, Community and Postmodernism in Contemporary Ethics*, Oxford: Polity Press.

Benyon, J. and D. Dunkerley (eds) (1999), *The Globalisation Reader*, London: Athlone.

Bernstein, R.J. (1991), *The New Constellation: The Ethical-Political Horizons of Modernity/Postmodernity*, Cambridge: Polity Press.

Bhagwati, J. (2002), 'Globalisation and appropriate governance', The 2000 WIDER Annual Lecture, Helsinki, http://www.wider.unu.educ.

Blackburn, R. (ed.) (1990), *Restructuring the Labour Market*, London: MacMillan.

Bickford, S. (1997), *Anti-Anti Identity Politics: Feminism, Democracy and the Complexities of Citizenship*, London: Hypatia.

Blackhurst, R. (1997), 'The capacity of the WTO to fulfil its mandate', in A. Krieger (ed.), *The WTO as an International Organisation*, Chicago: University of Chicago Press, pp. 87–104.

Blank, R.M. (1994), *Social Protection versus Market Flexibility*, Chicago, University of Chicago Press.

Blank, R.M. (2000), 'Fighting poverty: lessons from recent US history', *Journal of Economic Perspectives*, **14**, 3–19.

Blitz, J. (2003), 'Leap of faith', *The Financial Times Magazine*, Issue No 1.

Blumenberg, H. (1995), *The Legitimacy of the Modern Age*, London: MIT Press.

Bobbio, R. (1987), *The Future of Democracy*, Oxford: Polity Press.

Boggs, C. (2000), *The End of Politics; Corporate Power and the Decline of the Public Sphere*, London: The Guildford Press.

Bowles, G. and Wesskopf, J. (1983), *Beyond the Wasteland, A Democratic Alternative to Economic Decline*, London: Verso.

Bowles, S. and H. Gintis (1986), *Democracy and Capitalism: Property, Community and the Contradictions of Modern Social Thought*, London: Routledge and Kegan Paul.

Boyarin, D. and J. Boyarin (1993), 'Diaspora: generational ground of Jewish identity', *Critical Inquiry*, **19** (4), 693–725.

Boyte, H. (1993), 'Reinventing citizenship', *The Kettering Review*, http://www.public-work.org.

Brandt, W. (1980), 'North-South a programme for survival', *Brandt Report*, London: Pan.

Brecher, J. et al. (1993), *Global Visions: Beyond the New World Order*, Boston: South End Press.

Brecher, J. and T. Costello (1995), *Globalisation From Below*, Cambridge: Boston Press.

Bridges, T. (1994), *The Culture of Citizenship: Inventing Postmodern Civic Culture*, New York: State University of New York Press.

Brinkley, J. (1998), *Liberalism and Its Discontents*, Cambridge: Harvard University Press.

Brittan, S. (1977), *The Economic Consequences of Democracy*, London: Maurice Temple Smith.

Brittan, S. (1988), *A Restatement of Economic Liberalism*, London: MacMillan.

Bronner, E. (ed.) (1997), *Twentieth Century Political Theory – A Reader*, London: Routledge.

Brosman, P. (2003), 'The minimum wage in a global context', in J. Michie (ed.), *The Handbook of Globalisation*, Cheltenham, UK and Northampton, MA, USA: Edward Elgar.

Brown, B.S. (1991), *The US and the Politicization of the World Bank*, London: Kegan Paul.

Bulmer, M. and A.M. Rees (eds) (1996), *Citizenship Today: The Contemporary Relevance of T.H. Marshall*, London: UCL Press.

Burgess, S., K. Gardiner and C. Prooper (2001), 'Why rising tides don't lift all boats', CASE discussion paper No. 46, London School of Economics, London.

Bussemaker, J. (ed.) (1999), *Citizenship and State Welfare in Europe*, London: Routledge.

Butcher, H. (ed.) (1993), *Community and Public Policy*, London: Pluto Press.

Cardoso, F. (2001), 'Democracy as a starting point', *Journal of Democracy*, **12** (1), 5–14.

Carnoy, M. (ed.) (1993), *The New Global Economy in the Information Age: Reflections on a Changing World*, Pennsylvania: Pennsylvania State University Press.

Carter, A. and G. Stokes (ed.) (2002), *Democratic Theory Today: Challenges for the 21st Century*, Cambridge: Polity Press.

Castels, S. and A. Davidson (eds) (2000), *Citizenship and Immigration: Globalisation and the Politics of Belonging*, Basingstoke: MacMillan.

Castells, M. (1997), *The Information Age: Economy, Society and Culture*, Oxford: Blackwell.

Castells, M. (2000), *End of Millennium*, Oxford: Blackwell Publishers.

Centre for Public Integrity (2004), 'The water barons', http://www.store.publicintegrity.org.

Centre for Responsive Politics (2003), 'Rebuilding Iraq – the contractors', http://www.opensecrets.org/news, 28 April, 2003.

CEPR (1999), 'The Full Monty', *European Economic Perspectives*, **2**, 5–6.

Cerny, P. (1996), 'What's next for the State?', in E. Kofman and G. Youngs (eds), *Globalization: Theory and Practice*, London: Pinter.

Cesarini, D. and M. Fulbrook (1996), *Citizenship, Nationality and Migration in Europe*, London: Routledge.

Christian Aid (2003), 'Too hot to handle? The absence of trade from PRSPs', http://christian-aid.org.uk/indepth/0304toohot/intro.htm.

Clark, T. (2001), 'The limits of social democracy? Tax and spend under Labour 1974–79', IFS working paper 01/04, London, http://www.ifs.org.uk.

Clement, B. (1997), 'Income distribution and social expenditure in Brazil', IMF working paper 97/120, Washington DC.

Clifford, J. (1997), *Routes: Travel and Translation in the late 20th Century*, London: Harvard University Press.

Coates, D. (2000), *Models of Capitalism: Growth and Stagnation in the Modern Era*, Oxford: Polity Press.

Congressional Budget Office (2001), 'Historical effective rates 1979–1997', http://www/cbo.gov, May.

Connolly, W.E. (1983), *The Terms of Political Discourse*, Oxford: Martin Robertson.

Connolly, W.E. (1991, 1994), *Identity/Difference: Democratic Negotiations of Political Paradox*, Ithaca, US and London, UK: Cornell University Press.

Corbacho, A. and G. Schwarz (2002), 'Mexico: experiences with pro poor policies', IMF working paper, Washington DC, January.

Cornia, G.A. and S. Kiiski (2001), 'Trends in income distribution in the post-World War II period', UNU/WIDER discussion paper No. 89, Helsinki.

Cornia G.A. and S. Reddy (2001), 'The impact of adjustment related social funds on income distribution and poverty', WIDER discussion paper No. 1, UNU/WIDER, Helsinki.

Corporate Europe Observatory (2001), 'TABD in troubled water', http://www.corporateeurope.org.

Craypo, C. and F. Wilkinson (2003), 'The low road to competitive failure – immigrant labour and emigrant jobs in the USA', in J. Michie (ed.), *The Handbook of Globalisation*, Cheltenham, UK and Northampton, MA, USA: Edward Elgar.

Crick, B. (2000), *Essays on Citizenship*, New York: Continuum.

Crouch, C. and W. Streeck (1998), *Political Economy of Modern Capitalism: Mapping Out Convergence and Diversity*, London: Sage.

Dahl, R.A. (1989), *Democracy and its Critics*, London: Yale University Press.

Dahl, R.A. (2000), *On Democracy*, London: Yale University Press.

Dahrendorf, R. (1988), *The Modern Social Conflict: An Essay on Political Liberty*, London: Weidenfeld and Nicholson.

Danford, A. (1998), *Japanese Management Techniques and British Workers*, New York: Mansell.

Dancher, K. and R. Burbirch (eds) (2000), *Globalise This: The Battle Against the WTO and Corporate Rule*, Monroe, Maine: Cornia Coverage Press.

Danziger, S. and P. Gottschalk (eds) (1993), *Uneven Tides: Rising Inequalities in America*, New York: Russell Sage Foundation.

Davidson, A. (2000), 'Democracy, class and citizenship in a globalising world', in A. Vandenberg (ed.), *Citizenship and democracy in a Global Era*, London: MacMillan Press.

Deacon, B. with M. Hulse and P. Stubbs (1997), *Global Social Policy*, London: Sage.

Denninger, K. and L. Squire (1998), 'New ways at looking at old issues, inequality and growth', *Journal of Economic Development*, **57**, 259–287.

Department of Social Security (1999), *Households Below Average Income 1979–1998*, London: The Stationery Office.

Desai, A. (2002), *We are the Poors: Community Struggles in Post Apartheid South Africa*, London: Monthly Review Press.

Dicken, P. (1999), *Global Shift: Transforming the World Economy*, London: Paul Chapman Publishing.

Dixon, J. and J. Macarov (1998), *Poverty: A Persistent Global Reality*, London: Routledge.

Dollar, D. and A. Kraay (2001), *Growth is Good for the Poor*, Washington DC: World Bank, http://worldbank/research.

Dollar, D. and P. Collier (2001), *Globalisation Growth and Poverty: Building An Inclusive World Economy*, Oxford: Oxford University Press.

Doyal, L. and I. Gough (1991), *A Theory of Human Needs*, London: MacMillan.

Drew, E. (2000), *The Corruption of American Politics: What Went Wrong and Why*, London: New York Press.

Dunn, J. (2001), *The Cunning of Unreason: Making Sense of Politics*, London: HarperCollins.

Eatwell, J. (1998), *Understanding Globalisation*, Stockholm: Swedish Ministry for Foreign Affairs.

Eatwell, J. and L. Taylor (2000), *Global Finance and Risk: The Case for International Regulation*, Oxford: Polity Press.

Economic Commission for Latin America and the Caribbean (ECLAC) (1997), 'The Equity Gap', Latin America, the Caribbean and the Social Summit, March.

Edelman, M. (1977), *Political Language:Words that Succeed and Policies that Fail*, London: Academic Press.

Edwards, R. and J. Glover (eds) (2001), *Risks and Citizenship*, London: Routledge.

Eistenstein, Z. (1989), *The Female Body and the Law*, Berkeley: University of California Press.

Elgin, P. (2002), 'Controlling corruption: a key to development-orientated trade', Carnegie Endowment for International Peace, November, Issue No. 4.

Epstein, G. (2003), 'The role and control of multi-national corporations in the Global Economy', in J. Michie (ed.) (2003), *The Handbook of Globalisation*, Cheltenham, UK and Northampton, MA, USA: Edward Elgar.

Esping-Andersen, G. (1996a), *The Three Worlds of Welfare Capitalism*, Cambridge: Polity Press.

Esping-Andersen, G. (1996b), *Welfare States in Transition, National Adaptations in Global Economies*, London: Sage.

Faulks, K. (2000), *Citizenship*, London: Routledge.

Featherstone, M. (1990), *Globe Culture: Globalisation and Modernity*, London: Sage.

Foreman-Peck, J. (1995), *A History of the World Economy: International Economic Relations since 1850*, New York: Harvester Wheatsheaf.

Forrester, V. (1999), *The Economic Horror*, Oxford: Polity Press.

Foucault, M. (1975), *Discipline and Punish: The Birth of the Prison*, Harmondsworth: Penguin

Foucault, M. (1986), 'Disciplinary power and subjection', in S. Lukes (ed.), *Power*, Oxford: Blackwell.

Friedman, M. (1962), *Capitalism and Freedom*, Chicago: University of Chicago Press.

Friedman, T. (1999), *The Lexus and the Olive Tree*, New York: Farrrar, Strauss and Giroux.

Galbraith, J.K. (1986), 'Power and organisation', in S. Lukes S (ed.), *Power*, Oxford: Blackwell.

Galbraith, J. K. (1992), *The Culture of Contentment*, Harmondsworth: Penguin Books, Harmondsworth.

George, S. (1988), *A Fate Worse Than Debt: a Radical Analysis of the Third World Debt Crisis*, London: Penguin.

George, S. (1992), *The Debt Boomerang*, London: Pluto Press.

George, V. and Taylor Gooby P. (eds) (1996), *European Welfare Policy: Squaring the Welfare Circle*, Basingstoke: Macmillan.

Giddens, A. (1993), *Modernity and Self Identity: Self and Society in the Late Modern Age*, Oxford: Polity Press.

Giddens, A. (1995), *Beyond The Left and Right*, Stanford: Stanford University Press.

Giddens, A. (1999), *Runaway World: How Globalisation is Reshaping Our Lives*, London: Profile.

Giddens, A. (ed.) (2001), *The Global Third Way Debate*, Oxford: Polity Press.

Gills, B.K. (ed.) (2000), *Globalisation and the Politics of Resistance*, Basingstoke: Palgrave, MacMillan.

Gilroy, P. (1987), *There Ain't No Black in the Union Jack, The Cultural Politics of Race and Nation*, London: Hutchinson.

Gilroy, P. (1993), *The Black Atlantic Double Consciousness and Modernity*, London: Harvard University Press.

Ginsburg, N. (1992), *Divisions of Welfare*, London: Sage.

Glennister, H. (2000), 'US poverty studies and measurements: the last 20 years', CASE discussion paper No, 42, London School of Economics, London.

Glyn, A. and B. Sutcliffe (1992), 'Global but leaderless', in R. Miliband and L. Panitch (eds), *The Socialist Register*, pp. 76–95.

Goodman, A. and S. Webb (1994), *For Richer for Poorer: The Changing Distribution of Income in Britain*, London: Institute of Fiscal Studies.

Gorjanicyn, K. (2000), 'Citizenship and culture in contemporary France extreme right interventions', in A Vanderberg (ed.), *Citizenship and Democracy in a Global Era*, Basingstoke: MacMillan.

Gough, I. (1979), *The Political Economy of the Welfare State*, London: MacMillan.

Gould, C.C. (1990), *Rethinking Democracy*, Cambridge: Cambridge University Press.

Gould, C.C. and P. Paquino (2001), *Culture Identity and the Nation State*, Lanham, MD: Rowman.

Gray, J. (1991), *Liberalisms: Essays in Political Philosophy*, London: Routledge.

Gray, J. (1998), 'False dawn, the delusion of global capitalism', New York: The New Press.

Gregg, P. and J. Wadsworth (eds) (1999), *The State of Working Britain*, Manchester: Manchester University Press.

Grieve Smith, J. (1997), *Full Employment: A Pledge Betrayed*, London: MacMillan.

Gross, M.L. (1996), *The Political Racket: Deceit, Self Interest and Corruption in American Politics*, New York: Ballantine Books.

Gupta, S., M. Verhoeven and E. Tiongson (2001), 'Public spending on health care and the poor', IMF working paper 01/27, Washington DC.

Habermas, J. (1975), *Legitimation Crisis*, Boston, MA: Beacon Press.

Habermas, J. (1984), *The Theory of Communicative Action*, Vol. 1, Boston, MA: Beacon Press.

Habermas, J. (1987), *The Philosophical Discourse of Modernity*, Cambridge: Cambridge University Press.

Hannerz, U. (1990), 'Cosmopolitans and locals in world culture', in M. Featherstone (ed.), *Globe Culture: Globalisation and Modernity*, London: Sage, pp. 237–252.

Hansen, R. (1999), 'Against social solidarity and citizenship: justifying social provisionin Britain and France', in J. Bussemaker (ed.) (1990), *Citizenship and State Welfare in Europe*, London: Routledge.

Hayward, S.F. (2001), *The Age of Reagan: The Fall of the Old Liberal Order 1964–1980*, California: Prima Publishing.

Havel, V. (1990), *Disturbing the Peace*, London: Faber and Faber.

Hayek, F.A. (1944), *Road to Serfdom*, London: Routledge and Kegan Paul.

Hayek, F.A. (1982), *Law, Legislation and Liberty*, London: Routledge and Kegan Paul.

Held, D. (1999), 'The transformation of political community: Rethinking democracy in the context of globalisation', in I. Shapiro and C. Hacker-Cordon (eds), *Democracy's Edges*, Cambridge: Cambridge University Press.

Held, D. (1993), *Prospects for Democracy*, Oxford: Polity Press.

Held, D. (ed.) (1991), *Political Theory Today*, Oxford: Polity Press.

Held, D. and C. Pollitt (ed.) (1996), *New Forms of Democracy*, London: Sage.

Held, D., A. McGrew, D. Goldblatt and J. Perraton (2000), *Global Transformations: Politics, Economics and Culture*, Cambridge: Polity Press.

Heller, A. (1990), *Can Modernity Survive?*, Oxford: Polity Press.

Heller, A. and F. Feher (1988), *The Postmodern Political Condition*, Oxford: Polity Press.

Helleiner, G. (2000), 'Markets politics and globalisation: can the global economy be civilised?', UNCTAD 10th Raul Prebeisch Memorial Lecture, UNCTAD New York: United Nations Publications, http://www.unctad.org/en/docs/prebeisch.

Heller, A. (1990), *Can Modernity Survive?*, Oxford: Polity Press.

Hertz, N. (2001), *The Silent Takeover, Global Capitalism and the Death of Democracy*, London: William Heineman.

Herz, J. (1951), *Political Realism and Political Idealism*, Chicago: University of Chicago Press.

Hills, J. (ed.) (1996), *New Inequalities: The Changing Distribution of Income and Wealth in the UK*, Cambridge: Cambridge University Press.

Hills, J. (2000), 'Taxation and the enabling state', CASE discussion paper No. 41, London School of Economics, London.

Hindess, B. (1993), 'Citizenship in the modern West', in B. Turner (ed.), *Citizenship and Social Theory*, London: Sage.

Hines, C. (2003), 'Time to replace globalisation with localisation', in J. Michie (ed.), *The Handbook of Globalisation*, Cheltenham, UK and Northampton, MA, USA: Edward Elgar.

Hirschman, A. (1970), *Exit, Voice and Loyalty*, Cambridge: Harvard University Press.

Hirst, P. (1998), *How Global is Globalisation and where does the UK fit in?*, London: Goldsmith College.

Hirst, P. and G. Thompson (1999), *Globalisation in Question: The International Economy and the Possibility of Governance*, second edition. Cambridge: Polity Press.

Hirst, P. and G. Thompson (2003), 'The future of globalization', in J. Michie (ed.), *Handbook of Globalisation*, Cheltenham, UK and Northampton, MA, USA: Edward Elgar.

HMSO (2000), 'Eliminating world poverty: making globalisation work for the poor', White Paper on International Development, Cm 5006, London: HMSO.

Hobsbawm, E.J. (1979), *Labouring Men: Studies in the History of Labour*, London: Weidenfield and Nicholson.

Hobsbawm, E.J. (1995), *The Age of Extremes: The Short Twentieth Century*, London: Abacus.

Holden, B. (1988), *Understanding Liberal Democracy*, Oxford: Phillip Allan.

Holstein, W.J. (1990), 'The stateless corporation', *Business Weekly*, 14 May, pp. 98–100.

Honig, B.(1993), *Political Theory and the Displacement of Politics*, London: Cornell University Press.

Horsman, M. and A. Marshall (1994), *After the Nation State: Citizens, Tribalism and the New World Disorder*, London: HarperCollins.

Hutton, W. and A. Giddens (ed.) (2000), *On The Edge: Living with Global Capitalism*, London: Jonathan Cape.

IATP (2003), 'US dumping on world agricultural markets: can trade rules help farmers? institute for agriculture trade policy', Cancun Papers, No. 1, Minnesota.

IFS (Institute for Fiscal Studies) (2003), 'A survey of the UK tax system', updated November 2003, http://www.ifs.org.uk.

International Labour Organisation (ILO) (1976), *Meeting Basic Needs: Strategies for Eradicating Mass Poverty and Unemployment*, Geneva: ILO.

Isin, F.E. and P. Wood (1999), *Citizenship and Identity*, London: Sage.

Jacobs, D. (2000), 'Low inequality and low re-distribution: an analysis of income distribution in Japan, South Korea and Taiwan compared to Britain', CASE discussion paper No. 33, London School of Economics, London.

Jay, P. (2000), *Roads to Riches: Or The Wealth of Man*, London: Phoenix.

Jenkins, S. (1996), *Accountable to None: The Tory Nationalization of Britain*, Harmondsworth: Penguin.

Jones, M. (ed.) (1998), *Globalisation, Human Rights and Civil Society*, St Leonards, NSW: Prospect Media.

Joseph Rowntree Foundation (1998), 'Income gap remains wide despite mid-1990s fall in inequality', http://www.jrf.org.uk.

Kateb, G. (1989), 'Democratic individualism and the meaning of Rights', in N. Rosenblum (ed.), *Liberalism and the Moral Life*, London: Harvard University Press.

Kay, J.A. (2003), *The Truth about Markets, their Genius, their Limits, their Follies*, London: Allen Lane.

Keen, S. (2001), *Debunking Economics: The Naked Emperor of the Social Sciences*, London: Pluto Press.

Khor, M. (2000), 'Globalisation and the South – some critical issues', discussion paper No. 147, UNCTAD, Geneva, Switzerland.

Kiely, R. (ed.) (1998), *Globalisation and the Third World*, New York: Routledge.

Klein, N. (2001a), *No Space, No Choice, No Jobs, No Logo*, London: Flamingo.

Klein, N. (2001b), 'Farewell to "the end of history" organization and vision in anti-corporate movements', in L. Panitch and C. Leys (2001), *A World of Contradictions*, London: The Merlin Press.

Klein, N. (2003), 'No peace without a fight', *The Nation*, 13 March.

Kofman, E. and G. Youngs (1996), *Globalisation: Theory and Practice*, London: Pinter.

Krieger, A. (ed.) (2000), *The WTO as an International Organisation*, Chicago: University of Chicago Press.

Krugman, P. (2002), 'For Richer the magazine', *The New York Times*, 20 October.

Kukathas, C. and P. Pettit (1990), *Rawls: A Theory of Justice and its Critics*, Cambridge: Polity Press.

Kuttner, R. (2000), 'The role of government in the global economy', in A. Giddens and W. Hutton (eds), *On The Edge*, London: Jonathan Cape.

Kuznets, S. (1955), 'Economic growth and income inequality', *American Economic Review*, **45**, 1–28.

Kymlicka, W. (1989), *Liberalism, Community and Culture*, Oxford: Clarendon Press.

Kymlicka, W. (1990), *Contemporary Political Philosophy: An Introduction*, Oxford: Clarendon Press.

Kymlicka, W. and W. Norman (2000), *Citizenship in Diverse Societies*, Oxford: Oxford University Press.

Landes, D.S. (1969), *The Unbound Prometheus: Technological Change and Industrial Development in Western Europe from 1750 to the Present*, Cambridge: Cambridge University Press.

Layard, R. (2003), *Happiness: Has Social Science a Clue?*, London: Centre for Economic Performance.

Lee, S. (2003), 'The political economy of the Third Way: the relationship between globalisation and national economic policy', in J. Michie (2003), *The Handbook of Globalisation*, Cheltenham, UK and Northampton, MA, USA: Edward Elgar.

Lefort, C. (1986), *The Political Forms of Modern Society, Bureaucracy, Democracy Totalitarianism*, Oxford: Polity Press.

Leisink, P. (1999), *Globalisation and Labour Relations*, Cheltenham, UK and Northampton, MA, USA: Edward Elgar.

Lister, R. (1997), *Citizenship: Feminist Perspectives*, Basingstoke: MacMillan.

Lukes, S. (ed.) (1986), *Power*, Oxford: Blackwell.

Lyon, D. (1994), *Postmodernity*, Oxford: Oxford University Press.

Lyotard, J.F. (1984), *The Postmodern Condition: A Report on Knowledge*, G. Bennington and B. Massumi (trans), Minneapolis: University of Minnesota Press.

MacEwan, A. (1999), *Neo-liberalism or Democracy? Economic Strategy, Markets and Alternatives for the 21st Century*, London: Zed Books.

MacIntyre, A. (1981), *After Virtue, A Study in Moral Theory*, London: Duckworth.

MacPherson, C.B. (1984), *Democratic Theory: Essays in Retrieval*, Oxford: Clarendon Press.

Mayer, J. (2000), 'Globalisation and technology transfers in low income countries', discussion paper No. 150, UNCTAD, Geneva, Switzerland.

Mayer, J. (2001), 'Technology diffusion: human capital and economic growth in developing countries', discussion paper No. 154, UNCTAD, Geneva, Switzerland.

Mann, M. (1987), 'Ruling class strategies and citizenship', *Sociology*, **21** (3), 339–54.

Marshall, T.M. (1992), *Citizenship and Social Class*, London: Pluto.

McIntyre-Mills, J. (2000), *Global Citizenship and Social Movements*, Amsterdam: Harwood.

Mestrovic, S.G. (1993), *The Barbarian Temperament, Towards a Postmodern Critical Theory*, London: Routledge.

Michie, J. (ed.) (2003), *The Handbook of Globalisation*, Cheltenham, UK and Northampton, MA, USA: Edward Elgar.

Mishra, R. (1999), *Globalisation and the Welfare State*, Cheltenham, UK and Northampton, MA, USA: Edward Elgar.

Mokyr, J. (1992), *The Levers of Riches: Technological Creativity and Economic Progress*, Oxford: Open University Press.

Monbiot, G. (2001), *The Captive State*, London: Pan Books.

Monbiot, G. (2003), 'Out of the wreckage', *The Guardian*, Tuesday 25 February.

Moore, M. (2003), *A World without Walls: Freedom, Development, Free Trade and Global Governance*, Cambridge: Cambridge University Press.

Mouffe, C. (ed.) (1992), *Dimensions of Radical Democracy*, London: Verso.

Mullard, M. (1993), *The Politics of Public Expenditure*, London: Routledge.

Mullard, M. (1995), *Policy Making in Britain*, London: Routledge.

Mullard, M. (2001a), *New Labour New Thinking*, New York: Nova.

Mullard, M. (2001b), 'The language of public expenditure', *Political Quarterly*, October.

Mullard, M. and S. Lee (1997), *The Politics of Social Policy in Europe*, Cheltenham, UK and Northampton, MA, USA: Edward Elgar.

Mullard, M. and P. Spicker (1998), *Social Policy in a Changing Society*, London: Routledge.

Mullard, M. and H. Butcher (1993), 'Citizenship and democracy', in Butcher, H. et al (eds), *Community and Public Policy*, London: Pluto Press.

Mullard, M. (1997), 'Discourses on Citizenship', in M. Mullard and S. Lee (eds), *The Politics of Social Policy in Europe*, Cheltenham, UK and Northampton, MA, USA: Edward Elgar.

Murray, C.A. (1996), *The Underclass: The Developing Debate*, London: Institute of Economic Affairs.

Nedelsky, J. (1990), *Private Property and the Limits of American Constitutionalism*, Chicago: University of Chicago Press.

Nickell, S. (2001), 'Has UK labour market performance changed?', *Bank of England Quarterly Bulletin*, Autumn.

Norris, C. (1993), *The Truth about Postmodernism*, Oxford: Blackwell.

Nozick, R. (1974), *Anarchy, State and Utopia*, NewYork: Basic Books.

Nozick, R. (1984), 'Moral constraints and distributive justice', in M. Sandel (1984), *Liberalism and its Critics*, Oxford: Blackwell.

Ohmae, K. (1990), *The Borderless World*, London: Collins.

Ohmae, K. (1995), *The End of the Nation State: The Rise of Regional Economies*, London: Free Press.

O'Brien, M. and S. Penna (1998), 'Oppositional postmodern theory and welfare analysis', in J. Carter (ed.), *Postmodernity and Fragmentation of Welfare*, London: Routledge.

O'Connor, J. (1973), *The Fiscal Crisis of the State*, New York: St Martin's Press.

O'Sullivan, N. (ed.) (2000), *Political Theory in Transition*, London: Routledge.

OECD (1996a), 'Globalisation: what challenges and opportunities for governments?', Paris: OECD.

OECD (1996b), *Globalisation and linkages in 2020*, Paris: OECD.

OECD (1998), *Globalisaion and the Environment*, Paris: OECD.

Offe, C. (1985), *Disorganised Capitalism: Contemporary Transformations of Work and Politics*, Oxford: Polity Press.

Pack, H. (2001), 'Industrialisation options for poorest countries', United Nations Occasional Papers, United Nations, New York.

Palast, G. (2002), *The Best Democracy Money Can Buy*, London: Pluto Press.

Palma, G. (2003), 'National inequality in the era of globalisation: what do recent data tell us?', in J. Michie (ed.), *Handbook on Globalisation*, Cheltenham, UK and Northampton, MA, USA: Edward Elgar.

Pangle, T. (1993), *The Ennobling of Democracy: The Challenge of the Postmodern Age*, London: Johns Hopkins University Press.

Parekh, B. (1995), 'Ethnocentricity of the nationalist discourse', *Nations and Nationalism*, **1**, 25–52.

Pateman, C. (1989), *The Disorder of Women*, Cambridge: Polity Press.

Panitch, L. and C. Leys (eds) (2001), 'A world of contradictions', *Socialist Register 2002*, London: Merlin Press.

Perkin, H. (1969), *The Origins of Modern English Society 1780–1880*, London: Routledge and Kegan Paul.

Perraton, J. (2003), 'The scope and implications of globalisation', in J. Michie (ed.) *The Handbook of Globalisation*, Cheltenham, UK and Northampton, MA, USA: Edward Elgar.

Phelps Brown, E.H. (1977), *The Inequality of Pay*, Oxford: Oxford University Press.

Phillips, A. (1991), *Engendering Democracy*, Oxford: Polity Press.

Phillips, A. (1993), *Democracy and Difference*, Cambridge: Polity Press.

Phillips, A. (ed.) (1998), *Feminism and Politics*, Oxford: Oxford University Press.

Plattner, M. (ed.) (2001), *The Global Divergence of Democracy*, Baltimore: Johns Hopkins University Press.

Plattner, M. (2002), 'Globalisation and self government', *Journal of Democracy*, **13** (3), July, 54–67.

Polanyi, C. (1957), *The Transformation of Society*, Boston, MA: Gower Beacon Press.

Polaski, S. (2003), 'Serious flows in US – Singapore Trade Agreement', Carnegie Endowment for International Peace Brief, April, http://www.ceip.org.

Politi, D. (2003), 'Privatising water: what the European Commission don't want you to know', International Consortium of Investigative Journalists, Washington DC, April, http://www.icij.org.

Pollock, C. and D. Price (2000), 'GATS and the NHS', *The Lancet*, December, pp. 1–9.

Poulantzas, N. (1980), *State, Power and Socialism*, London: Verso.

Public Citizen (2001), *Down on the Farm: NAFTA Seven Years War on Farmers and Ranchers in the US, Canada and Mexico*, Washington DC: Public Citizen Global Trade Watch.

Ravallion, M. and G. Datt (1999), *When is Growth Pro-Poor*, Washington DC: World Bank.

Ravallion, M. (2002), 'How not to count the poor?', *A reply to Reedy and Pogge*, Columbia University, http://www.socialanalysis.org.

Rawlingson, K. and C. Whyley (1999), *Wealth in Britain: A Lifecycle Perspective*, London: Policy Studies Institute.

Rawls, J. (1986), *A Theory of Justice*, Oxford: Oxford University Press.

Rawls, J. (1993), *Political Liberalism*, New York: Columbia University Press.

Reddy, S. and T. Pogge (2002), 'How not to count the poor', *A reply to Ravallion*, Columbia University, http://www.socialanalysis.org.

Reddy, S. and T. Pogge (2003), *How Not to Count the Poor*, Columbia University, http://www.social analysis.org.

Rengger, N.J. (1995), *Political Theory, Modernity and Postmodernity*, Oxford: Blackwell.

Rhodes, M. (1996), *Globalisation and West European Welfare States*, Florence: European University Institute.

Rhodes, M. (1997), *Globalisation, Labour Markets and Welfare States*, Florence: European University Institute.

Rifkin, J. (1995), *The End of Work, The Decline of the Global Labour Force and the Dawn of the Market Era*, New York: Putnam Books.

Roche, M. and R. Van Berkel (1997), *European Citizenship and Social Exclusion*, Aldershot: Ashgate.

Rodrik, D. (1999), *Making Open-ness Work, The New Global Economy and the Developing Countries*, Washington DC: Overseas Development Council.

Rorty, R. (1982), *Consequences of Pragmatism*, Minneapolis: University of Minnesota Press.

Rorty, R. (1989), *Contingency, Irony and Solidarity*, Cambridge: Cambridge University Press.

Rose, R. (1984), *Understanding Big Government*, London: Sage.

Rose, R. and G. Peters (1979), *Can Governments go Bankrupt?*, London: MacMillan

Rosenblum, N. (ed.) (1989), *Liberalism and the Moral Life*, London: Harvard University Press.

Sandel, M. (1988), *Liberalism and Its Critics*, Oxford: Blackwell.

Sandel, M. (1998), *Democracy's Discontents: America in Search of a Public Philosophy*, London: Harvard University Press.

Sartori, G. (1987), *The Theory of Democracy Revisited*, Parts One and Two, New Jersey: Chatham House Publishers.

Sawyer, M. (1976), 'Income distribution in OECD countries', *OECD Economic Outlook*, July.

Schklar, J. (1989), 'The liberalism of fear', in N. Rosenblum (ed.), *Liberalism and the Moral Life*, London: Harvard University Press.

Schumpeter, J.A. (1987), *Capitalism, Socialism and Democracy*, London: Unwin.
Schweitzer, M.E. (2001), 'Ready willing and able? Measuring labour availability in the UK', mimeo, Bank of England, London.
Scruton, R. (1984), *The Meaning of Conservatism*, London: MacMillan.
Sen, A. (1999), 'Democracy as a universal value', *Journal of Democracy*, **10** (3), 3–17.
Sen, A. (2002), 'How to judge globalisation', *The American Prospect*, **13** (1).
Selbourne, D. (1997), *The Principle of Duty: An Essay on the Foundations of the Civic Order*, London: Abacus.
Sennet, R. (1979), *The Fall of Public Man*, London: Faber and Faber.
Sennet, R. (2000), 'Home and office: two sources of identity', in W. Hutton and A. Giddens (eds), *On The Edge*, London: Jonathan Cape.
Shapiro, I. (2003), 'Federal income taxes as a share of GDP Drop to Lowest Level since 1942', Centre on Budget and Policy Priorities, http://www.cbpp.org/pub.
Shapiro, I. and C. Hacker-Cordon (eds) (1999), *Democracy's Edges*, Cambridge: Cambridge University Press.
Shiva, V. (2000), 'Poverty and globalisation', *The Reith Lectures*, BBC, http://news.bbc.co.uk/hi/english/staticevents/reith 2000 Lecture 5.
Sinclair, S. (2003), 'The WTO and its GATS', in J. Michie (ed.), *The Handbook of Globalisation*, Cheltenham, UK and Northampton, MA, USA: Edward Elgar.
Singh, A. and A. Zammit (2003), 'Globalisation, labour standards and economic development', in J. Michie (ed.), *The Handbook of Globalisation*, Cheltenham, UK and Northampton, MA, USA: Edward Elgar.
Smith, A.D. (1995), *Nations and Nationalism in a Global Era*, Cambridge: Polity Press.
Solomon, R. (2001), 'Participation in people's budget: The Rio Grande Do Sol experience', speech to Port Allegre Social Forum, April.
South Centre (1995), *Reforming the United Nations: A View from the South*, Geneva: South Centre.
Soysal, Y. (1994), *Limits of Citizenship: Migrants and Postnational Membership in Europe*, London: University of Chicago Press.
Squires, J. (ed.) *Postmodernism and the Rediscovery of Values*, London: Lawrence and Wishart.
Stiglitz, J. (1998), 'More instruments and broader goal – moving towards the post Washington consensus', WIDER Annual Lecture No. 2, Helsinki, UNU/WIDER.
Stiglitz, J. (2002a), 'Globalism's discontents', *The American Prospect*, **13** (1), 1–10.
Stiglitz, J. (2002b), *Globalization and Its Discontents*, London: Allen Lane.
Strange, S. (1986), *Casino Capitalism*, Oxford: Blackwell.
Strange, S. (1995), 'The defective state', Journal of the American Academy of Arts, **124** (2), 55–74.
Strange, S. (1996), *The Retreat of the State: The Diffusion of Power in the World Economy*, Cambridge: Cambridge University Press.
Strange, S. (1998), *Mad Money*, Manchester: Manchester University Press.
Strange, S. (1998), 'The future of global capitalism: or will divergence persist forever?', in C. Crouch and W. Streeck (eds), *Political Economy of Modern Capitalism*, London: Sage.
Strange, S. and F. Sabelli (1994), *Faith and Credit: The World Bank's Secular Empire*, Harmondsworth: Penguin.
Streeten, P. (2001), *Globalisation: Threat or Opportunity*, Copenhagen: Copenhagen Business School Press.
Sutcliffe, B. and A. Glyn (2003), 'Measures of globalisation and their misinterpreta-

tions', in J. Michie (ed.), *The Handbook of Globalisation*, Cheltenham, UK and Northampton, MA, USA: Edward Elgar.

Swank, D. (2001), 'European welfare states: regionalization, globalization, and social policy change', paper presented at the 2001 Annual Meeting of the American Political Science Association, San Francisco, USA.

Swann, D. (1988), *The Retreat of the State: Deregulation and Privatisation in the UK and US*, London: Harvester Wheatsheaf.

Sykes, R., B. Palier and P. Prior (2001), *Globalisation and the Welfare State: Challenges and Change*, London: Palladin.

Talmon, J.L. (1991), *Myth of the Nation and Vision of Revolution: Ideological Polarization in the 20th Century*, London: Transaction Publishers.

Tanzi, V. (1998), 'Fundamental determinants of inequality and the role of government', IMF working paper 103/98, Washington DC.

Taylor, C. (1979), *Hegel and Modern Society*, Cambridge: Cambridge University Press.

Taylor, C. (1994), *Sources of the Self, The Making of the Modern Identity*, Cambridge: Cambridge University Press.

The Commission on Global Governance (1995), *Our Global Neighbourhood*, Oxford: Oxford University Press.

Thompson, E.P. (1976), *The Making of the English Working Class*, Middlesex: Penguin.

Thurow, L.G. (2000), *Building Wealth: The New Rules for Individuals, Companies and Nations in a Knowledge Based Economy*, New York: HarperCollins.

Tilly, C. (1996), *Citizenship, Identity and Social History*, New York: Cambridge University Press.

Todaro, M. (2000), *Economic Development*, seventh edition, Edinburgh: Pearson Education.

Toulmin, S. (1992), *Cosmopolis: The Hidden Agenda of Modernity*, Chicago: University of Chicago Press.

Townsend, P. and D. Gordon (eds) (2002), *World Poverty: New Policies to Defeat an Old Enemy*, Bristol: The Policy Press.

Turner, B.S. (1990), 'Outline of a theory on citizenship', *Sociology*, **24** (2), 189–218.

Turner, B.S. (1993), *Citizenship and Social Theory*, London: Sage.

Turner, B.S. (2000), 'Liberal citizenship and cosmopolitan virtue', in A. Vandenberg (ed.) (2000), *Citizenship and Democracy in a Global Era*, London: MacMillan.

UNDP (1996), *Human Development Report 1996: Economic Growth and Human Development*, New York: United Nations.

UNDP (1997), *Human Development Report 1997: Human Development to Eradicate Poverty*, New York: United Nations.

UNDP (1998), *Human Development Report 1998: Consumption for Human Development*, New York: United Nations.

UNDP (1999), *Human Development Report 1999: Globalisation with a Human Face*, New York: United Nations.

UNDP (2000), *Human Development Report 2000: Human Rights and Human Development*, New York: United Nations.

UNDP (2001), *Human Development Report 2001: Making Technologies Work for Human Development*, New York: United Nations.

UNCTAD (1997), *Trade and Development Report 1997*, New York: United Nations.

UNCTAD (2000), *The Least Developed Countries Report*, New York: United Nations.

UNCTAD (2001), *Trade and Development Report 2001: Global Trends and Prospects*, New York: United Nations.

UNCTAD (2002), *UNCTAD Annual Report 2002*, Geneva: United Nations.

UNICEF (1995), *Poverty, Children and Policy: Responses for Brighter Future*, Florence: UNICEF-ICDC.

UNICEF (1997), *Children at Risk in Central and Eastern Europe: Perils and Promises*, Florence: UNICEF-ICDC.

United Nations (2000), *We The Peoples' The Role of the United Nations in the 21 Century*, http://www.un.org/millenium.

Upchurch, M. (ed.) (1999), *The State of Globalisation*, New York: Mansell.

Van Steenbergen, J. (1994), *The Condition of Citizenship*, London: Sage.

Vandenberg, A. (ed.) (2000), *Citizenship and Democracy in a Global Era*, London: MacMillan.

Veblen, T. (1970), *The Theory of the Leisure Class, An Economic Study of Institutions*, London: Unwin Books.

Voet, R. (1998), *Feminism and Citizenship*, London: Sage.

Vogel, U. (1989), 'Is citizenship gender specific?', a paper presented to Political Studies Association Conference (PSA), Manchester, April.

Walby, S. (1994), 'Is citizenship gendered?', *Sociology*, **28** (2), 379–95.

Wallace, H. and W. Wallace (ed.) (1996), *Policy-making in the European Union*, Oxford: Oxford University Press.

Wallerstein, E. (1991), *Geopolitics and Geo-culture*, Cambridge: Cambridge University Press.

Warren, M. (2002), 'Deliberative democracy', in A. Carter and G. Stokes (eds), *Democratic Theory Today*, Oxford: Polity Press.

Waters, M. (1995), *Globalisation*, London: Routledge.

Weisbrot, M., D. Baker, R. Naiman and G. Neta (2000), *Growth Maybe Good for the Poor – But Are IMF and World Bank Policies Good for Growth?*, http://cepr.net/response.

Weisbrot, M. (2002), 'Why globalisation fails to deliver', *The Observer*, Sunday 28 July.

Weiss, L. (1998), *The Myth of the Powerless State: Governing The Economy in a Global Era*, Cambridge: Polity Press.

Wellmer, A. (1985), 'The dialectic of modernity and post modernity', *Praxis International*, **4**, January.

White, S.K. (1988), *The Recent Work of Jurgen Habermas: Reason, Justice and Modernity*, Cambridge: Cambridge University Press.

White, S.K. (1995), *Political Theory and Postmodernism*, Cambridge: Cambridge University Press.

Whitefied, D. (1994), *Globalisation: The Future of the Welfare State and Public Service*, Sheffield: Sheffield Centre for Public Services.

WIR (2002), *World Investment Report 2002: Transnational Corporations and Export Competitiveness*, Geneva: United Nations.

Wolfe, A. (1977), *The Limits of Legitimacy: Political Contradictions of Contemporary Capitalism*, London: Collier Macmillan.

Wood, A. (1994), *North-South Trade: Employment and Inequality*, Oxford: Clarendon Press.

World Bank (1990), *World Development Report: Poverty*, Washington DC: World Bank.

World Bank (1993), *Poverty and Income Distribution in Latin America: The Story of the 1980s Report*, Washington DC: World Bank.

World Bank (1994), *Averting the Old Age Crisis*, Oxford: Oxford University Press.

World Bank (1995a), 'Distribution and growth', *World Bank Policy Bulletin*, **6** (3).

World Bank (1995b), *World Development Report 1995: Workers in an Integrating World*, Washington DC: World Bank.

World Bank (1995c), *Investing in People, The World Bank in Action*, Washington DC: World Bank.

World Bank (1998), *The World Bank Economic Report 1998*, Washington DC: World Bank.

World Bank (2000), *World Development Report 2000*, Washington DC: World Bank.

World Bank (2001), *World Bank Report 2001*, Washington DC: World Bank.

World Bank (2002), *World Development Report 2002: Building Institutions for Markets*, Oxford: Oxford University Press.

Young, H. (1989), *One of Us: A Biography of Margaret Thatcher*, London: MacMillan.

Index

accountability *see* transparency
advertising, election campaign 84
agriculture
    child labour in 131–2
    MNCs access to government and
      44
    NAFTA and 114
    subsidies x, 22–3, 29, 104, 154
    WTO intellectual property rights
      enforcement and 143–4
Americanisation
    globalisation defined in terms of 40
    secular democracy and market
      liberalism 69–70
Amoore, L. 77
Annan, Kofi 17, 98
anti-globalisation
    democratic response, as 76–7
    forms of 9–12, 27
    protest strategies 150–51
    strategy requirements 178
    terrorism and 30–31
    see also globalisation;
      globalisations sceptics
anti-politics
    citizenship and 52
    democracy and 35–6
anti-Semitism, public citizen and 57
Arestis, P. 93
asbestos, trade barriers and 113
Atkinson, A. 6–7

bananas, trade barriers and 113
Baqir, R. 160
Barber, B.R. 74, 119, 120, 128
Bauman, Z.
    anti-globalisation and 77
    citizen's income and 52
    immortality of nationhood and 153
    insecurities and the end of ideology
      and 89
    modular man and 74–5

political economy of uncertainty
    and 21
    post-engagement and 87
    postmodern ethics and 183–4
    postmodern mind and 151
    self-constitution and 152
    welfare state failure and 67
BCRA (Bipartisan Campaign Reform
    Act 2001) 33
Beck, U. 40–41, 132–3, 152, 190
Beer, S.H. 71, 83
Beetham, D. 32, 34–5
Bernstein, R.J. 83, 151, 181
Bhagwati, J. 101–2, 118–19
Blair, Tony 137–8, 185, 186
Blitz, J. 138
Bobbio, R. 55, 83, 85
Boggs, C. xii–xiii
borderless economy
    capital mobility and 165–6
    markets and 128
    nature of 1–2
    networks compared 5
    political problems of 91
Bourdieu, P. 22
Bowles, S. 81
Boyte, H. 51
Bretton Woods era vii–viii
Bridges, T. 67
Brinkley, J. 73
Brittan, S. 84
Brosman, P. 5–6
budget
    deficits 16, 136–7, 189–90
    process, participation in 23–4
    see also fiscal policy
bureaucracy, democratic failings and
    85
Bush, George W. 136–7, 187

capital mobility
    borderless economy and 165–6